$15.00

LANCASHIRE IN DECLINE

A Study in Entrepreneurship, Technology, and International Trade

By Lars G. Sandberg

Few if any industries have a history as dramatic and exciting as the cotton textile industry of Lancashire, England, which between the middle of the eighteenth century and the early years of the twentieth underwent a spectacular and unprecedented growth, only to enter a sharp and disastrous decline following the First World War that led to its eventual collapse.

The industry was one of the first to successfully employ machinery and mechanical power in the manufacturing process, and indeed it can be argued that it was the world's first modern industry. Some have seen it as the major factor in Great Britain's emergence as the world's leading industrial power, and there is no question that a causal relationship existed between the health of the industrial economy and the state of the empire and nation. During the period in which the industry flourished, it brought a general prosperity to the entire British economy; and when it began to fail, severe depression afflicted the whole of society.

Not surprisingly perhaps, little serious criticism of the cotton textile industry was voiced during the period of its success. Throughout most of the nineteenth century, the charges of contemporary observers were limited to allegations of social abuse: the inhumane treatment of the women and children who worked in the mills, the length and hardships of the working day, and the absence of adequate sanitary facilities for the workers. It was only in the last quarter of the century, when the economic slowdown had obtained for some time and the political threat posed by Imperial Germany had become

(Continued on back flap)

LANCASHIRE IN DECLINE

LANCASHIRE IN DECLINE

a study in entrepreneurship,

technology, and international trade

BY LARS G. SANDBERG

OHIO STATE UNIVERSITY PRESS: COLUMBUS

Copyright © 1974 by the Ohio State University Press
All rights reserved

Library of Congress Cataloging in Publication Data

Sandberg, Lars G
  Lancashire in decline.

  Bibliography: p. 263
  1. Cotton trade—Lancashire, Eng.
2. Cotton manufacture—Lancashire, Eng.
3. Cotton machinery. I. Title.
HD9881.8L3S25   338.4'7'6772'094272   73-18435
ISBN 0-8142-0199-7

Manufactured in the United States of America

TO MY MOTHER AND FATHER

TABLE OF CONTENTS

viii) *CONTENTS*

LIST OF TABLES

x) *TABLES*

LIST OF FIGURES

ACKNOWLEDGMENTS

By far the greatest debts, both intellectual and personal, that I have incurred in the writing of this book are owed to Professor Alexander Gerschenkron. Without his help and encouragement, this project would probably never have reached fruition. I have also received many valuable suggestions at the various seminars and workshops at which parts of the book have been presented. In particular, I have benefited from comments by Donald McCloskey, Peter McClelland, and Richard Sylla. Finally, one of the readers consulted by the Ohio State University Press, who remains anonymous to me, made a large number of very useful suggestions for improving the original manuscript. None of these persons, of course, are responsible for any remaining errors of commission or omission. In addition, I would like to thank the *Quarterly Journal of Economics* and the *Journal of Economic History* for granting me permission to republish material from articles of mine that previously appeared in those journals. Finally, the Oxford University Press has granted me permission to reprint Figure 1.

PART I

ENTREPRENEURSHIP AND TECHNOLOGY

1

INTRODUCTION

Few if any industries have a history as interesting and exciting as that of the Lancashire cotton textile industry.[1] Over one hundred and fifty years of spectacular and usually steady growth was, after World War I, followed by an even more spectacular and steady decline. Shirtsleeves to shirtsleeves in two centuries.

Both in its rise and in its decline, the Lancashire cotton textile industry was of great importance not only to the British economy but to the whole world. Indeed, it can be argued cogently that it was the world's first modern industry. Certainly it was one of the first industries successfully to employ machinery and mechanical power. As for the industry's role in the emer-

[1] Throughout this study, the Lancashire cotton textile industry and the British cotton textile industry are referred to as if they were identical. Strictly speaking, of course, they are not, and never were, the same thing. It is true that Lancashire has persistently dominated the British cotton textile industry. The concentration of activity in Lancashire increased throughout the nineteenth century, reaching a peak just before World War I. In 1838, 59% of all British cotton textile workers were employed in the county of Lancashire; by 1898–99, this figure had increased to 75.7%. If the neighboring county of Cheshire is included, the figure for 1838 increases to 73% and that for 1898–99 becomes 82.2%. As a percentage of all cotton workers in England and Wales (i.e., excluding Scotland), the combined county figures were 86.1% in 1838 and 87.1% in 1898–99 (S. J. Chapman, *The Lancashire Cotton Industry*, p. 149). This joint figure for England and Wales reached a high of 89.8% in 1911 (R. Robson, *The Cotton Industry in Britain*, p. 31).

TABLE 1

BRITISH CONSUMPTION OF RAW COTTON AND EXPORTS OF COTTON
TEXTILES IN VARIOUS YEARS

Year	Cotton Consumption (millions of lbs.)	Cloth Exports (millions of linear yds.)	Exports (millions of £)	% of All Exports
1760	3.4	n.a.	0.3	3
1781–83	8.7	n.a.	n.a.	n.a.
1800	52	65.5	n.a.	n.a.
1810	124	212.2	n.a.	n.a.
1814	74	192.3	20.0	43.9
1820	120	251.0	16.5	45.3
1830	248	441.6	19.4	50.7
1840	459	790.6	24.7	48.1
1850	588	1,385.2	28.3	39.6
1860	1,084	2,776.2	52.0	38.3
1870	1,075	3,267.0	71.4	35.8
1880	1,361	3,724.6	75.6	33.9
1890	1,664	5,125.0	74.4	28.2
1900	1,737	5,031.7	69.8	24.0
1910	1,632	6,017.6	105.3	24.5
1913	2,178	7,075.3	126.5	24.1
1920	1,726	4,435.4*	401.4	30.1
1930	1,272	2,490.5	87.6	15.3
1939	1,317	1,426.4	49.1	11.2
1955	778	533.9	116.8	4.8

SOURCES: Robson, *The Cotton Industry in Britain*, pp. 331–35 and P. Deane and W. A. Cole, *British Economic Growth, 1688–1959*, p. 185. Cotton yarn exports were generally growing faster than raw cotton imports but less rapidly than cloth exports. See Robson.

*Square yards.

gence of Great Britain as the premier industrial power in the world, Walt Rostow has given it the singular honor of being the "leading sector" in the world's first "take-off."[2] Although the usefulness of Rostow's categories has frequently been questioned, his choice of a leading industry for Great Britain is generally accepted.[3]

The data presented in Tables 1 and 2 are intended to give the reader some idea of the rapid rate at which the British cotton textile industry grew between 1760 and 1913 as well as of the industry's importance to the British economy as a

[2] W. W. Rostow, *The Stages of Economic Growth*, pp. 52–55.

[3] A possible exception can be found in P. Deane and W. A. Cole, *British Economic Growth, 1688–1959*, esp. pp. 290–99. These authors seem to be undecided between the rival candidacies of the iron and cotton industries.

TABLE 2

EMPLOYMENT IN THE BRITISH COTTON TEXTILE INDUSTRY
IN VARIOUS YEARS

(in thousands of workers)

Year	Factory Workers	Handloom Weavers
1810	100	200
1814	110	216
1820	126	240
1830	185	240
1840	262	123
1850	331	43
1860	427	10
1870	450	
1880	483	
1890	529	
1901	523	
1907	577	
	Insured Workers	
1923	568	
1929	555	
1933	500	
1936	421	
1939	378	

SOURCE: B. R. Mitchell (with the collaboration of P. Deane), *Abstract of British Historical Statistics*, pp. 187–88.

whole. Roughly speaking, British cotton consumption increased fifteen times between 1760 and 1800. It then further increased nine times between 1800 and 1840 and doubled between 1840 and 1860. After stagnating during the 1860s, largely as a result of the American Civil War, cotton consumption once more doubled by 1913. During this period, the most rapid rate of growth was achieved during the years between 1780 and 1800. The most important growth probably occurred between 1820 and 1850, however, since this was the period during which all the processes of the industry were brought into the factory. After 1860, the rate of growth of cotton consumption was clearly lower than it had been earlier. Nevertheless, the growth rate was certainly respectable all the way up to World War I.

The export figures are in some ways even more spectacular than the cotton consumption figures. The rate of increase in the yardage of cloth and the poundage of yarn exported was generally higher than the rate of growth of cotton consumption. As for the share of cotton goods in total British exports, the figures are impressive, to say the least. This is true despite the fact that the relatively high import content of cotton textile exports tends to exaggerate the importance of these exports.[4]

British cotton textile exports reached their relative high point in 1830. In that year, they constituted no less than 50.7% of all British exports. That was the only year that their share was above one-half, but even in 1913 it was almost one-quarter.

Since cotton textiles was the first industry to be converted to modern factory production, the share of cotton factory employment in total British factory employment has been decreasing almost from the beginning of the Industrial Revolution. Nevertheless, a very large, if declining, percentage of all British factory workers were engaged in the cotton textile industry throughout the nineteenth century. For most of the period leading up to World War I, cotton textiles was the leading British industry in terms of value added. It was only toward the end of the period that it was passed by the combined engineering trades.[5]

Just as rapid growth and prosperity in Lancashire gave the whole British economy a boost, so depression in cotton textiles was a terrible drag. The suffering experienced during the "cotton famine" that occurred during the American Civil War was largely confined to the cotton-producing areas,[6] but the depression of the interwar period (i.e., the period between the two World Wars) affected the whole economy. This time the depression was permanent and required a major reallocation

---

[4] During the nineteenth century, the cost of the imported raw cotton represented an average of about 40% of the value of the industry's final product (Deane and Cole, *British Economic Growth*, p. 187). Such a large import content was probably a good deal higher than the average for all British exports. Thus, cotton textile exports represent a somewhat smaller percentage of British value added exported than of total British goods exported. For most purposes, the former percentage is a better measure of economic importance than is the latter percentage.

[5] Deane and Cole, *British Economic Growth*, p. 192.

[6] W. O. Henderson, *The Lancashire Cotton Famine, 1861–1865*, chap. 2.

of capital and labor. This reallocation proved to be a very drawn-out and painful process. To a large extent, of course, the difficulties of readjustment were a result of the concentration of the industry in Lancashire and Cheshire. The problem was further exacerbated by the poor performance of Britain's other staple industries: in particular, wool textiles, coal mining, and shipbuilding. Indeed, the poor performance of the entire British economy during the interwar period can largely be attributed to cotton, wool, coal, and shipbuilding.

As was the case with British industry in general, the economic performance of the cotton textile industry was not seriously criticized by contemporary observers at least until the end of the nineteenth century. During most of that century, attacks on the cotton industry and its leaders were limited to its treatment of women and children, the length of the working day, sanitary conditions, and other basically *social* problems. The competence of British management and the superiority of British workers was taken for granted. It was only after the economic slowdown (or "climacteric") of the last quarter of the nineteenth century had persisted for some time and the economic and political threat from Imperial Germany had become obvious that Britain began its pre–World War I orgy of economic self-criticism. Even then, however, the cotton textile industry and its managers, workers, and trade unions were treated relatively gently. Thus, for example, E. A. Pratt in his stinging indictment of the economic behavior of the British trade unions does not have a single critical word to say about the cotton textile unions; this despite the great numerical and economic strength of these unions.[7] Similarly though Melvin Copeland noted that British cotton firms were not adopting ring spinning and automatic weaving at anything near the American rate, he did not take this as a sign of managerial ineptness or technological conservatism.[8]

To a large extent, this relatively favorable treatment was

[7] E. A. Pratt, *Trade Unionism and British Industry.* This book is principally a reprinting of a series of articles Pratt had published in the *London Times* between 18 November 1901 and 16 January 1902.

[8] See M. T. Copeland, *The Cotton Manufacturing Industry of the United States,* chap. 4.

undoubtedly a result of the industry's continued expansion and success. Thus, it is not surprising that the attitude of journalists, economists, and economic historians all hardened as they watched the industry flounder and eventually collapse during the interwar period. This disaster made it much more interesting and fashionable to search for a villain.

As far as economists and economic historians are concerned, an important turning point occurred in 1933 with the publication of G. T. Jones's book *Increasing Returns*.[9] Jones argued forcefully that there had been no improvement whatsoever in the manufacturing efficiency of the Lancashire cotton textile industry between 1885 and 1910. Indeed, he maintained that efficiency had actually declined somewhat between 1900 and 1910.[10] In Massachusetts, on the other hand, Jones found considerable improvement in cotton-manufacturing efficiency between 1885 and 1910.[11] I believe that these findings, which to my knowledge have gone completely unchallenged for thirty-six years, were of the greatest importance in causing economic historians to reassess the performance of the British cotton textile industry in the period between 1880 and World War I. In particular, they came to the virtually unanimous conclusion that British entrepreneurs and managers were seriously at fault in not following the example of their American brethren in a wholehearted adoption of ring spinning and automatic weaving. Indeed, this failure was now taken as a sign, not to say proof, of irrationality and technological backwardness. The explicit, or sometimes implicit, conclusion of this line of analysis is that Britain would have been able to improve her efficiency significantly, as America had done, had she adopted the new American machines. This in turn, would have helped stem the relative decline (in terms of her share of total world production and total world trade) of Lancashire between 1880 and 1913, and would have resulted in at least a somewhat better performance during the interwar period.

[9] G. T. Jones, *Increasing Returns*. The work was edited by Colin Clark, Jones having been killed in an automobile accident in 1928.

[10] Jones, *Increasing Returns*, pp. 117, 274.

[11] Ibid., pp. 289–90.

This claim that there was poor management in the cotton textile industry is part and parcel of a more general attempt to explain Britain's relative economic decline after circa 1870 in terms of "entrepreneurial failure." This explanation was introduced into the scholarly world by the distinguished trio of Marshall, Veblen, and Hobson.[12] Its essence has been succintly expressed by T. H. Burnham and G. O. Hoskins in their study of the British iron and steel industry. After a highly subjective and definitely qualitative evaluation of the extenuating circumstances, they concluded that "if a business deteriorates it is of no use blaming anyone except those at the top."[13] Clearly, this is the economic equivalent of the political call to "throw the rascals out."

The most influential current exponents of the entrepreneurial failure theory are David Landes and Derek Aldcroft.[14] Aldcroft in particular has presented a broad indictment of late nineteenth-century British businessmen. He accuses them of five failures:

1. They did not adopt the best available techniques of production in many industries. Prominently mentioned among these non-adopted techniques are ring spinning and automatic weaving in cotton textiles.

2. They neglected science and research.

3. They put their money into the old staple industries and neglected new industries with a better future.

4. They were bad salesmen.

---

[12] See A. Marshall, "Fiscal Policy of International Trade" in *Official Papers*, p. 405, *Principles of Economics*, p. 298 ff., and *Industry and Trade*, p. 86 ff.; T. Veblen, *Imperial Germany and the Industrial Revolution*, p. 128; and J. Hobson, *Incentives in the New Industrial Order*, pp. 78–83.

[13] T. H. Burnham and G. O. Hoskins, *Iron and Steel in Britain, 1870–1930*, p. 271.

[14] See esp. D. S. Landes, "Some Reasons Why," pp. 553–84, in "Technological Change and Development in Western Europe, 1750–1914," chap. 5 in H. J. Habakkuk and M. Postan, eds., *The Cambridge Economic History of Europe*, vol. 6, reprinted with revisions and extensions in Landes, *The Unbound Prometheus.* Also D. H. Aldcroft, "The Entrepreneur and the British Economy, 1870–1914."

5. They did not do enough to establish international cartels to extract monopoly profits from the world at large.[15]

The first part of this book is an attempt to see whether in fact British cotton textile firms were irrational and "technologically backwards" in the period after 1880. A secondary question is the extent to which any mistakes they may have made concerning the new technology could have affected Lancashire's competitive position.

The criteria for rationality will be cost minimization and profit maximization. That is, given the technology available at the time and making reasonable assumptions about future economic and technological developments, could the British cotton textile managers have lowered their costs, and thereby raised their profits, by adopting machinery or techniques that they in fact neglected? A similar question is: Did they invest in machinery and other equipment that yielded a lower rate of return than did other available but neglected investment opportunities? Efficiency and rationality are thus defined strictly in an economic, not a general, sense. A faster or less labor intensive machine is not necessarily more profitable than its slower or more labor intensive alternative. Furthermore, what is most profitable at one time and in one place is not necessarily most profitable at a different time and in a different place.

In looking at the performance of the British cotton textile industry, I am limiting myself to the aggregate results. Did the industry taken as a whole act in a rational way? The bahavior of individual entrepreneurs and firms is of little or no concern; any industry is bound to contain some firms that are being mismanaged. As long as there are a substantial number of firms who make the right decision, however, even if it is a result of pure luck, and the industry is reasonably competitive, strong forces will be at work to make the industry as a whole behave properly. The growing profits of those who choose

[15] Aldcroft, "The Entrepreneur and the British Economy," pp. 116–18 and 121–23. For a review of the literature and a longer discussion of the issue of entrepreneurial performance in late Victorian and Edwardian England, see D. N. McCloskey and L. G. Sandberg, "From Damnation to Redemption: Judgments on the Late Victorian Entrepreneur."

the right alternative must give other firms a good reason for emulation. As for those who cannot be persuaded by potential profits, bankruptcy and forced exit is a likely result.

In case the reader should object that I am cheating by looking only at aggregate behavior, let me defend myself by pointing out that it is exactly this kind of aggregate rational behavior that the adherents of the entrepreneurial failure hypotheses deny, both in the British economy as a whole and in the cotton textile industry. Indeed, David Landes explicitly considers, and then rejects, competition as a major force for ensuring aggregate technological rationality.[16]

The first problem examined in the book concerns spinning technology. I begin by trying to determine if the difference in choice of spinning technique made by British and American manufacturers when they were installing new equipment in the period just before World War I can be explained by differing economic conditions. I have included American, as well as British, behavior in this study for two reasons. First of all, most critics of British investment policy contrast it unfavorably with American behavior. Second, and more important, a model that can explain differential behavior in two different countries is much more convincing than one that deals only with a single country.

The analysis presented in chapter 2 leads me to conclude that both British and American cotton manufacturers, at least as a general rule, were rational in their choice of spinning techniques. In chapters 3 and 4, I then go on to examine whether differing economic conditions can explain the difference in British and American behavior with regard to the junking of old, mule-type spinning equipment and with regard to the choice between plain (power) looms and automatic looms. Unfortunately, these questions cannot be answered as authoritatively as the previous one. The difficulty arises because these later decisions come down to whether or not to make a capital investment. These investment opportunities were more fre-

---

[16] See Landes, *The Unbound Prometheus*, pp. 354–55. Landes points to the "long run" nature of adjustments in competitive industries and then repeats Keynes's quip that "in the long run we are all dead."

quently accepted in America than in Great Britain. In order to judge the rationality of these actions, I estimate the rate of return on the investment opportunities present in the two countries. The range of the results, as well as the probable size of the errors of measurement, however, makes it impossible to state with complete confidence that everyone acted in an entirely rational manner. On the other hand, the evidence by no means proves, or even indicates, irrationality. Furthermore, the data clearly show that if the British should in fact have acted differently, their failure to do so could not possibly have played a major role in Lancashire's decline.

Chapter 5 deals with over-all technological improvement in Lancashire and Massachusetts. Basically it is a reassessment and correction of Jones's calculations. I have no serious criticism of his calculations of efficiency improvement in Massachusetts, but I believe that his results for Lancashire are very misleading. My reworking of his model and his data leads me to conclude that efficiency in the Lancashire cotton textile industry did in fact increase between 1885 and 1910, although not as rapidly as it did in Massachusetts. In particular, I replace the decrease Jones found for the 1900–1910 period with a rate of increase similar to that he reported for the 1885–1900 period. This difference in findings is partly the result of defects in Jones's model. The most important change, however, results from the fact that he incorrectly spliced a price series for cotton cloth at the turn of the century.

In addition to considering over-all efficiency, I also estimate the change in output per unit of labor input for both Lancashire and Massachusetts. As was to be expected, these labor productivity series show more improvement in both regions than do the over-all efficiency series. As in the case of over-all efficiency, labor productivity increased more rapidly in Massachusetts than in Lancashire. I argue, however, that the more rapid rise in both over-all efficiency and in labor productivity in Massachusetts can be explained by economic factors without recourse to theories of technological backwardness or managerial incompetence in Lancashire.

Chapter 6 contains a brief survey of investment, or rather disinvestment, in Lancashire between the World Wars. The general conclusion is that the choice of which type of equipment to junk was made in a reasonable manner.

Chapter 7, which concludes Part I of the book, contains some final observations on technological change and entrepreneurship in Lancashire.

Having examined and rejected the hypothesis that managerial and technological failure were principal causes of Lancashire's fall, I devote Part II of the book to the alternate theory. That is, Lancashire's decline, and eventual fall, was principally the result of a decline in exports brought about by forces outside Lancashire's control. Chapter 8 consists of a survey of Lancashire's export experience between 1815 and the outbreak of World War I, and chapter 9 examines the period from 1914 up through 1938.

The gist of the argument presented in these chapters is that Lancashire's relative decline after 1880 and her virtual collapse during the interwar years were both the result of two separate developments. The first of these was the rapid spread of cotton manufacturing to all parts of the world. In most cases, this spread was accompanied and encouraged by tariff protection and other forms of government assistance. In addition, national governments virtually without exception showed a strong determination not to allow imports to endanger the position of a previously established domestic cotton textile industry.

The second development was a shift in comparative advantage in cotton textiles away from highly industrialized countries toward areas that were just beginning to industrialize. On the international scene, this movement consisted principally of Britain's losing her dominant position as a cotton textile exporter to countries such as Italy, India, and especially Japan. At the same time, a similar movement was occurring within the highly protected American market. Here the new cotton industry of the previously unindustrialized southern states was gaining the upper hand over the long-established New England cotton textile industry.

Chapter 10 attempts to explain these trends in terms of economic variables. It is argued that they can in fact be explained by a number of characteristics of the manufacturing process involved in cotton textiles. The most important of these are low transportation costs (both differential and absolute), limited economies of scale, and low capital and skill intensity.

Finally chapter 11 contains a few concluding remarks on the study as a whole.

2

AMERICAN RINGS AND
ENGLISH MULES

Before proceeding to a detailed analysis of alternative spinning techniques, it seems appropriate to interject a very brief description of the principal steps required to convert raw cotton into finished cloth.[1]

FROM RAW COTTON TO CLOTH: A DIGRESSION

Raw cotton arrives at the mill in bale form. The cotton seeds have been removed by a cotton gin, but there is generally a good deal of dirt mixed in with the fibers. The bale is normally picked apart by hand and is fed into a machine called a bale breaker. It is common practice to mix the cotton from several bales at this stage by putting in armfuls first from one bale and then from another. The purpose of this is to get the mixture of cottons that is necessary to achieve the desired product.

This chapter is a revised and considerably expanded version of my paper "American Rings and English Mules: The Role of Economic Rationality," *Quarterly Journal of Economics,* February 1969.

[1] For a somewhat more detailed account, see L. H. C. Tippett, *A Portrait of the Lancashire Cotton Textile Industry,* chap. 3; or Robson, *The Cotton Industry in Britain,* chap. 1.

It is possible, however, to delay the mixing until the immediately succeeding steps.

The bale breaker, as well as the succeeding machines—the opener, the scutcher, and the card—work on the general principle of pulling the cotton through sets of spikes. Some of these spikes are set in place and some are attached to revolving cylinders. The principal effects of passing the cotton through these machines are to open the cotton fibers, to allow the dirt to fall out, and to remove extremely short and broken fibers.

When the cotton emerges from the scutcher, it is called a lap. A lap can best be visualized as a very wide, very thick, and very loose blanket. This lap is fed into a card, which continues the process of cleaning and separating the fibers. In addition, the card stretches the lap in a ratio of about 100 to 1, making it more compact. The result is called a card sliver.

This card sliver is put into a drawing frame. The drawing frame consists simply of sets of rollers (or cylinders) moving at different speeds. As the sliver passes through the machine, it is stretched, thereby straightening the cotton fibers and causing them to lie parallel to each other. In order to increase the uniformity of the sliver, a given drawing frame is simultaneously fed a number of card slivers. By setting the relative speeds of the first and last sets of rollers equal to the number of card slivers being fed into the machine, the resulting product (a draw frame sliver) will be of the same thickness as the original card slivers. A different speed ratio will, of course, result in a different thickness. Repeating the process of drawing results in a more uniform thickness and in straighter and more parallel fibers.

At this point, it is possible to spin the cotton directly. The usual procedure, however, is and long has been to convert it into roving before spinning. This is done on a speed frame, which continues the attenuating process and, in addition, imparts a small amount of twist to the cotton.

The next step is spinning. In this process, the roving (or draw frame sliver) is further attenuated and a great deal of twist is imparted. The degree of stretching and the amount of twist are, of course, two of the principal determinants of the type of yarn that results.

This yarn may be bleached and dyed before further processing. This is usually done with yarn destined for knitting. Most yarn that is to be woven into cloth is not so treated at this stage, however. Instead, it is directly prepared for the loom. The first step in this process is to rewind the yarn. At this stage, it is possible to remove inferior sections of yarn.

After rewinding, the treatment of the yarn differs, depending on whether it is to be used as warp or woof (filling) in weaving. The yarn to be used as woof is wound onto small bobbins that will fit into the loom shuttles. The warp yarn (which is going to be stretched in the loom) is wound onto loom beams and sizing is applied to protect it from the friction and pulling to which it will be subjected during weaving. This process uses machines called beamers, tapers, and slashers.

In the loom, the warp is stretched out in parallel and the woof is introduced between the strands of warp by moving the shuttle back and forth through the warp. The result of this process (assuming that unbleached yarn is used) is called gray cloth. Some of this cloth may be sold directly to consumers (e.g., the North Chinese peasants have used it to make their familiar padded winter clothing), but most is subjected to further processing (or finishing). This may include bleaching, dyeing, or some form of printing.

Of these processes, spinning and weaving are by far the most important. The United States Tariff Board in its 1912 report on the cotton textile industry found that in Great Britain, in a new set of mills converting raw cotton into gray cloth, 63.7% (by value) of the required textile machinery consisted either of looms or spinning frames. Even more striking is the fact that 74.7% (by number) of the total labor force required to operate these mills was directly involved in operating the spinning and weaving equipment. This last percentage is even higher if general maintenance and supervisory personnel are excluded from the total.[2] Roughly speaking, spinning and weaving thus account for two-thirds of the processing required to make gray cloth out of raw cotton.[3] This dominance, together

---

[2] United States Congress, House of Representatives, United States Tariff Board, *Cotton Manufactures*, pp. 808–14 (hereacter cited as "U.S. Tariff Board").

[3] The mill in question used plain power looms. Had automatic looms been used

with the fact that the most important technical innovations in the cotton industry during the period being studied occurred in spinning and weaving, justify the great stress I put on these particular processes.

SPINNING TECHNIQUES

Since the second half of the ninetheenth century, two different types of machines have been widely used to spin cotton yarn.[4] These are the mule—or more properly, the self-acting mule—and the ring (see Figure 1). The mule was invented by Samuel Crompton in 1779. It was given the name *mule* because it combines the spinning-with-rollers principle of Richard Arkwright's water frame with the moving carriage of James Hargreave's spinning jenny.

The mule consists of a bank of rollers (or cylinders) that are fixed in place and a movable carriage on which the spindles are located. The drawing or stretching begins when the roving is passed through sets of rollers going at different speeds, just as they do in the card. More stretch is added by having the carriage move away from the bank of rollers. While the carriage is thus moving away from the rollers, the spindles on the carriage are rapidly revolving, thus imparting twist to the yarn. When the carriage has reached the end of its track, the spinning stops and the finished yarn is wound onto a bobbin as the carriage returns to its original position.

The mule was an almost instant success, even in its original hand-operated version. Its desirability became even greater after the invention of the self-acting mule by Richard Roberts in 1825. This new machine made the various actions of the mule automatic, thereby greatly increasing the number of mule spindles per operator. In addition, it reduced the level of skill necessary to operate the mule. In this new version, the mule

---

instead, the machinery percentage given above would have been somewhat larger, but the employment percentage would have been somewhat smaller.

[4] For a technical description of mule and ring spinning, see J. Jewkes and E. M. Gray, *Wages and Labor in the Lancashire Cotton Spinning Industry*, chap. 1; or J. E. Winterbottom, *Cotton Spinning Calculations and Yarn Costs*.

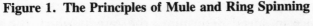

Figure 1. The Principles of Mule and Ring Spinning

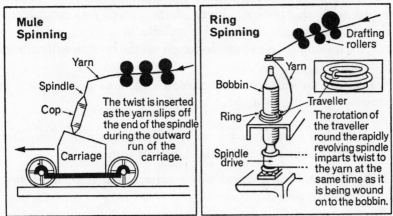

SOURCE: Tippett, *A Portrait of the Lancashire Textile Industry*, p. 61. Permission to reprint granted by Oxford University Press.

came to dominate world factory cotton spinning around the middle of the nineteenth century.[5]

The dominance of the (self-acting) mule was, however, soon challenged by the development of ring spinning. The ring is essentially an improved verion of the throsle which, in turn, is an improvement of Arkwright's water frame. After leaving the rollers, which have stretched it, the yarn goes to the spindle located directly below the rollers. Each spindle has a ring around its base and on each ring there is a not-quite-closed wire loop called a traveler. The ring itself is nothing more or less than a track for the traveler. The yarn passes through this traveler and is then attached to a bobbin which, in turn, is attached to the spindle. As the spindle, and the attached bobbin, turn (the ring remaining in place) the impetus of the yarn makes the traveler race around on the ring (its track). The rotation of the spindle imparts a twist to the yarn. The tension of the twisted yarn, however, puts drag on the traveler causing it

[5] Even in the United States the mule was more important than the ring before the Civil War (see Copeland, *The Cotton Manufacturing Industry of the United States*, p. 68).

to move slightly slower than the spindle and bobbin. This difference in speed determines the rate at which the yarn is wound onto the bobbin. Thus, if the traveler is completing 1% fewer rotations than is the spindle in a given period of time, then every turn of yarn collected on the bobbin will contain 99 twists.

Three major differences between ring and mule spinning immediately come to mind:

1. Mule spinning (even on the self-acting mule) requires more skill and strength than ring spinning.[6]

2. Mule spinning results in a softer yarn than does ring spinning.

3. Mule spinning is intermittent, whereas ring spinning is continuous.

THE CHALLENGE OF THE RINGS

Not only was ring spinning invented and perfected in the United States,[7] it was also in the United States that this technique first rose to economic prominence. As early as 1870, ring spinning had become the most important form of spinning in the United States. In that year, there were a total of 3.7 million ring spindles and 3.4 million mule spindles installed in the United States.[8] Since, for a given fineness (count)[9] of yarn, output per ring spindle exceeds output per mule spindle, a comparison of the numbers of the two types of spindles installed tends to understate the importance of ring spinning. By 1905, of the 23.1 million installed spindles in the United States, 17.9 million were rings.[10] This trend, of course, contin-

[6] The particular trick is to mend broken threads while the carriage is in the process of backing away from the rollers (see Tippett, *A Portrait of the Lancashire Textile Industry*, p. 62).

[7] It was invented in 1831 by a certain Mr. Jenks (see Copeland, *The Cotton Manufacturing Industry of the United States*, pp. 9, 66).

[8] Ibid., p. 70.

[9] The "count" of a yarn is defined as the number of hanks, at 840 yards each, per pound.

[10] Copeland, *The Cotton Manufacturing Industry of the United States*, p. 70.

ued; and by the outbreak of World War II, mule spinning was virtually extinct in the United States.

Ring spinning was also introduced into other parts of the world, but at a slower pace than in the United States. If modern cotton industries outside the United States are divided into three general groups—non-European (principally those in Japan, China, and India), continental European, and British— then the percentage of ring spindles installed at any given point in time decreased in the order listed above. That is, Great Britain, with the largest cotton industry in the world, was last among all important cotton industries in the introduction of ring spindles.[11] As late as 1913, there were 45.2 million mule spindles but only 10.4 million ring spindles in Great Britain.[12]

Although some contemporary observers, notably M. T. Copeland,[13] pointed out that Great Britain had certain special advantages in mule as opposed to ring spinning, the British lag in ring spinning has usually been taken as a sign of technological conservatism, not to say backwardness. The list of recent economic historians that are more or less critical of Britain's lag in ring spinning includes Rockwood Chin, Charles P. Kindleberger, Roland Gibson, A. L. Levine, A. E. Musson, and R. S. Sayers.[14]

This view has been reinforced by subsequent developments, in that ring spinning has proved indeed to be the wave of

[11] Robson, *The Cotton Industry in Britain*, p. 355; for other references, see chap. 4.

[12] Ibid.

[13] Copeland, *The Cotton Manufacturing Industry of the United States*, pp. 71–73.

[14] R. Chin, *Management, Industry, and Trade in Cotton Textiles*, p. 85; C. P. Kindleberger, "Foreign Trade and Economic Growth: Lessons from France and Britain, 1850–1913," p. 297, and *Economic Growth in France and Great Britain, 1850–1950*, p. 273; R. Gibson, *Cotton Textile Wages in the United States and Great Britain*, p. 76; A. L. Levine, *Industrial Retardation in Britain, 1880–1914*, p. 34; A. E. Musson, "The Great Depression in Britain, 1873–1896: A Reappraisal," p. 207; R. S. Sayers, *A History of Economic Change in England, 1880–1939*, p. 101.

An interesting recent opponent of this position is R. E. Tyson. Tyson, however, does nothing beyond summarizing the unfortunately rather general and qualitative argument made by Copeland in 1912 (see R. E. Tyson, "The Cotton Industry," in D. H. Aldcroft, ed., *The Development of British Industry and Foreign Competition, 1875–1914*, p. 122). Nevertheless, Tyson's argument (or rather, Copeland's) has been accepted by his editor, D. H. Aldcroft (ibid., p. 34).

the future and in that the British cotton textile industry has experienced a sharp decline ever since the end of World War I. Neither of these later trends, however, in any way proves that the British made a mistake, or were irrational, in not introducing more ring spindles before World War I. Under the conditions then prevailing with regard to factor costs, as well as the technical capabilities of the ring spindles then being built, the British may well have been acting rationally.

The question whether the difference in the ratio of rings to mules in Great Britain and the United States in some given year was justified by differing factor costs and market conditions is, however, extremely difficult to answer. Phrased in this form, the question presents several formidable obstacles to quantitative analysis. First of all, as will be discussed below, the relative efficiency of ring and mule spindles varied for different counts of yarn. Thus, a detailed knowledge of the counts of yarn spun in the United States and in Great Britain would be needed. Although it is generally presumed that Great Britain devoted a larger percentage of her spindles to high-quality yarn than did the United States,[15] no sufficiently detailed information is available for the pre–World War I period. Furthermore, installing rings when a new plant was built, or when old mules were physically worn out, was quite a different thing from throwing out technically well-functioning mules and replacing them with rings. Thus, the optimal mix of rings and mules depended not only on the distribution of counts spun but also on the past rate of expansion of the industry. The faster the recent rates of expansion had been, the more rings one would expect. The rate of expansion in earlier (pre-ring) years would also play a role, but not an easily quantifiable one, because it would influence the rate of physical obsolescence of previously installed mules. Finally, the situation is further complicated by differences in factor costs in the two countries. These differences mean that the profitablilty of replacing mules by rings on a given count differed in the two countries. Not only does this mean that the same count might sometimes rationally have been spun by different methods in the two countries,

[15] See, for example, Copeland, *The Cotton Manufacturing Industry of the United States*, p. 71.

but also that mules would be judged ready for the scrap heap at different ages in the two countries. There is, thus, no doubt that in the pre–World War I period it paid to keep old mules longer in Great Britain than in the United States. Any calculation of this effect on the optimal combination of rings and mules in the two counries would require a detailed knowledge of the distribution of mule spindles by age in the two countries, as well as a huge amount of information about the effect of age and obsolescence on the costs of mule spinning. In addition, of course, the unavailable information on the distribution of counts spun would be needed. Clearly these obstacles require that the original question be rephrased in a more convenient form.

Because it is clear that rings were considered more suitable for low- as opposed to high-count yarn, I have decided to concentrate my attention on the counts at which new investment generally shifted from mules to rings in each of the two countries. That is, the central question of this chapter will be: Can rational economic forces explain why American firms generally installed rings to spin all yarns up to count X while British firms shifted to the installation of mules at count Y, lower than X?

The years for which this question will be investigated is the period immediately preceeding World War I. This period has the advantage that a good deal of information is available for it. Unfortunately, some of the information on the technical characteristics of mules and rings needed for this analysis is only available for a later period. This later period is not a good one for the study as a whole, however, principally because of the chaotic state of the British cotton textile industry that has prevailed ever since the end of World War I. The extremely depressed conditions that have existed since then are clearly not conducive to a study of investment behavior and technological change.

It must be admitted, however, that the problem as I have rephrased it leaves something to be desired. It concentrates attention on "up-to-date" firms that are in fact installing new spindles, but says little about the possibility that there were more firms in Great Britain than in the United States that held on to uneconomical mule spindles past the time when they should have been replaced. (This problem, however, will at least implicitly be considered in chapter 3.) Another, although somewhat less important, problem is that there may have been more mules installed for counts below the "cutoff" point that is established for mule installations in Great Britain than was the case in the Unitd States.

ACTUAL OBSERVED INVESTMENT BEHAVIOR

The first problem of this analysis is to determine if there really were fairly sharp cutoff points between rings and mules when new spindles were being installed in the United States and Great Britain, respectively, and if so, at what counts these cutoff points occurred. In his excellent study of the American cotton textile industry published in 1912, Melvin Copeland reports, "Not much yarn finer than 40's, and very little higher than 60's is produced upon the ring-frame in Europe, whereas practically all warp yarn, even up to 120's, is spun upon that machine in America." [16]

This statement is well supported by other evidence available from the same period. The works by Uttley and Young are full of examples of high-quality yarn spun on rings in the United States.[17] Not only is this true with regard to warp, but it also seems to be the case for weft,[18] although the references to high-quality weft being spun on mules are somewhat more common than the same situation with regard to warp yarn. On the other hand, there are no references to any yarn below 40 being spun on mules.[19]

As for new installations, the U.S. Department of Commerce reports that, between 1900 and 1914, only 981,023 new mule

[16] Ibid., p. 301.

[17] T. W. Uttley, *Cotton Spinning and Manufacturing in the United States of America,* pp. 9, 11, 16, 22, 23, 29, 31, 32, 34, 49, 54, 56, 60; and T. M. Young, *The American Cotton Industry,* pp. 10, 16, 18, 19, 24, 35, 61, 68, 73, 86, 88, 97, 110.

[18] Warp, also known as twist, is the yarn that is stretched in the loom. Weft, also known as filling, is the yarn inserted into the warp by means of the shuttle. Warp has to be stronger than weft.

[19] See previous references in Uttley, *Cotton Spinning and Manufacturing in the United States of America;* and Young, *The American Cotton Industry.*

spindles were installed in the United States as opposed to 11,888,587 new ring spindles.[20] Further confirmation of the low number of new mule spindles being installed can be obtained from the U.S. *Census of Manufactures* for 1914, where it is stated that "the installation of these [mule] spindles has practically ceased."[21] It is also clear that the small number of mules still being put in were intended to make very-high-quality yarns. In fact, the 1905 *Census of Manufactures* concluded that the only reason any mules at all were being installed was that "there are some [high] qualities of yarn which cannot be made successfully by ring spinning."[22]

There is equally good evidence that there was little or no yarn of a count above the lower 40s spun with rings in Europe in general or in Great Britain in particular. Thus, the various available descriptions of ring spinning costs generally go up to, but not above, the middle 40s.[23] Perhaps the most important evidence that rings were indeed being installed in Great Britain for yarns up to the lower 40s but very seldom above that range comes from the Universal Wage List for Ring Spinning, which was adopted in 1912 and which covered virtually all British ring spinning.[24] Because the number of spindles tended by a spinner increased as the count of the yarn spun increased, the list was designed to give a lower piece rate per spindle as the count spun increased. This accommodation is made for counts up to and including 43, but then stops abruptly. This is true despite the fact that the tendency toward more and more spindles per spinner continued on past the 40s and that the adjustment would have created no great computational problems.[25] The only reasonable conclusion is that the list ends because there were virtually no spinners working on higher counts.

[20] United States Department of Commerce, Bureau of Foreign and Domestic Commerce, *The Cotton Spinning Machinery Industry*, Miscellaneous Series, No. 37, p. 77.

[21] United States Bureau of the Census, *Census of Manufactures, 1914*, 2:38.

[22] United States Bureau of the Census, *Census of Manufactures, 1905*, 3:42.

[23] See, for example, W. A. G. Clark, *Cotton Fabrics in Middle Europe*, Bureau of Manufactures, Special Agents Series, No. 24, p. 130.

[24] Jewkes and Gray, *Wages and Labor in the Lancashire Cotton Spinning Industry*, pp. 117, 128.

[25] Ibid., p. 121.

The evidence thus presented makes it clear that at least some rings were being installed for counts up to the lower 40s, but virtually none for counts above that. This is of little value, however, unless it can at least be shown that installations below 40 were not unusual occurrences. Ideally, it would be desirable to be able to answer exactly the questions raised above about the extent to which firms did not install rings for counts below the cutoff point (that is, below the vicinity of 40 to 43) and to what extent firms held on to economically obsolete mule-spinning equipment. Although it is not possible to answer these two questions definitely, I do believe there are enough data to show that in this period it was the general practice in Great Britain to install rings for the spinning of counts up to around 40 when new capacity was, in fact, being created.

Between 1907 and 1913, the number of installed mule spindles in Great Britain increased from 43.7 million to 45.2 million, and the number of ring spindles increased from approximately 8.3 million to 10.4 million.[26] The implications of this information depend largely on the distribution of counts being spun. Unfortunately, even a rough indication of yarn qualities spun cannot be made for any period before 1924. Information, however, is available for that and subsequent years. Of the total of 1,395 million pounds of yarn spun in 1924, 1,022 million pounds were of a count below 41, 314 million pounds between 41 and 80, 56 million pounds were between 81 and 120, and 3.6 million were above 120.[27] Combining this data with what appear to be reasonable assumptions about the distribution of yarn within the above categories[28] and taking account of the lower output per spindle achieved at higher

[26] The 1907 figure is based on extrapolation of exact figures on type of spindles received on about 80 percent of all spindles in the 1907 census of production. In all probability, this procedure gives a slight upward bias to the number of rings installed in 1907, thus biasing downward the number of new rings installed between 1907 and 1913. See British Census Office, *Census of Production, 1907,* 1:293. The source of the 1913 figures is Robson, *The Cotton Industry in Britain,* p. 355.

[27] Robson, *The Cotton Industry in Britain,* p. 343.

[28] It is assumed that the category up to 40s can be replaced with the single count of 20, and the succeeding categories can be replaced with the single counts 53, 93, and 140, respectively.

counts, the division of "mule equivalent"[29] spindles used to spin yarn above and below a count of 40 would be 65% and 35%, respectively.

If this spindle division is applied to the 1907–13 period, together with the assumptions that capacity grew at the same rate for all counts and that all new spindles designed for a count of 40 or below were rings, the result is that enough new rings were installed to replace about 15% of the mules that were being used for sub-40 yarn in 1907. Given the well-known physical endurance of the mule frames and the general prosperity of the British cotton textile industry during this period, such a rate of replacement seems very reasonable.

This calculation, however, has some serious limitations. First of all, the assumption made about the distribution of yarns within the count categories might be somewhat off the mark. An even more serious problem arises from the data themselves. The year 1924 was not in the period 1907–13, and it takes some pretty strong assumptions to switch data from one to the other. It is quite possible that the average count of yarn produced in 1907–13 was lower than the average count produced in 1924. I have no direct evidence on this. It might be noted, however, that in the years following 1924 there was almost certainly a reduction in the average count spun.[30]

This problem of a change in the average count spun raises yet another question. My calculation assumed that capacity was increasing at an equal rate for all counts. This, of course, need not have been the case. The average count spun may either have been increasing or decreasing, just as well as remaining constant. Any such change in the average count spun would naturally throw my calculations off the mark. Here again, little direct evidence is available. My own studies, however, have allowed me to compute a quality index for British cotton goods

[29] In accordance with the accepted practice of this period, a ring spindle is assumed to be the production equivalent of 1 1/3 mule spindles. As will be shown below, this is not strictly correct because the ratio of the two varies with the count spun. For purposes of this rough calculation, however, this assumption seems good enough.

[30] Robson, *The Cotton Industry in Britain*, p. 343.

(yarn and cloth) exports for this period. This index indicates that there was little or no change in the average quality of British cotton goods exported during the 1907–13 period.[31] During the years in question, exports amounted to over three-fourths of total British cotton goods production.[32]

One final problem with this calculation should also at least be mentioned. The question is, if rings were more profitable than mules at low counts, why were not the mules employed on low counts converted to higher counts, thus eliminating the need for new investment in mules to increase high-quality capacity, and replaced with new rings? The principal answer to this question is that a mule designed for low counts is not the same machine as a mule designed for high counts. In particular, low-count mules have longer "draws,"[33] making them inappropriate for high-count work.

This is not to say that there was no shifting of mules to higher counts when rings were introduced. Mules designed for counts at or just below 40 may well have been shifted up a bit. There is no reason, however, to expect this to have been happening in the 1907–13 period. The conditions that made it profitable to install rings up to at least a count of 40 had existed for some years before this period, and there was no reason to postpone such a shift until after 1907.

These limitations on the above calculations mean that it cannot be claimed that in the 1907–13 period virtually every new spindle installed to make yarn up to a count of 40 in Great Britain was a ring and that the mules being used for low counts were being depreciated at a relatively brisk rate. What can be maintained, however, is that a very large percentage of the spindles installed for counts up to 40 were rings and that virtually no rings were installed at counts above the low 40s.

[31] L. G. Sandberg, "Movements in the Quality of British Cotton Textile Exports," pp. 1–27.

[32] See the annual trade returns in the Trade and Navigation Accounts of the *British Parliamentary Papers*, and Robson, *The Cotton Industry in Britain*, Table 1.

[33] Jewkes and Gray, *Wages and Labor in the Lancashire Cotton Spinning Industry*, p. 5.

THE RELATIVE ADVANTAGES OF RINGS OR MULES
IN THE UNITED STATES AND GREAT BRITAIN

The purpose of this section is to examine the differences that existed in the benefits to be derived from replacing mules with rings in the United States and the benefits to be derived from doing so in Great Britain. The discussion will be divided into two parts, the first dealing with factor costs and the second with such problems as the role of labor unions and the technological interrelationships between ring spinning and automatic weaving.

Factor Costs

Labor Costs. The principal advantage of ring as opposed to mule spinning was that the former used unskilled or semiskilled female labor whereas the latter used highly skilled males. In addition, there were differences in the amounts of spinning, preparatory, and auxiliary labor[34] used in the two methods.

Good estimates of the spinning labor costs of the two methods of producing yarn in this period are available for both the United States and Great Britain in Copeland's book. Copeland presents a range of spindles per operator and a range of wages per operator.[35] I have focused attention on the high estimates for both the number of spindles tended and the weekly wage. In fact, it would not matter very much if I had used the lower estimates for both, or if I had chosen a middle position. I chose to use the upper limits because these figures are most likely to apply to the new equipment in which I am principally interested.[36]

[34] Preparatory and auxiliary labor principally carded and roved the cotton before it was spun and collected (doffed) and handled the yarn after spinning.

[35] Copeland, *The Cotton Textile Industry of the United States*, pp. 298–300.

[36] In the calculations below, I shall be implicitly assuming that the wage rates per hundred spindles per week that I calculated from Copeland's data are applicable to work of a count around 40. Fortunately, in mule spinning the number of spindles tended per worker and the pay per spindle tended is virtually independent of the count spun. This assumption is, therefore, automatically satisfied for mule spinning. The number of rings tended and the wage per ring spindle, however, clearly tend to decrease with increasing counts. Thus, some error may enter if

Taking account of the difference in ring spindle speed in the United States and Great Britain and allowing for the difference in productivity between ring and mule spindles at a count of around 40, the spinning labor cost for ring spinning turns out to have been about 50 cents per week, per hundred "mule equivalent"[37] spindles in both countries. For mule spinning, the cost was around $1.65 per hundred actual mule spindles per week in Great Britain and $2.15 in the United States. This in turn implies that, at a count of 40, ring-spinning labor cost per pound of yarn was about 1.6 cents lower in Great Britain and about 2.4 cents lower in the United States than the cost of mule-spinning labor.

Although rings generally required less actual spinning labor than did mules, rings did require a little bit more roving and doffing labor.[38] This difference, however, is a very small fraction of the difference in spinning labor, especially if measured in terms of wage payments, amounting to perhaps a mill (one-tenth of a cent) per pound of 40 yarn. Furthermore, it is by no means clear that there was any important difference in the cost of providing these services in the United States and in Great Britain. These costs can thus safely be ignored in analyzing the relative advantages of ring and mule spinning in the United States and Great Britain.

Capital. Mule and ring spinning appear to have been of almost exactly the same capital intensity per unit of output

---

my figures really apply to some count other than 40. In the case of Great Britain, the error can hardly be very large because I used the top of the scale in number of spindles tended and there was virtually no ring spinning done above 40. In the United States, however, ring spindles were used at higher counts, and I again took the top of the scale. In fact, however, not very much really high-quality yarn was spun in the United States by any method, and the testimony of contemporary observers indicates that the high number of spindles per operator that I used for the United States was reached at counts not far exceeding 40 (see Young, *The American Cotton Industry;* and Uttley, *Cotton Spinning and Manufacturing in the United States*). It is unthinkable that this error could have underestimated ring spinning costs in the United States by more than 10 or 15%, and it would take an error of the order of 100% to affect my conclusions.

[37] I have converted ring spindles into mule equivalents so that the cost comparisons can be based on equal quantities of output.

[38] Copeland, *The Cotton Manufacturing Industry of the United States,* p. 69; and Winterbottom, *Cotton Spinning Calculations and Yarn Costs,* p. 213. Winterbottom was lecturer in cotton spinning at the Municipal School of Technology in Manchester during the period covered in this study.

in the production of yarns of a count around 40.[39] Below this count, mules tended to be more capital intensive; and above it, rings were more capital intensive. This rough equality around 40 was the result of higher machinery costs for ring spinning, including some extra roving equipment, offset by the space-saving achieved in ring spinning.[40] In view of this, it is difficult to believe that any difference in interest rates could have had much to do with America's greater propensity to install rings. Certainly, if rings stopped being profitable in Great Britain at a count of 40, no reasonable change in the interest rate could have made them profitable.

It does seem apparent, however, that mule-spinning machinery was more expensive relative to ring-spinning machinery in the United States than in Great Britain. Evidence for this comes primarily from the fact that between 1900 and 1914, 77.6% of all new mule spindles installed in the United States were imported from Great Britain, but only small quantities of other types of cotton textile machinery were imported.[41] This, of course, was not due to any inherent inefficiency in mule manufacturing in the United States, but rather to the fact that so few mules were being installed that it was not profitable for American producers to make mule-spinning frames.[42] It is difficult to tell how much of a difference there was in the relative prices of the two types of machinery, but this must have given some further impetus to ring spinning in the United States. On the other hand, it should be remembered that ring spinning tended to save capital in the form of buildings and required extra capital for machinery. In view of the fact that construction was relatively cheaper than machinery in the United States as compared with Great Britain,[43] this would tend to favor the use of the "construction intensive" mule process in the United States.

Fuel and lubricants. Here again, the costs appear to be virtually

[39] Winterbottom, *Cotton Spinning Calculations and Yarn Costs*, pp. 213, 272, 273.

[40] Ibid.

[41] *The Cotton Spinning Machinery Industry*, Table 44, p. 77.

[42] Because America was a high-cost, protected producer of textile machinery, there was no hope of capturing an export market for mule frames.

[43] Young, *The American Cotton Industry*, p. 9.

the same for the two methods. Sources can be found that disagree about which method saved fuel.[44] In any case, the difference was very small when expressed in terms of cents per pound of yarn. This means, of course, that any effect of different fuel prices in the two countries on the choice of spinning technique must have been infinitesimal.

Transportation. Transportation is treated as an input because the yarn had to be moved before it could be woven into cloth. The difference in transportation costs between rings and mules arises because mule yarn was spun either on a bare spindle or on a paper tube, whereas ring yarn had to be wound on a heavy wooden bobbin. Fortunately, the warp yarn could be rewound. The weft, however, had to be shipped on the bobbin.[45] Copeland quotes with approval an estimate that the paper tubes added only 10% to the freight costs, whereas the wooden bobbins added 200%. Furthermore, the bobbin had to be returned.[46]

The reason this difference in transportation costs affected Great Britain and the United States differently is that the American industry was vertically integrated whereas the British industry was not. Thus, much more yarn transportation was required in Great Britain than in the United States. In addition, Britain had a large export trade in yarn.

Fortunately, a good estimate can be made of the level of these extra transportation costs. Reliable information is available on the cost of shipping yarn in Lancashire in 1907 over the average distance yarn was in fact shipped.[47] If the 200% cost increase figure is used together with an allowance for the extra cost of returning the wooden bobbins, it appears that shipping ring weft within Lancashire cost about three mills more per pound of yarn than shipping mule weft. This cost differential, of course, did not apply to yarn produced in integrated plants.

[44] Winterbottom, *Cotton Spinning Calculations and Yarn Costs*, pp. 272, 273; and W. A. G. Clark, *Cotton Textile Trade in the Turkish Empire, Greece, and Italy*, Bureau of Manufactures, Special Agents Report No. 18, pp. 89, 90.

[45] Copeland, *The Cotton Manufacturing Industry of the United States*, pp. 69, 72.

[46] Ibid., p. 69.

[47] W. Whittam, *Report on England's Cotton Industry*, Bureau of Manufactures, Special Agents Report No. 15, p. 32.

It is impossible to give a single cost estimate for exports, since it depended on the destination of the yarn. This extra cost of exporting ring rather than mule weft, however, could clearly be very high or even prohibitive. Nevertheless, the effect of this cost differential is severely limited by the fact that in this period only 10 to 15% of total British yarn production was being exported.[48] This means that no more than 5 to 8% of all the yarn produced was weft for export. Since there were many more mules working at all counts than were needed to produce this percentage, there was probably little effect on investment behavior. Presumably, the export transportation disadvantage of ring weft resulted mainly in the concentration of the production of sub-40 weft for export on mules installed in the pre-ring period.

Other Factors Affecting the Choice of Spinning Method

Labor Unions. The literature on the history of the American cotton textile industry is full of statements to the effect that the disruptive and belligerent attitude of the American mule spinners' unions was a major factor in encouraging the shift to ring spinning. Thus, it is reported that it was after the strike of January 1898 (led by the mule spinners) that the treasurer of the highly efficient and well-managed Pepperell Manufacturing Company, of Biddeford, Maine, "made plans to get rid of all the mule frames eventually and to put in ring frames."[49] Earlier, the cotton manufacturers of Fall River, Massachusetts, had been "particularly anxious to introduce ring spindles" as a result of the strikes of 1870 and 1875.[50] A more general comment to the same effect appears in the 1905 *Census of Manufactures:*

But there are reasons, not unconnected with the labor problem, which render manufacturers desirous of using frames [i.e.,

[48] See Robson, *The Cotton Industry in Britain,* p. 333.

[49] E. H. Knowlton, *Pepperell's Progress,* p. 171.

[50] R. Smith, *The Cotton Textile Industry of Fall River, Massachusetts,* p. 100. See also R. K. Lamb, "The Development of Entreneurship in Fall River, 1813–1859," p. XII–8.

rings] rather than mules whenever it is [technically] practical to do so.[51]

These observations must, however, be viewed with at least some reservations. In all cases there were other good reasons for introducing rings. Furthermore, the manufacturers had every interest in making the workers fear that aggressive union action would result in technological unemployment. Nevertheless, there can be no doubt that American manufactures had a strong aversion to unions and that the mule spinners were probably the most efficient and powerful cotton textile union, at least until the absolute number of installed mule spindles started to decline around 1900. It is also clear that the mule spinners union tended to encourage at least temporary organization among the other workers and that it was largely responsible for many strikes.[52] Thus, the desire to break the power of the union by replacing the obstreperous mule spinners with docile girl spinners probably did have at least some effect in encouraging the adoption of ring spinning in the United States.

In the case of Great Britain, there was also a sharp contrast between the powerful and well-organized mule spinners and the weakly organized ring spinners.[53] The British employers, however, appear to have been better adjusted to the fact of having to face unions than were American employers. The British mule spinners' union was far from the only strong British cotton union.[54] Even more important, the British mule spinners were mainly dedicated simply to raising their own wages. To the extent that they succeeded in this endeavor, they may, of course, have helped the cause of ring spinning; but any such effect has already been considered in the section on relative wages.

Relation of ring yarn to automatic looms. The period under discussion in this paper was also a period during which large

[51] *Census of Manufactures, 1905,* 3:42.

[52] Knowlton, *Pepperell's Progress,* pp. 170–71; and Smith, *The Cotton Textile Industry of Fall River, Massachusetts,* p. 100.

[53] See H. A. Turner, *Trade Union Growth, Structure, and Policy,* p. 143.

[54] E.g., Copeland, *The Cotton Manufacturing Industry of the United States,* pp. 306–8, 291–92.

numbers of automatic looms were installed in the United States. Automatic looms, however—or at least these automatic looms— required the greater strength of ring as opposed to mule yarn.[55] This complementarity between ring spinning and automatic weaving meant that the existence of ring spinning made the introduction of automatic looms more appealing and, similarly, plans to install automatic looms depended on the availability of ring spinning.[56] There may have been, therefore, some American manufacturers for whom a desire to introduce automatic looms made ring spinning relatively more advantageous as compared with mule spinning than would otherwise have been the case. For the most part, however, ring spinning clearly preceded automatic weaving.[57] With regard to Great Britain, this interdependence between ring spinning and automatic looms can be ignored for purposes of this paper because automatic looms did not begin to appear there in significant numbers until the 1930s.[58]

The Role of Cotton Prices

This discussion of factor costs and other considerations has shown that in virtually every category the advantage of replacing mules by rings was greater in the United States than in Great Britain. This situation combined with the generally accepted fact, to be discussed in greater detail below, that the relative advantage of ring as opposed to mule spinning declined as the count spun increased, generally accords well with the observed fact that Great Britain stopped installing rings at a count of about 40, but the United States continued installing rings at much higher counts. It says very little, however, about whether the British cutoff line logically should have been drawn exactly where it was drawn. Some information on this problem can be obtained from the structure of cotton prices.

[55] I. Feller, "The Draper Loom in New England Textiles, 1894–1914: A Study of Diffusion of an Innovation," p. 331.

[56] Ibid., p. 333.

[57] See Copeland, *The Cotton Manufacturing Industry of the United States*, pp. 70, 87; and Robson, *The Cotton Industry in Britain*, p. 355.

[58] In 1937, only 3% of all British cotton looms were automatic (Robson, *The Cotton Industry in Britain*, p. 210).

Cotton prices played an important role in the choice of spinning technique because of the technological fact that, for a given count of yarn, ring spinning required a longer cotton staple than did mule spinning. Figure 2 is designed to show what lengths of fiber were "suitable" for different counts.[59] Clearly, this chart is not exact for all conditions, nor is the lower limit for fiber length as exactly defined in fact as it is in the diagram.[60] Thus, for example, humidity can affect the staple length needed. More important, to some limited extent lack of staple length can be compensated for by lowering the spindle speed, increasing the skill and/or the quantity of the labor used, and by accepting a lower-quality product.[61] All of these alternatives involve increased costs, however, and can only increase the maximum count for a given staple length by a limited amount. Thus, Figure 2 certainly represents a useful approximation of staple length requirements.

Unfortunately, the compiler of the information used to produce Figure 2 considered only ring twist, mule twist, and mule weft; he neglected to include ring weft. This could be interpreted to mean that ring weft required the same staple length as ring twist. This was almost certainly not true, however. Most observers were of the opinion that, for a given count, a shorter staple could be used to produce weft than was needed for twist, both on mules and rings.[62] Indeed, the evidence seems to indicate that the difference in length was pretty much the same regardless of the spinning method used.[63] If this is correct, it means that the mule twist requirements would be the same as the ring weft requirements. I will, therefore, treat the difference between the staple length needed for mule

[59] Winterbottom, *Cotton Spinning Calculations and Yarn Costs*, p. 236.

[60] In fact, Figure 2 is based on the following simplified equations:
$$\text{Length of staple in inches, for ring twist} = 0.35 \sqrt[3]{\text{count}}.$$
$$\text{Length of staple in inches, for mule twist} = 0.325 \sqrt[3]{\text{count}}.$$
$$\text{Length of staple in inches, for mule weft} = 0.30 \sqrt[3]{\text{count}}.$$
See Winterbottom, *Cotton Spinning Calculations and Yarn Costs*, p. 236.

[61] The principal reason for needing longer staple on rings than on mules was that the former put more strain on the yarn, thus increasing breakages (see Copeland, *The Cotton Manufacturing Industry of the United States*, p. 68).

[62] P. H. Nystrom, *Textiles*, pp. 71–72.

[63] Ibid.

Figure 2. Cotton Staple Lengths "Suitable" for the Spinning of Various Yarns

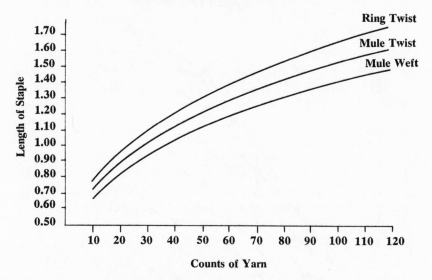

Source: Winterbottom, *Cotton Spinning Calculations and Yarn Costs,* p. 235.

twist and mule weft as representing the difference between ring weft and mule weft.

This difference in the required staple length enters as a factor in the choice of spinning technique because the price of cotton generally increased as its staple length did. This is shown in Figure 3, which contains cotton prices in New Orleans on 1 April 1913. This year and date were deliberately chosen as representing a season and period when the market was "normal."[64] In particular, the compiler of these data reports that the big jump in price occurring between staple lengths

---

[64] Winterbottom, *Cotton Spinning Calculations and Yarn Costs,* p. 234. It would have been better, of course, had this data referred to Liverpool prices. Because cotton brokerage was a competitive business (see for example, G. C. Allen, *British Industries and Their Organization,* pp. 204–5), however, the price difference between New Orleans would only reflect transport and Liverpool handling costs. The only reasonable differences in these costs would be higher insurance and inventory costs (interest) on the more expensive types. This would tend to slightly *increase the absolute* price differentials as the cotton was moved from New Orleans to Liverpool.

**Figure 3. Prices of Various Cottons by Quality
and Staple Length, New Orleans,
1 April 1973**

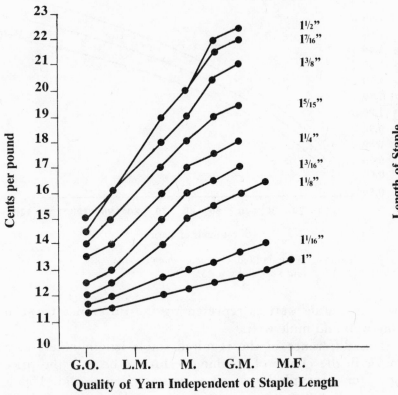

SOURCE: Winterbottom, *Cotton Spinning Calculations and Yarn
Costs,* p. 234.

of 1 1/6 inches and 1 1/8 inches was "common at all times."[65]
The exact size of the price-jumps between different staple
lengths must have varied somewhat, depending on harvest
conditions as well as peculiarities of final demand for cotton
products; but Figure 3 can certainly be taken as representative
of the period just preceding World War I.

Figure 3 does not include the very longest staple cottons.

[65] Ibid.

It should thus be added that at the very top of the scale the jump was from cotton of about 1 3/4 inches to about 2 inches, with virtually nothing in between, and an increase in price amounting to around 5 or 6 cents per pound at July 1914 prices.[66]

Combining Figures 2 and 3, it is possible to compute the differential cotton cost in spinning with rings as opposed to mules. A literal application of the technical information in Figure 2 results in Figure 4 for ring twist versus mule twist and Figure 5 for ring weft versus mule weft.

It must be noted that the results obtained above are based on the price differentials existing for cotton of a quality, independent of staple length, listed as "medium" or better. For cotton of a lower quality, the differentials shown in Figures 4 and 5 would have been somewhat smaller. In all probability, however, only limited amounts of poor-quality cotton were used for yarns finer than 40. There seems to be little point to using such poor material for such fine yarn and cloth. Indeed, this lack of demand probably is the reason why the staple price differential on poor cottons was so small. Nevertheless, it may well be that this small differential on poor cottons has something to do with those few rings that were used to spin yarns above 40 in Great Britain and in Continental Europe.

It is clear that Figure 2, and therefore Figures 4 and 5, are primarily based on technological rather than economic considerations. Since cotton prices were not quoted continuously by length, but by steps of 1/16 inch, rational producers would be prepared to accept somewhat higher costs in order to avoid the next step on the staple progression. Rather than immediately going to the longer staple when the count they were spinning required it if they were to continue with the exact production methods used at a slightly lower count, they would try to keep on using the lower staple by altering their production methods somewhat. They would presumably keep doing this for higher and higher counts until the extra cost of these production changes equaled the cost of using the more expensive longer-staple cotton with the more efficient, regular production meth-

[66] J. A. Todd, *The World's Cotton Crops*, p. 17.

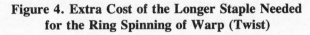

**Figure 4. Extra Cost of the Longer Staple Needed
for the Ring Spinning of Warp (Twist)**

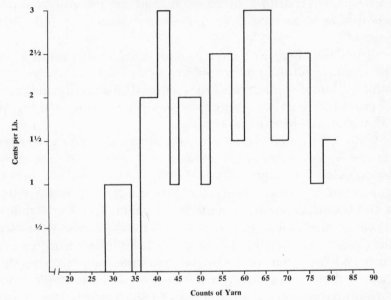

od. That is, they would substitute other inputs for fiber length until it became more economical to raise the fiber length. Another possibility might be to mix cottons of different staple lengths.

This possibility of using a shorter staple than was technologically ideal means that the cost differential that occurs at a count of 28 in Figure 4 might indeed have started to appear at that count, but it would have been the extra cost of *not* using 1 1/16-inch cotton on rings. Only once the cost of *not* using 1 1/16-inch cotton equaled the difference in cost between 1- and 1 1/16-inch cotton would the producer switch. This means that the cost differential would only reach the one cent per pound figure, which occurs immediately at a count of 28 in Figure 4, at some higher count. The next step in staple length, from 1 1/16 inch to 1 1/8 inch, would be delayed even longer, both when using rings and when using mules, because it involved an even larger increase in cotton

**Figure 5. Extra Cost of the Longer Staple Needed
for the Ring Spinning of Weft**

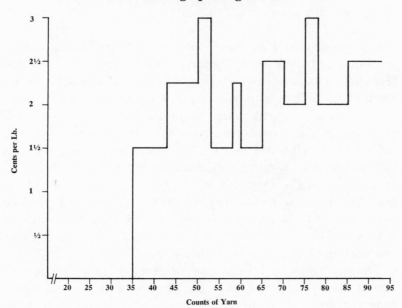

price. The possible mixing of different cottons would give similar results.

It is thus clear that diagrams of the extra cost imposed on ring spinning because of the need for a longer staple would in fact differ somewhat from Figures 4 and 5. The following differences would certainly be involved:

1. The cost differences would still start at approximately the same counts, but they would rise gradually, not perpendicularly.

2. The peaks on the diagrams would be pushed out to somewhat higher counts. This would be particularly true of the two-cent and three-cent peaks. This, of course, is because these peaks depend on a change-over from 1 1/16- to 1 1/8-inch cotton, the step producers rationally must have wanted to delay the most.

3. Generally speaking, the peaks will be lowered and the troughs raised. Thus, the diagrams would generally be smoothed out.

It is possible to draw some conclusions of relevance to this analysis from these rather general comments. First, the differential in cotton costs between rings and mules for warp yarn probably starts to appear at a count of about 28 and then increases to a peak somewhat below three cents per pound, probably in the vicinity of 45 to 50. In all probability, the difference reaches two cents in the low 40s. Second, the cost differential does not drop significantly below two cents again, at least not in the range shown in Figure 4. As for weft, the cost differential starts at about a count of 35 and rises to more than two cents in the 50s. It probably reaches two cents in the upper 40s. The differential then stays at least as high as one and one-half cents for higher counts.

The discussion so far has only dealt with counts below 100. This is the area relevant for Great Britain. In the United States, however, the only count range where mules appear to have been installed was above 100. The question thus arises as to whether cotton price differentials can explain at least the partial return to mules at very high counts.

On the whole, it can be expected that price differentials of two or even three cents continued out well beyond a count of 90. This continued gap resulted from the need to resort to Egyptian and "regular" Sea Island cotton for ring twist in the 80 to 100 range.[67] Above that range, however, it eventually became necessary to use "Best Sea Island" cotton. In view of the very large difference in the count that could be spun by the two methods at these high counts,[68] the differential must at some point have been between using Best Sea Island on rings or distinctly inferior types of cotton on mules. The cost differential can be estimated to be five or six cents per pound and sometimes even more. Once the count is high enough, however, even the mule would require Best Sea Island. After

[67] Ibid.
[68] Ibid.; and Winterbottom, *Cotton Spinning Calculations and Yarn Costs*, p. 52.

this point, the cost differential would be very much reduced, at least if the ring was physically capable of spinning such extremely fine yarn. This evidence appears to be consistent with rational manufacturers installing both mules and rings for very high counts.

Relative Factor Costs as a Function of Counts Spun

I have repeatedly stated that expert opinion in the period being studied unanimously held that ring spinning was relatively less suited to high than to low counts. It is now necessary to look at this proposition in more detail. Changes in the relative advantage of ring and mule spinning as the count increases can be expected to result from changes in the relative cost of the raw material and other inputs on the one hand and the quality of the product on the other hand.

Input Costs. In the previous section, the relative costs imposed by the cotton needed for ring and mule spinning were studied as a function of the count of the yarn spun. It appears that this cost difference did increase with the count, at least in moving from low to medium and high counts.

The other important inputs to be examined are labor and capital. It is quite clear from all contemporary evidence that labor input per pound of yarn increased faster on rings than on mules as the count increased. Even with a constant capital/labor ratio, this would also imply that the capital cost of ring spinning increased faster than that of mule spinning. In fact, however, the capital/labor ratio increased faster in ring than in mule spinning.[69] In ring, unlike mule, spinning, the number of spindles per operative increased as the count increased. The difference in capital costs thus increased even faster than implied by the changing ratio of spinning labor input.

Before jumping to the conclusion that this evidence proves that the cost of ring spinning increased faster than the cost of mule spinning, it must be remembered that mule spinners

---

[69] Jewkes and Gray, *Wages and Labor in the Lancashire Cotton Spinning Industry,* p. 121.

were more expensive than ring spinners. Thus, an equal percentage increase in the number of spinners' hours per pound of yarn would increase the saving per pound of yarn to be derived from using rings rather than mules.

Although a good deal of vague information on the relationship between the count of yarn spun and labor input is available for the pre–World War I period, careful studies of this relationship were only carried out in a later period. Two such studies, one based on interwar conditions and one based on 1949 conditions, are available.[70] Happily, the two studies present almost identical results with regard to the relationship of output per man-hour in spinning and the count of yarn spun. I therefore used the results of these studies to calculate cost differentials.

It is, of course, unfortunate that these studies do not refer to the exact period under study. Encouragement, however, can be taken from the fact that no noticeable change occurred between the 1930s and 1949. More important, virtually all the mules studied, and the great majority of the rings, were in fact installed before World War I. If there is any bias in using these past period studies, it is probably in underestimating the labor required on high-count rings.[71]

In addition to an estimate of output per man-hour, I also needed an estimate of changes in the spindles-per-man ratio in ring spinning. I obtained an estimate of this from the structure of piece rates in the British Universal Ring Spinning List of 1912.[72] This structure was specifically designed to reflect the fact that spinners working on higher counts were able to tend more spindles. On the basis of this information, I calculated the saving per pound of yarn in spinning labor and capital charges that resulted at various counts from using rings instead of mules. Assuming a waste rate of 5 to 10%, the saving per pound of cotton used would be 5 to 10% less than the results shown in Table 3.

[70] See British Ministry of Production, *Report of the Cotton Textile Mission to the United States of America*, and Productivity Team, *Cotton Spinning*.

[71] Such a bias might be expected because technical change on the ring generally is credited with making it effective at higher and higher counts.

[72] Jewkes and Gray, *Wages and Labor in the Lancashire Cotton Spinning Industry*, p. 121.

TABLE 3

DIFFERENCE IN LABOR AND CAPITAL COSTS

(in U.S. cents)

	Count								
	40	50	60	70	80	90	100	110	120
Great Britain	1.6	1.7	1.8	1.8	1.8	1.6	1.5	1.2	0.8
United States	2.4	2.6	2.9	2.9	3.0	3.0	2.9	2.7	2.3

NOTE. This calculation is based on the assumption that the capital costs of mules and rings were the same at a count of 40. Account has been taken of the somewhat greater speed of rings in the United States as compared with Great Britain. The generally accepted figure of 10% for loss, depreciation, and upkeep of machinery (see Winterbottom, *Cotton Spinning Calculations and Yarn Costs*, p. 271) is used. In addition, the interest cost of the money invested is set at 10%. While the cost differential at a count of 40 is independent of these percentages, the cost differentials at higher counts would be higher if lower interest rates were used and lower at higher interest rates.

There is some reason to believe that the rate of growth of the capital differential is underestimated. This bias results because high-count mules have shorter "draws" than do low-count mules and, therefore, occupy less space. This is not the case with rings.

Quality Differentials

There remains the question of the quality of ring versus mule yarn. There is a great deal of talk, especially in British writings, concerning the superior quality of mule yarn. Clearly, however, British comments on this subject are of questionable value. After all, one can be counted on to claim superiority for the product one concentrates on. I have also been unable to find any data that show a price differential between yarns of the same count, made of cotton of the same quality (here defined to exclude staple length), differing only in the method of production.

Nevertheless, there do seem to have been some differences between the two types of yarn. Thus, Copeland, an American, remarks: "Mule yarn, however, is superior . . . ," and "the harder ring-spun yarn is better adapted for warp than for weft."[73]

My general conclusion in this matter is that mule yarn probably did have some superior qualities. It is not clear whether this advantage became greater in a technical sense as the count increased. What is clear, however, is that the *importance* of this difference increased with the count. For the low-quality cloth usually made with low-count yarns, this minor difference

[73] Copeland, *The Cotton Manufacturing Industry of the United States*, p. 68.

in the yarn probably did not matter much. As the quality of the cloth increased with the count, however, differences in the yarn undoubtedly took on added importance. Quality differences thus probably did make the ring somewhat less well adapted to high than low counts as well as more suited to warp than weft. This difference in suitability for warp and weft probably played a role in what appears to have been the greater staying power of old American mules in weft as opposed to warp spinning.

COSTS AND BENEFITS

Having estimated the various costs and benefits involved in choosing between mules and rings, we may now evaluate the results.

Taking into account all these different costs (including labor, fuel, transportation, and capital) with the single exception of cotton, it seems that in Great Britain the saving per pound of cotton spun on rings rather than mules was about 1.5 cents for warp and 1.2 cents for weft at a count of 40. This saving rose to about 1.7 and 1.4 cents respectively at a count of around 70 and then declined slightly. On the other hand, the increase in costs due to the longer staple required by ring as opposed to mule spinning for twist (i.e., warp) rose from zero at counts below 28 to about 2 cents around 40. It then remained at that level. For weft, the differential probably reached 2 cents around 50. It thus appears that in Great Britain rings were preferable for warp production up to a count perhaps of a little below 40, but for weft they were probably to be preferred even for counts in the low 40s. In cases where the spinner contemplated using low-quality cotton, rings may have been better even at slightly higher counts. It does not appear that rings ever became profitable again at higher counts. This conclusion is reinforced by the fact that a growing effective quality differential probably worked against ring yarn at higher counts.

When these results are compared with the actual behavior of British manufacturers, they appear to have behaved in a rational manner. At the very least, these results should throw the burden of proof onto those who maintain that the British were irrational in their choice between rings and mules.

In the case of the United States, the cost advantage per pound of yarn was over 2 cents at a count of 40 and then rose to around 3 cents. In view of these results, it is understandable that ring spinning was used for much higher counts in the United States than in Great Britain. At the same time, the cost differential is down to 2.3 cents per pound at a count of 120 and heading lower. In view of this fact and the high price differentials encountered for very long staple cotton, it is also not surprising that some mules were being installed to spin very fine yarn. Indeed, my reaction is that surprisingly few new mules were installed in the United States. Although the quantitative data are not strong enough to prove the point, I suspect there may have been some substance to the many comments by contemporary observers that employer dislike of unions caused them to avoid mule spinning.

Having completed this study of the choice of spinning technique by British and American manufacturers, I made a simplified analysis of French and German behavior. This latter analysis was based on the data concerning spinning wages and the number of spindles tended given by Copeland for France and Germany.[74] In addition, I assumed that the relation between the quantity of labor and capital used and the count being spun that applied to Great Britain also applied to France and Germany. On this basis, I computed the difference in labor and capital costs per pound of yarn spun on rings rather than mules for France and Germany. The results of this calculation (see Table 4) indicate that French and German manufacturers should have stopped installing rings at a count very slightly below the British cutoff point.[75]

---

[74] Ibid., pp. 299–300.

[75] This difference is due almost entirely to the fact that German and French mule spinners received somewhat lower wages per hundred spindles than did the British mule spinners. Copeland himself, however, reports that the French and German mule spinners, unlike the French and German ring spinners, were less skilled than their British counterparts (ibid., pp. 300–301). He thus feels that the German and French spinners would not have earned any more in England than at home. This, in turn, implies that British mule-spinning wages were not really higher per unit of output. If this is the case, then French and German

TABLE 4

DIFFERENCE IN LABOR AND CAPITAL COSTS

(in U.S. cents)

	Count								
	40	50	60	70	80	90	100	110	120
France	1.3	1.3	1.3	1.2	1.1	.8	.5	.1	−.3
Germany	1.2	1.2	1.2	1.1	1.0	.7	.3	0	−.5

How does this compare with actual behavior? The information available is not good enough to detect the kind of very minor deviation from English behavior that my results appear to call for. The general conclusion of the literature is that the Continental countries resembled England in that they installed very few rings for counts above the mid-40s.[76] Furthermore, the fact that, by 1913, 54% of all German spindles and 46% of all French spindles were rings indicates that, at the very least, a very large percentage of the spindles installed for counts below 40 must have been rings.[77]

These results may be taken as at least prima facie evidence that German and French cotton manufacturers were also rational in their choices of spinning techniques. Perhaps more important, it increases the confidence that can be put into the analysis as a whole. Clearly, it would have been very strange if British and American manufacturers were found to be rational, but French and German manufacturers were not.

---

cotton manufacturers were in the same position as their British brethren when it came to choosing between spinning techniques.

[76] See, for example, Copeland, *The Cotton Manufacturing Industry of the United States*, p. 301.

[77] Robson, *The Cotton Industry in Britain*, p. 355. The higher percentage of rings in Germany and France than in Great Britain seems very reasonable on the basis of the higher-quality goods that were produced in Great Britain and the higher rates of growth in spinning capacity that France and Germany had experienced in the period since the large-scale introduction of rings into Europe had begun.

3

RINGS AND MULES: PART TWO

Because our figures show that low-count rings were a better new investment than low-count mules in Great Britain, the question naturally arises as to whether they were so much better that well-functioning sub-40 mules should have been junked and replaced with rings. The standard way of phrasing this decision problem is to say that if the total cost of the new method is less than the variable cost of the old method, then the old method should be thrown out.[1] Any calculation of total costs, however, includes some essentially arbitrary allowance for depreciation and capital costs. Therefore, I feel it is more illuminating to determine what rate of return on invested capital is consistent with equating the total cost of the new method (i.e., the rings) with the variable cost of the old method (i.e., mules). That rate, of course, is the rate of return that would be earned on the capital needed to replace the old method with the new (for a given level of output). The question of rational economic behavior arises in the context of whether actual observed behavior is consistent with this rate of return. In this particular case, the relevant question is: Did the British

[1] See W. E. G. Salter, *Productivity and Technical Change,* pp. 55–58.

cotton manufacturers pass up an investment opportunity that would have yielded a remarkably high rate of return on invested capital when they failed to replace their well-functioning sub-40 mules with rings in the period before World War I?

Unfortunately, it is not possible to reach as definite a conclusion with regard to this question as was possible in the case of choosing between ring and mule spinning for new installations. The difficulty arises because the errors involved in measuring the rate of return on the money needed to replace the mules are relatively large. This would not matter if the rate of return estimated for this investment was clearly so very high or so very low that no reasonable error of measurement could change the basic conclusion. The results are not this clear-cut, however. Thus, the evidence is not sufficiently strong to exclude the *possibility* that British cotton-spinning firms may have shown "excessive" conservatism or caution in not junking their low-count mules in the pre–World War I period. It is also *possible* that they made other investments that earned a lower rate of return than that which they would have obtained on money put into replacing their low-count mules. On the other hand, the magnitude of the numbers involved makes it extremely unlikely that this investment opportunity was so good that failure to take advantage of it was of more than marginal importance to profits. Excessive caution is a possibility, blindness to change and opportunity is not.

Equally important, it is clear that the failure to junk sub-40 mules before World War I could not possibly have had a significant effect on the competitive position of the British cotton textile industry. At the very worst, this failure could have been offset by a wage cut in spinning of a few percent. Much larger wage cuts were in fact obtained during the interwar period.

SAVINGS AND COSTS OF CONVERTING
FROM MULES TO RINGS

The labor saving to be derived from replacing mules with rings can be obtained from the data presented in chapter 2. In Table 5, I have calculated this saving in labor costs per ring

TABLE 5

LABOR COST SAVING PER RING SPINDLE PER WEEK
AT VARIOUS COUNTS
(in U.S. cents)

Count	United States	Great Britain
10	1.81	1.28
20	1.69	1.19
30	1.67	1.14
40	1.65	1.12
50	1.62	1.09
60	1.60	1.07
70	1.57	1.04
80	1.55	1.02
90	1.52	.99
100	1.49	.96
110	1.46	.93
120	1.43	.90

spindle per week for different counts of yarn, both in the United States and in Great Britain.

A much more difficult problem is to accurately calculate the costs of replacing mules with rings. Finding the cost of the spinning equipment itself is not much of a problem. According to the United States Tariff Board, the unit cost of ring-spinning equipment in Great Britain right before World War I was around $1.80 per spindle.[2]

In order to obtain an internal rate of return on this investment, I applied the formula

$$C = \frac{S_i - D_i}{r}$$

where

C is the unit cost of the ring-spinning equipment,

S_i is the annual labor cost saving per ring spindle (assumed constant over time),

D_i is the annual charge for "depreciation, upkeep, and obsolesence" on the ring-spinning machinery (10 per-

[2] U.S. Tariff Board, pp. 463–65.

cent of original unit cost, a constant amount over time), and

r is the internal rate of return.

This formula views S_i as a permanent stream of income that can be maintained forever so long as D_i is reinvested in the equipment each year. This may be a slightly unorthodox view of D_i, but I do not think it an unreasonable one.[3]

This particular approach to D_i could possibly evoke the objection that if new rings depreciate and become obsolete, so do old mules. That is, depreciation and obsolescence should affect both alternatives similarly over time, leaving the cost difference between the two approximately the same. This objection, however, fails to note that if the old mules are retained (at zero cost) and then become even more worn and out of date, they can be replaced with brand new, modern rings at any time without loss. This clearly is not the case with somewhat worn and somewhat outdated rings that were recently installed (at considerable cost). Alternatively, it can be said that if both rings and mules, once they have been installed, deteriorate over time, then the longer conversion from mules to rings is delayed, the greater will be the eventual cost reduction. D_i

---

[3] Another approach to this calculation, which would give similar results, is to estimate the expected lifetime of the new spinning equipment and then to apply the formula

$$C = \sum_{i=1}^{n} \frac{S_i}{(1 + r)^i} :$$

where n is the expected lifetime of the equipment. In this case S_i has to include any possible increase in upkeep costs. On the other hand, no explicit calculation of depreciation allowances is needed since the lifetime of the equipment is limited. The reason I preferred not to use this approach is that though I have no truly accurate measure of how long the ring-spinning equipment was expected to last, or how S_i might decline as the ring spindles aged, I do have good information on the actual rates charged for depreciation, obsolescence, and upkeep.

It should also be noted that my assumption (in the text) that S_i will remain constant over time means that there is no possibility that two investments with the same internal rate of return will have different present value to cost ratios. If S_i had varied over time it would have been possible for two investments costing the same and having the same internal rate of return to have different present values.

can thus be seen as the opportunity cost incurred by converting now instead of in the future.

The results of this calculation indicate that capital used to replace mules with rings in Great Britain in the production of 10-count yarn would have earned a net return of about 26% per annum. At a count of 40, the net return would have been 21%. Turning down such an attractive investment opportunity might well be considered an act of economic irrationality.

The problem is much more complicated than this, however. The conversion from mules to rings would result in a number of other costs, most of which are not incurred when a whole new plant is built. Some of them are:

1. The cost of halting production in the entire plant while the new ring spindles are being installed.

2. The cost of alterations that have to be made in other machinery and in the building (which can be a serious problem). W. E. G. Salter has pointed out that the "inadequacy of existing buildings for modern methods is a simple but extremely common form of technical complementarity."[4]

3. The cost of the extra preparatory equipment required by the ring spindles.[5]

4. The loss that would undoubtedly be encountered on the disposition of the inventory of spare parts held for the mule spindles.

5. The cost of the suboptimal results that would probably be achieved in the first months of operating the new equipment.

6. The cost in money, trouble, and time that would be involved in recruiting and training the female ring spinners to replace the male mule spinners. The dismissal of the mule spinners might also increase the probability

[4] Salter, *Productivity and Technical Change*, p. 85. Salter specifically refers to the problems of the British cotton textile industry.

[5] Winterbottom, *Cotton Spinning Calculations and Yarn Costs*, pp. 213, 272, 273.

of a strike by the rest of the work force. Trouble would seem especially likely if only part of the mules in a mill are replaced at one time.[6]

The difficult problem, of course, is to estimate the level of these costs. Very little of the detailed information needed to make a hard calculation exists. Any such estimate is therefore only an educated guess. Nevertheless, in this case it is essential that the attempt be made. These costs were very real and to assume them away, and then to conclude that the British spinning firms ignored an investment opportunity that would have yielded a net return of between 21 and 26% per annum, would quite simply be wrong. I have, therefore, made what I consider to be a set of fairly conservative estimates of these costs. Because these adjustments in fact reduce the net rate of return to a level sufficiently low to make this investment opportunity relatively unprofitable, the reader can also view the adjustments I make to be what is necessary to make conversion appear unattractive. To the extent the reader thinks that any of the extra cost estimates I make are excessive, he can scale them down and see what effect this has on the final net rate of return. After doing so, he will have to make up his own mind about the British manufacturers who, at least implicitily, decided that this rate of return was insufficient.

The first extra cost listed is that of closing down the whole plant while the new equipment was being installed. Conversion clearly was no snap operation. Not only did the old equipment have to be dismantled and the new equipment assembled but the building itself and the rest of the machinery also had to be adjusted. The power mechanism would, of course, have to be changed.[7] In addition, extra preparatory equipment had to be installed. Changes in the building would be required to accommodate the change in the ratio between preparatory and spinning equipment.[8]

[6] For a discussion of the hostility of the mule spinners to women spinners of any kind, see Turner, *Trade Union Growth, Structure, and Policy*, pp. 142–43.

[7] The mule required power to move back and forth as well as to turn rollers and spindles.

[8] See Salter, *Productivity and Technical Change*, p. 85; and Tippett, *A Portrait of the Lancashire Textile Industry*, pp. 85, 87 (caption 30).

It seems likely that a four-month shutdown is a conservative estimate for a total conversion. If a 10% rate of depreciation, loss, and upkeep and a 10% interest rate are combined with the cost of an English spinning mill (excluding the spinning equipment itself) as reported by the United States Tariff Board[9] in 1912, this shutdown period would have increased the cost per new spindle by about 41 cents.

The cost of the idle capital, however, is not the only cost incurred during a shutdown. In addition, there are personnel costs. Surely, the administrative and white collar workers would have to be kept on throughout the shutdown period. As for the operatives, other than the now-redundant mule spinners, the firm would face the alternatives of keeping them on the payroll or risking their dispersion.[10] Either possibility would be costly. Because the labor costs of spinning far exceeded the capital costs, I think it is a conservative estimate to say that the personnel costs of a shutdown were probably of the same magnitude as the costs of idle capital.

It was, of course, possible to replace the mules piecemeal. Such a procedure would have avoided the necessity of closing the mill completely. On the other hand, it would have resulted in lower production and general inconvenience for an extended period of time. In addition, labor troubles would probably have been more severe under such an arrangement. The temporarily remaining mule spinners would certainly have objected to a policy of gradual dismissal. Finally, the adjustments required in the arrangement of the building and the other equipment would probably have been done less efficiently if done in stages. It is thus by no means obvious that a step-by-step conversion would have been cheaper than a single sweeping overhaul.

The next cost to be considered is the cost of the alterations in the building and the power mechanism. An estimate of 15% of the original cost of the building and driving equipment (excluding the power plant) seems to be reasonable. Such a

[9] U.S. Tariff Board, p. 465. The other equipment has to be depreciated because it presumably deteriorated or at least became outmoded while standing idle.

[10] For a comment on the importance to one textile firm of keeping the operatives continually employed, see W. G. Rimmer, *Marshalls of Leeds: Flax-Spinners, 1788–1886*, p. 281.

figure would add roughly 40 cents to the cost per spindle.

The rings would also require somewhat more preparatory equipment.[11] Once again, a figure of 15% is certainly reasonable. This would add about 20 cents per spindle.

Finally, there is the question of the spare parts inventory. To some extent, this inventory could have been run down in anticipation of the changeover, and presumably some of it would be sold, although undoubtedly at a substantial loss. All in all, I believe that a probable loss equal to 50% of the normal spare parts inventory of a British mule spinning mill is not an unreasonable estimate. This would add approximately another 40 cents to the cost per spindle.[12]

The total of these extra costs, as I have estimated them, is $1.82 per spindle. This implies a total cost per new spindle of slightly over $3.60. In recalculating the internal rate of return according to the formula used above, C should thus be doubled. A serious question arises, however, as to what should be done about D_i. I have chosen to make the most conservative assumption possible and have limited depreciation allowances to the investment in machinery only. (For a discussion of the issues involved in this question, see Appendix A.)

On the basis of these conservative assumptions and estimates, I calculate that the rate of return on capital used to replace well-functioning mules with rings was approximately 12% per annum for count 10 yarn and slightly less for higher counts. At a count of 40, the net return was around 10% per annum. The generosity of these estimates is apparent from the fact that points 5 and 6 in the above list of costs have been ignored. The possible influence of point 5 is indicated by the fact that if during the first year of operation realized labor economies were held to one-half those shown in Table 1 for count 10 yarn (not an unreasonably pessimistic assumption), this would be the equivalent of *permanently* reducing the rate of return on the capital invested by almost 1 percentage point.

---

[11] Winterbottom, *Cotton Spinning Calculations and Yarn Costs*, p. 213.
[12] U.S. Tariff Board, p. 465.

THE PROBLEM OF CAPACITY UTILIZATION

At first glance, even 12% may seem to be a pretty good net rate of return on capital. In fact, however, it is not all that it seems to be. This calculation is based on an assumption of continual operation at 100% of capacity. In choosing between two equally capital intensive techniques, it does not matter whether 100% utilization is expected. In the case of a replacement decision, however, it matters a great deal because the option to retain the old equipment requires no capital at all.

Thus, the rate of return on capital used to replace mules with rings would be less than 12% if the new equipment were not used full time. In view of the prevalence of (usually organized) short-time operations, strikes and lockouts, not to mention the continuing fear of a cotton shortage,[13] no sane British cotton spinner could have expected continuous 100% utilization. At a 90% utilization rate, which must be considered a relatively optimistic expectation, the rate of return on count 10 yarn would fall from 12% to approximately 10.3%. At 75% utilization, the rate of return is around 8%, and at 50% utilization, it is around 3.3%.[14]

In view of the risks involved and the conservative nature of my calculations, I find it understandable that British cotton spinners generally did not consider the replacement of well-functioning mules with rings a particularly attractive investment. In the period just before World War I, leading Lancashire spinning firms were paying around 6% on preferred shares

[13] The much feared reoccurrence of a cotton famine became a reality during the last few years of World War I. As a result of a shipping shortage, raw cotton supplies at one time fell so low that output in the "American sector" of the industry was restricted to less than 40 percent of capacity (D. Henderson, *The Cotton Control Board*, p. 6). During this period of raw cotton shortage, output was regulated by the Cotton Control Board, which relied on rules limiting the percentage of its equipment a firm might operate or on a combination of this type of regulation with short-time work. Although profits were very high in the industry, especially in spinning (raw cotton prices were controlled, but output prices were not), this system certainly did not favor firms who had installed labor-saving, capital intensive equipment. For a more detailed discussion of this period, see Henderson.

[14] In 1930, capacity utilization in the British cotton-spinning industry fell to 58% and in 1931 was probably worse (see Robson, *The Cotton Industry in Britain*, pp. 344, 338).

and 5% on money deposits.[15] Thus, on the basis of the quantitative evidence available, the failure to junk mules can certainly not be taken as proof of mass irrationality or technical backwardness. On the other hand, these calculations and estimates in no way *prove* that there were not occasions when English cotton manufacturers missed a fairly good investment opportunity when they kept their mules in operation.

THE ROLE OF MACHINERY AGE

The above calculations are, of course, supposed to be based on a comparison of new rings with at least relatively new mules.[16] Older mules would presumably work less well because of wear and tear and might also be less well designed.[17] In addition, old mules would presumably be served by old preparatoty equipment and an old power plant. Thus, rings could be substituted for the mules at the same time as the other old equipment was switched. This would reduce the part of the cost of closing down the plant chargeable to the switch in spinning equipment.[18]

This discussion simply points out that as mules got older and older, a stronger case could be made for replacing them. Old mules were in fact scrapped in Great Britain, however, so that this observation in no way conflicts with observed behavior. It is, of course, true that the advantage of new rings over new mules at certain counts undoubtedly speeded up the

[15] United Textile Workers Association, *Inquiry into the Cotton Industry, 1921–1922,* pp. 17, 24.

[16] It should be noted, however, that all the biases involved in the calculation of the numbers in Table 5 tend to make the mules used in the comparison older than the rings used.

[17] Available information indicates that the average output per mule "side" (at a given count) was probably increasing by about 1 percent per annum between 1870 and World War I. This resulted from having more spindles per side and making them move faster. Not all of this gain accrued to the employer, however. Bigger and faster machines tended to require more labor input, and to the extent that output per unit of labor increased the employers had approximately to split this gain with the workers (see Jewkes and Gray, *Wages and Labor in the Lancashire Cotton Spinning Industry,* pp. 204–5).

[18] On the other hand, if the preparatory and other equipment was old but in reasonable condition, the manager might well want to postpone replacing the mules with rings in order to be able to switch all the equipment at one time.

rate at which old mules producing these counts were scrapped.
This can hardly be considered a startling revelation, however,
since it is a logical corollary of the superiority of new rings
over new mules.[19]

DIFFERENCES IN BRITISH AND AMERICAN BEHAVIOR

In the United States the labor-saving resulting from switching
to rings was greater than in Great Britain. It is also clear that
new rings had a greater advantage over new mules than was
the case in Great Britain. The rate of return on capital used
to replace well-functioning sub-40 mules with rings, however,
does not seem to have been higher in the United States than
in Great Britain. My calculations indicate that this rate of return
must have been almost identical in the two countries. The
principal reason for this was the high cost of machinery,
especially spinning machinery, in the United States.[20]

In the United States, unlike Great Britain, rings were generally
a better new investment than mules even for counts above
40.[21] The extra cotton costs involved in using high-count rings,
however, reduced this advantage below that enjoyed by new
rings over new mules at sub-40 counts. As a result, using capital
to throw out well-functioning mules used for counts above
40 was definitely not a good investment. Capital so used would
undoubtedly have failed even to return respectable depreciation
charges. This point, of course, does not affect the fact that
the possibility of using rings to advantage accelerated the rate
at which high-count mules were scrapped.

The difference in the rate of return to be gained from capital
used to finance the junking of mules at low, as opposed to
high, counts is in good accord with the observed fact that old

[19] The only situation in which the superiority of new rings over new mules
would not tend to accelerate the scrapping of old mules is one in which replacing
old mules with new rings costs sufficiently more than replacing old mules with
new mules to offset the advantage of new rings over new mules. In such a situation,
worn-out mules would presumably be replaced with new mules, but entirely new
installations would be equipped with new rings.

[20] See U.S. Tariff Board, pp. 462–65.

[21] See chapter 2.

mules remained in service for high counts long after they had been totally displaced in low-count production.[22]

There is one problem remaining, however. Although the rate of return on junking well-functioning sub-40 mules was about the same in the two countries, junking seems to have been much more prevalent in the United States than in Great Britain. The mere fact that sub-40 mules vanished earlier in the United States than in Great Britain does not prove very much. After all, it is undoubtedly true that it became rational to choose new rings over new mules earlier in the United States than in Great Britain. Nevertheless, the fact that there were virtually *no* sub-40 mules operating in the United States as early as 1900 indicates that there must have been a good deal of junking.[23] In addition, the literary evidence gives strong support to the willingness of American manufacturers to junk mules.[24]

It thus seems that American and British manufacturers reacted at least somewhat differently to what, as so far described, were similar economic situations. The question is whether this divergence can be explained without recourse to British "technological conservatism" or, conversely, to American "technological radicalism."

One possible cause of this divergence in behavior could have been a difference in interest rates. Interest rates, however, were if anything somewhat higher in the United States than in Great Britain.

DIFFERENCES IN CAPACITY UTILIZATION

A more important consideration is the fact that a British cotton manufacturer could expect to enjoy a lower average rate of capacity utilization on his new equipment than could his American counterpart. There can be little doubt that the

[22] See previous references (chapter 2) to Young, *The American Cotton Industry,* and Uttley, *Cotton Spinning and Manufacturing in the United States.*

[23] Ibid.

[24] See Knowlton, *Pepperell's Progress,* p. 171; Smith, *The Cotton Textile Industry of Fall River,* p. 100; Lamb, "The Development of Entrepreneurship in Fall River," p. XII-8; and *1905 Census of Manufacturers,* 3: 42.

British industry was more subject to excess capacity than was the American industry. This was mainly due to the fact that although both industries grew in spurts, the trend rate of growth was much more rapid in the United States. This meant that the level of demand reached in one spurt, and to which capacity had in all likelihood been adjusted, was more rapidly surpassed in the United States than in Great Britain. This is clear from the figures in Table 6 on cotton consumption in the two countries. In the thirty year period 1885–1914, there were not less than 20 years in Great Britain during which cotton consumption was below the previous peak level. In the United States, there were only 10 such years.[25] Since the United States got rid of many sub-40 mules before 1885, it can also be noted that between 1870 and 1884 there were only 5 such years.[26]

While there were still plenty of sub-40 mules in operation, and assuming a freely competitive environment, a ring-spinning firm might not have been *overly* concerned about the possibility of excess capacity in the industry. Such a firm presumably could count on using its lower variable costs to take business away from its mule-equipped competitors. This was probably the situation in United States up until the sub-40 mule approached extinction in that country. In Great Britain, however, the ability of the low-variable-cost producer to take orders away from his competitors was virtually foreclosed by the widespread practice of organized short-time work.[27]

Leading students of the cotton textile industry have referred

[25] See Mitchell, *Abstract of British Historical Statistics*, p. 460; and *U.S. Historical Statistics*, p. 654.

[26] U.S. Department of Commerce, Bureau of the Census, *Bulletin No. 160*, 1926, p. 50.

[27] Short-term work must be distinguished from production quotas, especially tradable quotas. Short-term work forced all (participating) firms to operate a short day. Robson notes specifically that it was a matter of having each plant operating for a reduced number of *hours* per week. Since all the workers were to work these hours, it even impeded the shifting of production between different machines in a given plant (see Robson, *The Cotton Industry in Britain*, p. 221; also see Turner, *Trade Union Growth, Structure and Policy*, pp. 337, 339, 346, 349). Turner notes (p. 349) that post-World War II workers were afraid to abandon the long tradition of short-time work which would have relaxed "labor restrictions in efficient ones (firms)." J. Jewkes and H. Campion note how short-time work after 1921 retarded labor movment out of the depressed cotton industry by making it possible for all workers to remain and still get some employment and income ("The Mobility of Labour in the Cotton Industry," p. 137).

TABLE 6

COTTON CONSUMPTION IN THE UNITED STATES AND
GREAT BRITAIN, 1885–1914

(in millions of pounds)

Year	United States*	Great Britain
1885	1,047†	1,298
1886	1,025	1,450
1887	1,103†	1,499
1888	1,155†	1,525
1889	1,259†	1,564†
1890	1,302†	1,664†
1891	1,423†	1,666†
1892	1,208	1,548
1893	1,150	1,434
1894	1,492†	1,603
1895	1,250	1,664
1896	1,421	1,637
1897	1,736†	1,618
1898	1,836†	1,761†
1899	1,844†	1,762†
1900	1,802	1,737
1901	2,040†	1,569
1902	2,094†	1,633
1903	1,990	1,617
1904	2,262†	1,486
1905	2,439†	1,813†
1906	2,487†	1,855†
1907	2,247	1,985†
1908	2,599†	1,917
1909	2,380	1,824
1910	2,357	1,632
1911	2,700†	1,892
1912	2,934†	2,142†
1913	2,971†	2,178†
1914	3,044†	2,077

SOURCE: U.S. Department of Commerce, Bureau of the Census, Bulletin 160, pp.49–50; Mitchell, *Abstract of British Historical Statistics*, p. 179.

*Figures for the United States were originally presented in running bales and have been converted to pounds at the rate of 478 lbs. per bale.

† New all-time high.

to organized short-time work by British spinning firms as the "normal response to a decline in demand"[28] and as "traditional policy" in the face of a fall in demand.[29] In the years leading

[28] Robson, *The Cotton Industry in Britain*, p. 221.

[29] Allen, *British Industries and their Organization*, p. 236.

up to World War I, organized short-time was practiced in British cotton spinning in 1897, 1900, 1903, 1904, and 1910.[30] In 1903, organized short-time was worked for four months; and in 1904, short-time work at about 70% of capacity was the rule for most of the year.[31] The fact that the short-time policy was supported by both the Employers Association and the trade unions increased compliance and made violation of the rules a risky activity.

In view of these facts, it seems clear that British firms were more likely to experience less than 100% capacity utilization of their equipment than were American firms. At the same time, I do not believe that this factor is important enough to explain all of the differences in behavior of American and British manufacturers with regard to their low-count mules.

DIFFERENCES IN EMPLOYER REACTION TO TRADE UNIONS

At this point, I have no choice but to claim that there were differences either in employer reaction to unions or to technical change in the two countries. Of these alternatives, the union explanation appeals to me for two reasons. First of all, the literary sources all report that employer antipathy to the mule spinners' unions was an important factor in explaining the rapidity with which the mule was replaced in the United States.[32] These, incidentally, are the very same sources that describe the willingness of American manufacturers to junk mules and on which I partly base my claim that American manufacturers did in fact junk well-functioning mules. Second, the union argument makes good economic sense.

It has already been noted that the American mule spinners' unions were troublesome in themselves and, more important, were a powerful catalyst in encouraging strikes and organization on the part of the other workers.[33] It is hardly surprising

---

[30] Robson, *The Cotton Industry in Britain*, p. 221; and Copeland, *The Cotton Manufacturing Industry of the United States*, p. 333.

[31] Robson, *The Cotton Industry in Britain*, p. 221.

[32] Knowlton, *Pepperell's Progress*, p. 171; R. Smith, *The Cotton Textile Industry of Fall River*, p. 100; Lamb, "The Development of Entrepreneurship in Fall River," p. XII-8; and *1905 Census of Manufacturers*, 3: 42.

if under these circumstances the prospect of getting rid of the mule spinners would make an otherwise mediocre investment opportunity appear attractive to American cotton manufacturers.

My argument with regard to the British manufacturers is virtually the opposite. Their mule spinners unions were more orderly and, furthermore, were not nearly as important in the leadership of general strikes and general unionism.[34] On the contrary, an attempt to replace the mule spinners with more docile girl ring spinners might well have increased the possibility of opposition from the other workers.

CONCLUSION

It thus seems likely that the differences in levels of capacity utilization and in labor organization probably caused American and British manufacturers to react somewhat differently to this particular investment opportunity. My information is not precise enough to say who came off better. Nor have I proved that attitudes toward change and innovation played no role whatsoever in this matter. What is clear from the order of magnitude of the numbers involved, however, is that neither country could have gained, or lost, very much from the difference in their behavior. At worst, the British ignored a marginally good investment opportunity. The worst possible for the Americans is that they took advantage of a marginally poor one.

Finally, a word has to be said about the relatively late adoption of rings, for any count, in Great Britain. The United States had more rings than mules as early as 1870, but in Great Britain rings did not have much practical effect until well after that date. The most that I can say is that some such gap is consistent with the greater relative advantage of rings under American conditions,[35] together with the unanimous opinion

[33] Knowlton, *Pepperell's Progress*, p. 171; and R. Smith, *The Cotton Textile Industry of Fall River*, p. 100.

[34] Turner, *Trade Union Growth, Structure and Policy*, p. 141.

[35] In fact, the relative advantage of rings in the United States as opposed to

of contemporary observers that ring technology was improving much faster than mule technology during the second half of the nineteenth century.[36] This, of course, by no means implies that there may not have been an information or learning gap between the United States and Great Britain.

Great Britain was probably even greater in the second half of the nineteenth century than is indicated by my calculations. These calculations are based on a period when America had gone over much more heavily to rings than had Great Britain. Unless the supply schedules for ring and mule spinners were both perfectly elastic (which they definitely were not) in both countries, this would imply that there was probably more downward pressure on mule spinners' wages and upward pressure on ring spinners' wages in the United States than was the case in Great Britain.

[36] See, for example, Copeland, *The Cotton Manufacturing Industry of the United States*, pp. 66–68.

4

LANCASHIRE AND THE AUTOMATIC LOOM

Besides ring spinning, the other great innovation in the cotton textile industry during the second half of the nineteenth century was automatic weaving.

Prior to the introduction of the automatic loom, the standard factory cotton-weaving equipment in both Great Britain and the United States, and everywhere else for that matter, was the plain power loom. This loom carries out the basic steps in weaving without manual assistance. If a warp thread breaks, however, the loom continues working. To prevent the quality of the cloth from deteriorating seriously, it is essential that such a break be noted promptly, the loom stopped, and the break repaired. In addition, plain power looms have to be stopped when the yarn in the shuttle is exhausted. The operator then has to replace the bobbin in the shuttle and rethread it.[1]

In 1894, the American textile machinery firm of George

---

[1] Threading the shuttle involves sucking the thread through an opening in the shuttle. Inevitably, this causes the weaver to inhale a good deal of dust. This operation is repeated approximately 500 to 1,000 times per day, so it is very unhealthy (Copeland, *The Cotton Manufacturing Industry of the United States*, p. 86).

Draper & Sons introduced the Northrop automatic loom. This loom solved the two problems of the plain loom just mentioned. The Northrop loom stops automatically when a warp thread breaks, and, without stopping, it automatically changes and rethreads the shuttle when it runs out of yarn. These automatic actions not only mean that an automatic loom has to stop less frequently than a plain loom but, more important, that an operator can tend many more automatic than plain looms. In order to achieve some part of the labor-saving advantage of this innovation without requiring the junking of well-functioning plain looms, the company developed a separate warp stop motion that could be installed on existing plain looms. By automatically stopping the loom when a warp thread breaks, this devise permits a somewhat larger loom/operator ratio.[2]

THE RATE OF ADOPTION OF AUTOMATIC LOOMS

There is no doubt that Great Britain lagged far behind the United States in the adoption of the Northrop and other automatic looms. As noted above, the Northrop loom (the first and easily the most important automatic loom) was first marketed in 1894. Although about three times as expensive as regular (plain) power looms, the labor-saving it permitted made the Northrop loom very attractive to American manufacturers. By 1901, some 46,000 Northrop looms had been sold by the Draper Company. Through 1914, American sales amounted to over 286,000 looms. In that year, approximately forty percent of all the looms in New England and fifty percent of all the looms in the South were Northrop looms.[3] This was true despite the fact that the Northrop loom was only slowly adapted to the production of the finer and more complicated types of fabrics.

No such rapid rate of adoption occurred in Great Britain.

---

[2] A more primitive type of warp stop-motion, suitable only for coarse weaving, had been available since before the Civil War. The considerable improvements needed in the warp stop mechanism for the purposes of the automatic loom, however, resulted directly in the development of a vastly better separate device (Copeland, *The Cotton Manufacturing Industry of the United States*, pp. 84, 86).

[3] Feller, "The Draper Loom in New England Textiles," pp. 324, 326.

The Northrop loom was first introduced in 1902,[4] and in 1904, the British Northrop Loom Company was established.[5] By 1914, however, this company employed only about 350 workers as compared with 40,000 for the entire British textile machinery industry and 12,000 for the single firm of Platts of Oldham.[6] Indeed, it is likely that even this small Northrop staff worked partly for export. The best estimate is that in 1914 there were at least 6,000, but certainly not more than 10,000 automatic looms in Lancashire.[7] This at a time when Lancashire had a total of not less than 805,000 looms of all kinds weaving cotton. Indeed, as late as 1936, there were only about 15,000 automatic looms in place in the United Kingdom.[8]

Between 1903, the year after the introduction of the Northrop loom into Great Britain, and 1914, the number of cotton looms in Lancashire increased by 157,000.[9] Even if it is assumed that as much as two-thirds of the cloth whose production in Great Britain was increasing was not suited to production on automatic looms,[10] well over 80% of the new looms installed in new weaving sheds to produce goods suited to automatic looms were, in fact, plain looms. Indeed, even this figure understates the case. If the main impediment to putting in automatic looms was that the types of cloth whose production was increasing were not suited to production on automatic looms, then there would undoubtedly still have been plenty of room for switching the

[4] D. A. Farnie, "The Textile Industry: Woven Fabrics," in C. Singer et al., eds., *A History of Technology*, 5: 586.

[5] S. B. Saul, "The Engineering Industry," in Aldcroft, ed., *The Development of British Industry and Foreign Competition, 1875–1914*, p. 195. When this company was formed, the American Draper company is reported to have taken 2/3 of the stock in return for rights and designs (ibid.). The law requiring foreigners holding British patents to either produce in Britain or give up the patent was not passed until 1907, so this legislation was presumably *not* the reason for the establishment of this company.

[6] Ibid., pp. 191, 195.

[7] U.S. Tariff Board, p. 494.

[8] Robson, *The Cotton Industry in Britain*, p. 340.

[9] Ibid.

[10] Irwin Feller estimates that "at least 60% of New England output was beyond the technical capabilities of the Draper loom—at least, again, as first marketed" ("The Draper Loom in New England Textiles," p. 331). The United States Tariff Board also states that the automatic loom was not well suited to the products of a "large portion" of English mills (see U.S. Tariff Board, p. 494).

production of goods that were suited to automatic looms from old plain looms to the new automatics and producing more cloth not suited to automatics on the plain looms thus released. This means that the well-known argument presented by Marvin Frankel that the unsuitability of existing British weaving sheds for the new machines blocked the spread of the automatic loom is not relevant to *this* period.[11] Although the problem is thus one of explaining why the automatic loom failed almost completely to catch on in Great Britain before World War I, even when entirely new weaving sheds were being built, it should be kept in mind that a number of attempts to use automatic looms were in fact made. This means that some experience with, and knowledge of, the performance of the Northrop loom under British conditions must have been gained.

INTERPRETATIONS OF BRITAIN'S LAG IN AUTOMATIC WEAVING

The standard reaction to Britain's lag in automatic weaving has been to call it an important failure and a major reason for the industry's decline. The blame for this failure is usually placed either on inefficient management or on obstructive unions, or else it is shared between the two groups in varying proportions. Management is frequently accused of a short-sightedness approaching myopia. Thus, for example, in a recent article stressing the failure of British entrepreneurship in general during the 1870–1914 period, Derek Aldcroft accussed British cotton-weaving management of ignoring the automatic loom despite the fact that this type of loom (according to Aldcroft) cut the cost of weaving approximately in half.[12]

[11] See Marvin Frankel, "Obsolescense and Technical Change in a Maturing Economy," pp. 313–14. I also doubt that Frankel's points about the need for ring yarn and the practices of converters (p. 313) can help explain the almost total failure to install any automatic looms in Great Britain before World War I. The same argument applies to the very interesting point made by the United States Tariff Board that many British weaving firms preferred soft mule yarn, unsuited for automatic looms, because it absorbed more sizing than did the harder ring yarn (U.S. Tariff Board, p. 494). This, of course, is not to say that these arguments might not have some relevance to the later experience of the British industry.

[12] Aldcroft, "The Entrepreneur and the British Economy, 1870–1914," p. 117. Aldcroft refers to a 1909 article by Melvin Copeland as the source of this information

The view expressed by Aldcroft is supported by many other prominent economic historians. Thus, in a book published in 1967, A. L. Levine states that "Lancashire" was complacent and obdurate in the face of the automatic loom. Levine also refers to an "ostrichlike or incorrect" attitude toward costs in connection with the automatic loom.[13] Other more moderate but still adverse comments are made by A. E. Musson, C. P. Kindleberger, and R. S. Sayers. J. H. Clapham makes the somewhat obscure remark that it was "unfortunate" that there were not more automatic looms in Great Britain before World War I.[14]

Other observers blame worker and union opposition to the new machines. Indeed, Roland Gibson virtually accuses the unions of destroying the industry by their opposition to the

---

on cost savings. What Copeland really says, however, is that the automatic loom (in America) reduced the *labor* cost of weaving by 50% ("Technical Developments in Cotton Manufacturing Since 1860," p. 146). Because the automatic (Northrop) loom cost about three times as much as a plain loom (both in the United States and in Great Britain), such a statement about labor cost proves nothing at all about total cost. In view of this fact, Aldcroft's statement about "costs" is very misleading. Even more remarkable, however, and a strong indication of the confused state of knowledge on this question, is the fact that Aldcroft has since completely reversed his position. In a 1968 publication, he states: "Moreover, the fact that some industrialists were slow to adopt new techniques does not necessarily mean that they were inefficient or lacked enterprise. One might, for example, criticize cotton manufacturers on the grounds that they ignored the ring spindle and automatic loom. But this was not due to conservatism on their part but rather to the fact that the new machinery was not really suitable to English conditions of manufacture" ("Introduction," in Aldcroft, ed., *The Development of British Industry and Foreign Competition, 1875–1914,* p. 34).

Aldcroft offers no evidence or reference to support this very strong assertion. Presumably, however, it is based on the study of the cotton industry by R. E. Tyson that is included in the book. As noted above, however, Tyson's discussion of spinning is only a summary of Copeland's argument of 1912, which, in turn, is much too general to support such a strong conclusion, although Copeland himself draws it (*The Cotton Manufacturing Industry of the United States,* p. 70). As for weaving, all Tyson does is to point out that the automatic loom offered "advantages and disadvantages," but he makes no systematic attempt to evaluate them. As I read him, Tyson does not draw any conclusions concerning whether or not the British cotton manufacturers should have installed more automatic looms (Tyson, "The Cotton Industry," p. 122). In fact, of course, his evidence and analysis (a total of six sentences) is grossly inadequate as a basis for any kind of conclusion on this very complex issue.

[13] Levine, *Industrial Retardation in Britain,* pp. 36, 125.

[14] Musson, "The Great Depression in Britain," p. 207; Kindleberger, "Foreign Trade and Economic Growth," p. 297, and *Economic Growth in France and Great Britain,* p. 273; Sayers, *A History of Economic Change in England,* p. 101; J. H. Clapham, *An Economic History of Modern Britain, Vol. III,* p. 177.

automatic loom.[15] The opposition of the unions is also stressed by Frank Taussig and the United States Tariff Board.[16] Finally, some writers avoid partisanship and blame both unions and management.[17]

ECONOMIC PERFORMANCE OF THE AUTOMATIC LOOM

Unfortunately, there is very little information available on the early British experience with automatic looms. Indeed, despite the extensive use of such looms in the United States during this period, there is also a shortage of hard facts about the American experience. Enough data are available, however, to permit some fairly reliable conclusions about the performance of the automatic loom in the United States. In addition, I feel that it is possible to modify the analysis to take account of British conditions with sufficient accuracy to draw at least some tentative conclusions about British behavior.

Performance in the United States

The most comprehensive and reliable information available concerning the operation of automatic looms in the United States appears in a book published by an Englishman, T. W. Uttley, in 1905.[18] While visiting New England in 1903, Uttley calculated the cost of producing 5,400 yards of 28-inch print cloth in a Burlington plant using Draper automatic looms and in a Fall River plant using plain looms. Adjusted for a mistake Uttley made in his depreciation figures,[19] the results are shown in Table 7.

---

[15] Gibson, *Cotton Textile Wages in the United States and Great Britain*, p. 76.

[16] Taussig, *Some Aspects of the Tariff Question*, pp. 283–85; U.S. Tariff Board, p. 494.

[17] See, for example, Chin, *Management, Industry, and Trade in Cotton Textiles*, pp. 55, 85; and Copeland, *The Cotton Manufacturing Industry of the United States*, p. 92.

[18] Uttley, *Cotton Spinning and Manufacturing in the United States*, p. 26. This information is also used by Irwin Feller in his article on the Northrop loom in New England. See also my "Comment" on Feller's article, pp. 624–27.

[19] This mistake was corrected by Irwin Feller ("The Draper Loom in New England Textiles," pp. 339–41).

TABLE 7

LABOR AND CAPITAL COSTS OF PRODUCING 5,400 YARDS OF CLOTH
ON DRAPER AND PLAIN LOOMS, WEEKLY BASIS, 1903

	Draper Loom	Plain Loom
Weavers	$10.227	$19.368
Weft carriers	.355	.203
Tackler	2.293	1.096
Oiler	.913	
Total labor cost	$13.788	$20.667
Interest at 6%	3.203	.931
Depreciation and Obso-lescense, 7%	3.737	1.085
Total Capital and Labor Costs	$20.728	$22.683

On the basis of these figures, Uttley and others[20] have
concluded that the automatic looms were preferable to the
plain looms as a new investment. This conclusion, however,
depends crucially on the rate of interest charged. The 6%
used by Uttley is based on his judgment and should not be
accepted without question. As with the problem of replacing
well-functioning mules with new rings, I think it is much more
useful to determine at what interest rate the information in
Table 7 indicates that an investor should be indifferent about
installing new automatic looms or new plain looms.[21] This
interest rate, of course, also represents the rate of return that
would be earned on the extra capital invested in automatic
looms (i.e., the cost of automatic looms minus the cost of the
plain looms) once it had been decided to invest in some kind
of loom. Thus, for example, in the above case, the automatic
looms were a better original investment than the plain looms
if the interest rate was below approximately 11.2%. This is
so because the extra capital invested in the plain looms would
earn a return of approximately 11.2% per annum. This, in
turn, means that if market conditions were such that the plain
looms would earn a return of 6%, then the automatic looms

[20] See Feller, "The Draper Loom in New England Textiles," p. 341, and my
"Comment," p. 624.

[21] I am assuming that the weaving shed is also new or else is equally well suited
to either automatic or plain looms.

TABLE 8

COMPARATIVE COSTS OF PRODUCING ONE POUND OF
CLOTH BY PLAIN AND BY AUTOMATIC WEAVING IN
ONE TEXTILE MILL, 1910–1911

	Automatic Looms	Plain Looms
Labor cost of yarn	$0.033012	$0.033254
Labor cost of weaving	.028110	.046250
Total labor cost	.061122	.079504
Works expense cost of yarn	.016719	.017036
Works expense cost of weaving	.013300	.014660
Total works expense	.030019	.031696
Depreciation cost	.017988	.018765
Total conversion cost	.109129	.129965
Cotton cost	.165067	.165067
Total cost per pound of cloth	.274196	.295032
Total cost per yard of cloth	.049494	.053255

would earn a total rate of return of approximately 9.7%. This is a weighted average of 6% on the capital needed for plain looms and 11.2% on the extra capital needed to have automatic looms instead.[22] If the plain looms could earn no return at all, then the total rate of return on the automatic looms would be approximately 8.0%, this being the weighted average of 0.0% and 11.2%.

Another set of data bearing on this problem is presented by the United States Tariff Board in its 1912 study of the cotton textile industry.[23] These data are presented in Table 8.

The data are of only limited use, however. The main trouble is that they say nothing about the cost of capital and that the depreciation item included clearly refers to the whole process of converting ginned cotton into gray cloth. I see no way of

[22] The two rates of return are combined (weighted by the cost of plain looms relative to the *incremental* cost of automatic looms) because it is only the *incremental* capital needed for automatic looms that has been found to yield 11.2% per annum. The cost of installing automatic looms is thus the cost of installing plain looms plus the incremental cost of the automatic looms.

[23] U.S. Tariff Board, p. 342.

calculating the capital costs of the two methods of weaving from this information.[24] In addition, the value of the data is called into serious question by the willingness of the Tariff Board to compare automatic looms (of necessity, modern) with plain looms installed before the Civil War.[25] Although the Tariff Board says nothing about the ages of the machines compared in Table 8, it seems quite likely that some such mismatch underlies these data.[26]

Nevertheless, I would argue that something can be salvaged from the board's data by considering only the reduction in labor costs resulting from the use of automatic looms. If this percentage of reduction is applied to the data provided by Uttley, it turns out that the total cost of automatic weaving was less than the total cost of plain weaving if the interest rate was below 14.5% (assuming Uttley's 7% depreciation rate and the other limitations listed above). This result can be taken as at least some evidence that Uttley's calculations were of the right order of magnitude.

These calculations indicate a rate of return on extra money spent on installing automatic instead of plain looms of between 11% and 15% per annum. In fact, however, there is good reason to believe that these numbers are somewhat exaggerated. Thus, it is clear that the automatic looms required more maintenance than did the plain looms.[27] In the case of Uttley's example, he reports that the automatic looms required "extra repairs, space, power, etc."[28] but these considerations were not included in his calculations.

In addition, of course, the 11% and 15% figures assume continual operation at 100% of capacity. Any slipping below 100% utilization would lower the cutoff point below the above figures. Finally, the 7% charged for depreciation and obsolescence is a very arbitrary figure. Any change in this number would, of course, result in an opposite change in the cutoff

[24] See my "Comment," pp. 626–27.

[25] U.S. Tariff Board, p. 470.

[26] See my "Comment," p. 627.

[27] This was even admitted by General Draper himself, although he tried to play it down (see Feller, "The Draper Loom in New England Textiles," p. 343).

[28] Uttley, *Cotton Spinning and Manufacturing in the United States,* p. 26.

point. In this connection, it might be noted that at least in regard to spinning and preparatory machinery, which was probably less subject to obsolescence than were looms during this period, the standard British practice was to charge 10% for depreciation, obsolescence, and repairs. It is by no means obvious that this 10% rate is evidence of excessive conservatism. The range of rationality with regard to rates of depreciation must certainly stretch at least from 7% to 10%. (For a discussion of the problem of determining appropriate rates of depreciation, see Appendix B).

Given these various considerations, a range of from 9% to 12% seems a better estimate of the rate of return on extra capital put into automatic looms than the original 11% to 15% range I calculated. This, of course, is not to deny that in some particular instances the rate of return might have been much higher. If it was noticeably lower, as it presumably was for those fabrics not "suited" to production on automatic looms, automatic looms would clearly not have been used.[29]

These calculations indicate rates of return on automatic looms consistent with their installation when capacity was expanded. This is indeed what appears to have happened in the United States during this period.[30] On the other hand, such rates

[29] It is likely that the longer work days customary in the South, as opposed to New England, tended to make the rates of return a bit higher there. As for wage levels, although the average wage was certainly lower in the South, the small-town location of most southern cotton mills probably made the marginal wage a good deal higher than the average wage. Thus, automatic looms may well have been somewhat more attractive in the South than in New England (Copeland, *The Cotton Manufacturing Industry of the United States*, pp. 39, 115–17).

[30] The number of automatic looms installed increased from 12,661 in 1899 to 136,322 in 1914 in the South and from 13,752 to 150,464 in the North. During the same period, the number of plain looms increased from 97,926 to 127,361 in the South and decreased from 285,133 to 229,713 in the North (Feller, "The Draper Loom in New England Textiles," p. 326). The entire decrease in the number of plain looms in the North occurred between 1909 and 1913, a period when the number of plain looms in the South remained constant. These years in all probability witnessed the replacement of plain looms in New England that had been installed well before 1895 and had finally stopped functioning satisfactorily. These numbers certainly give no evidence of any mass junking of well-functioning plain looms, as undoubtedly would have happened had the rates of return on automatics been much higher than those calculated above (the range for throwing out well-functioning plain looms and replacing them with automatics corresponding to the 11.2% and 14.5% figures calculated above is 5.9% to 8.3%). These numbers also indicate that only a relatively small portion of all the automatic looms installed in the United States before 1914 had to be installed in buildings that previously housed plain looms.

of return are somewhat less than sensational,[31] and can hardly have revolutionized productivity per unit of all inputs, as opposed to output per unit of labor, in the industry.[32]

The Automatic Loom under British Conditions

The principal problem in applying these data to the British pre–World War I experience is determining the extent of the labor-saving that was available in Great Britain from using automatic looms. Because there was very little experience with automatic looms in Britain before World War I, only scattered pieces of data are available on automatic weaving wages in this period. Furthermore, such data as exists are available only because these particular wages (i.e., the wages in a particular plant or company) were at issue in strikes and lockouts. Systematic data on the wages of automatic loom weavers in Great Britain are not available for any period before the middle 1930s. I feel, however, that these data can be used to get a general idea of the change in per-unit labor costs resulting from using automatic rather than plain looms, even in the pre–World War I period. I would argue further that any bias that results from using 1930s data is in favor of the automatic loom. This follows from the fact that by 1930 the automatic loom had at least grudgingly been accepted by the workers and had been incor-

[31] Peter McClelland has pointed out that this good, but not sensational, rate of return can be taken as evidence of a good pricing policy on the part of the Draper Company. By setting the price of the automatic loom, on which they had a patent monopoly, at a level that yielded a return just high enough to induce rapid adoption, the company must have come very close to maximizing its own profits. Assuming these actions were deliberate, the Draper Company did a beautiful job of extracting the monopoly profits available. The British price, however, was so high as to allow little or no adoption. The direct cause of this high price was that the North American Draper Company demanded such a large percentage of the (nominally independent) British Draper Company's profits in return for patents, designs, and so on (as noted above, the American Company took 2/3 of the shares in the British Company) that the British investors could not make a reasonable rate of return on their investment if looms were to be sold at a price low enough to induce rapid adoption in Great Britain. The rationale for this action by the American company, I suspect, was fear of a British price low enough to induce export to the United States.

[32] In this context, it is interesting to note that the figures on productivity change in the Massachusetts cotton textile industry to be presented in chapter 5 indicate that the rate of productivity increase was considerably greater between 1880 and 1895 than between 1895 and 1910. The latter period, of course, witnessed a very rapid adoption of automatic looms in Massachusetts.

porated into the "system." No longer was every introduction followed by disputes over wages and work loads. In the past, such disputes had frequently resulted in strikes.[33] In addition, it is perfectly clear that the possibilities for increasing the number of looms per weaver, a tendency clearly in evidence during the post–World War I period, were greater on automatic than on plain looms.[34]

Finally, all authorities agree that the automatic loom was being rapidly improved throughout this period, whereas the plain loom remained pretty much unchanged.[35] In the 1930s, about half of the automatic looms operating in Lancashire had been installed after World War I, whereas almost all the plain looms were pre–World War I.[36]

Very extensive data on weaving wages, both for automatic and plain looms, for the year 1936 are presented by E. M. Gray in his book *The Weaver's Wage*. The data presented by Gray indicate that there was a high concentration of weavers having 6 plain looms apiece or from 11 to 16 automatic looms apiece.[37] Those having fewer looms, he reports, were usually either learners or operators working on extremely wide looms or complex fabrics. On the other hand, those operating more looms usually had particularly narrow looms and simple fabrics.[38] The standard assignments clearly appear to have been 6 plain looms or between 11 and 16 automatic looms. For purposes of this analysis, I shall make the relatively conservative

[33] Gibson, *Cotton Textile Wages in the United States and Great Britain*, pp. 70–76.

[34] The British unions finally abandoned their policy of not more than four plain looms per man after World War I (Gray, *The Weaver's Wage*, p. 10). For a discussion of the American experience with increased work loads, see R. C. Nyman, *Union-Management Cooperation in the Stretchout*.

[35] See, for example, Tyson, "The Cotton Industry," p. 123.

[36] It might be noted that the fact that after World War I the number of automatic looms in Lancashire was increasing while the number of plain looms was decreasing—and decreasing at a fairly rapid rate (40% in the 1920s and 1930s [see Robson, *The Cotton Industry in Britain*, p. 330])—is difficult to explain unless (1) the automatic loom was getting more efficient at a faster rate than the plain loom, or (2) larger labor savings were available as a result of changing from plain to automatic looms than had previously been the case, or (3) previously mistaken entrepreneurs suddenly "saw the light" with regard to automatic looms. Of these possible explanations, I find the last one to be the least plausible.

[37] Gray, *The Weaver's Wage*, pp. 10, 35. The average appears to have been about 6 1/2 for men and 5 1/2 for women.

[38] Ibid., p. 9.

assumption that the average number of automatics tended was 14.

If we make a 10% allowance for the greater speed and output of the English over the American plain looms[39] and apply the loom-output ratio given for the United States by Uttley, these data indicate that the labor cost of weavers per unit of output on automatic looms in Great Britain was 67.9% of the cost of plain looms. The corresponding figure given for the United States in Uttley's example was 52.8%.

The second problem in this analysis is to determine the capital cost of plain and automatic looms in Great Britain. I have accepted the Tariff Board's assertion that plain looms were 24% cheaper in Great Britain than in the United States.[40] As for the ratio of the price of automatic looms to the price of plain looms, this is variously given as from 2.5/1 to 3/1.[41] This is virtually the same price ratio that existed in the United States. I therefore felt free to use the ratio of 2.75/1, given in Uttley's example.

If we assume that the wage rate per loom was the same in the United States and Great Britain, an application of the information about Great Britain discussed above to the Uttley data results in a rate of return on the extra capital invested in the automatic looms of 6.2% (assuming 100% capacity utilization and 7% for depreciation, obsolescence, and upkeep). In fact, however, wages were probably somewhat higher in Great Britain than in the United States.[42] A very generous allowance for this fact would raise the British rate of return from 6.2% to perhaps 10%.

This calculation, admittedly based on very scanty data, thus results in a rate-of-return range of 11% to 15% for the United States and a single and, in my opinion, very conservative estimate of 10% for Great Britain. The method of calculating the British number certainly makes it more like the upper than the lower of the American figures. Furthermore, as with spinning equipment, the problem of capacity utilization was more serious in

[39] See U.S. Tariff Board, pp. 490–92.

[40] Ibid., p. 465.

[41] Ibid., p. 494; and Farnie, "The Textile Industry: Woven Fabrics," p. 586.

[42] Copeland, *The Cotton Manufacturing Industry of the United States*, p. 303.

Great Britain than in the United States. As will be recalled, this results both from the slower growth of British output in this period and the predilection of the British for spreading available work regardless of the types of equipment in different plants. Thus, in a period of slack demand, a British weaving shed equipped with automatic looms might well have had trouble in making full use of its low variable cost advantage. In addition, Great Britain seems to have had rather more strikes. The strike problem is made even more serious when it is realized that, at least in Great Britain, the introduction of automatic weaving in itself was quite likely to bring on a strike.[43]

If 80% capacity utilization was expected,[44] the British rate of return on automatic looms would fall from 10% to about 6.6%. In addition, if 10% was allocated for depreciation, obsolescence, and upkeep, then the rate of return would be down to 3.6%—hardly an attrative investment.

A final reference should be made to the experience of the one British firm that employed automatic looms before World War I and whose experience is known in some detail. The reason this firm's experience is known, incidentally, is that it had so much labor trouble with its automatic weaving facilities. In 1903, Ashton Brothers of Hyde opened a good-sized automatic weaving shed, equipped with Northrop looms. After a dispute with its employees that almost resulted in a strike, the company obtained a one-year agreement concerning work loads and wages on the automatic looms. This settlement appears to have been slightly more favorable to the firm than the assumptions I have used in calculating the rate of return of automatic weaving in Great Britain. The workers were unhappy with this settlement once work began, however, and as soon as the agreement expired, they went on strike. The outcome of this strike, which began in May 1904 is, unfortunately, not

---

[43] See Gibson, *Cotton Textile Wages in the United States and Great Britain,* pp. 70–76.

[44] This percentage makes no allowance for the possibility that a strike could be brought on *because* of the introduction of the automatic looms. Such a strike would, of course, do even more to reduce the benefits of automatic looms; it would idle all the firm's equipment and its management and would do so only because the automatic equipment was introduced. Regular strikes would presumably idle all the firm's equipment regardless of whether it had automatic or plain looms.

known. In April 1908, however, another strike broke out at Ashton Brothers. Once again, the issue was work loads and wages on the automatic looms. After three months, the strike was settled with a 7.5% wage increase.[45] Although it is possible that this firm got a somewhat larger labor-saving from its automatic looms than I have assumed in my calculations,[46] any advantage they gained was accompanied by continual labor discord and two undoubtedly expensive strikes within the course of six years.[47] This could hardly have been either a very profitable experience for the firm or much of an inducement to other firms to adopt automatic looms.

THE WARP STOP MOTION

While discussing the role of the automatic loom in the pre–World War I period, some mention must also be made of the warp stop motion. This device could be attached to plain looms, in the United States at a cost of about $25.00;[48] and as noted above, it accomplished part of the purposes of the automatic loom. Almost never used in Great Britain, this device was widely adopted in New England as a modification to previously installed plain looms. New nonautomatic looms with warp stop motions, however, were not considered a viable alternative to new automatic looms.[49] Thus, though New England manufacturers preferred plain looms with warp stop

[45] *Cotton Factory Times,* July 24, 1908.

[46] It is only certain that they did so for the first year of their operations.

[47] Because Ashton Brothers put in their Northrop looms some time before the British Northrop Company was organized, it seems very likely their looms were imported from the United States. This means, however, that they must have paid the American price, which I have concluded was about 33% above the later British price, plus transport, for their Northrop looms. This, in turn, means that Ashton Brothers must have needed a very substantial decrease in labor costs in order to make the automatic looms a profitable investment. Probably they were hoping to get their work loads on automatic looms up to American standards. Such a move from 4 to around 20 looms per man would undoubtedly have made the investment in automatics very profitable. Unfortunately for the firm, they were unable to get terms anywhere near this standard, despite all the labor trouble and strikes.

[48] Feller, "The Draper Loom in New England Textiles," p. 344.

[49] Ibid., pp. 344–46.

motions to plain looms without them, they also preferred automatic looms to plain looms with warp stop motions.

Given this fact, if plain looms were preferable to automatic looms in Great Britain, it seems reasonable to expect that plain looms without warp stop motions would also be preferable to plain looms with warp stop motions. If this were not true, it would mean that the preference *ordering* of New England and British cotton manufacturers between plain looms with warp stop motions and automatic looms was not the same. Although such a situation is certainly possible, I do not think it reasonable, in the absence of any direct evidence, to assume that it existed.[50] Only if such an assumption is made can the non-use of the warp stop motion in Britain be taken as evidence of faulty management.

CONCLUSIONS ON THE RESPONSE OF BRITISH FIRMS
TO AUTOMATIC WEAVING

These calculations unfortunately cannot be taken as conclusive evidence of the complete rationality of British cotton manufacturers in their choice between plain and automatic looms. It is certainly possible that there were situations where automatic looms were a much more attractive investment than my calculations indicate. On the other hand, some few automatic looms were in fact installed in Great Britain before World War I.

Although I admit the possibility that British manufacturers in general were somewhat more conservative than their American counterparts with regard to weaving technology and that a few of them may have made a mistake in passing up the investment opportunity available in the form of the automatic loom, I think, however, the evidence makes it highly unlikely that the British cotton manufacturers as a group made some tremendously costly and remarkably stupid error in not going

[50] For the plain loom with warp stop-motion to be superior to the automatic loom in Great Britain, unlike the New England situation, would require that the ratio of the wage-saving on warp stop-motion to the wage-saving on automatics was considerably greater in Great Britain than in the United States. This, in turn, would require that British workers were relatively much more adept at, or fond of, the warp stop-motion as compared with the automatic loom than were American workers. Such a situation, though possible, does not seem likely.

over to automatic weaving on a large scale. On the contrary, a very reasonable defense can be made of the proposition that automatic looms did not appear to be, and in fact, were not, a particularly attractive investment opportunity in Great Britain before World War I.

I find this argument very comforting. To see why, just consider the consequences of rejecting it. Such a rejection would imply that British cotton manufacturers ignored a remarkably attractive investment opportunity when they failed to install large numbers of automatic looms. This, of course, means that they would have made a lot of money had they invested in automatic looms, and it certainly means that those few British manufacturers who did put in automatic looms must have made large profits. The 5,500 automatic looms in use in Lancashire in May 1911[51] were enough to equip at least 10 or 15 good-sized weaving sheds.[52] Within the small geographical area of Lancashire, there must thus have been a number of firms directly experiencing the advantages of the automatic loom. If this was really such a profitable investment, it is difficult to believe that the rest of the industry would not have acted on this knowledge. Because automatic looms constituted about 40% of the total investment in a weaving shed, a very high rate of return on automatic looms would inevitably have been strongly reflected in the overall profitability of the firms using them. Furthermore, if the automatics were so highly profitable, it seems inevitable that the firms using them would expand very rapidly, especially if the great majority of firms rejected this opportunity. Even if the banks ignored the automatic firms, despite what would have had to be sensational profits, the firms themselves would have had their large profits to expand with. There is, however, no evidence whatsoever indicating a rapid expansion of the automatic firms. Indeed, the relatively slow rate of growth of the number of automatic looms in operation makes it virtually impossible that these firms grew rapidly.

[51] U.S. Tariff Board, p. 465.
[52] See S. J. Chapman and T. S. Ashton, "The Sizes of Businesses Mainly in the Textile Industries," p. 486.

I find no greater comfort in the alternative hypothesis that though the automatic looms were indeed very profitable, the British weaving firms were so starved for capital and the capital market was so bad that the higher capital costs of the automatic loom prevented its introduction. First of all, it is difficult to believe that the capital market was so bad that it would not supply money for investments earning, let us say, 25% to 30% per annum. Second, though many Lancashire weaving firms were small and might have had trouble raising funds, there were also a number of large operations. In 1911, there were no fewer than 153 Lancashire firms operating more than 1,000 cotton looms.[53] In addition, there were a number of combined firms that both spun and wove and therefore operated with considerable capital. Indeed, if the weaving firms were excluded by a capital shortage from using automatic looms, one would certainly have expected the large spinning companies, such as the "Oldham Limiteds," who clearly had ready access to sources of capital, to move into automatic weaving. This, in turn, should have resulted in a growth of integrated firms, both in numbers and in market share. In fact, however, the opposite was happening. The number and market share of integrated firms were both declining in the pre–World War I period.[54] Under these circumstances, it is difficult to believe that an inefficient capital market could have prevented the adoption of the automatic loom had it really been a highly profitable investment; and if the automatic loom was to have done much for the international competitive situation of the industry, it would have had to have been highly profitable.

THE ROLE OF BRITISH UNIONS AND WORKERS

If, then, British manufacturers did not display extreme and illogical conservatism in ignoring the automatic loom, the British worker still requires examination. The defenders of the British unions maintain that the unions did not oppose the automatic loom per se, but acted only to keep work loads and wages on

[53] Ibid., p. 531.
[54] Ibid., pp. 491–92.

automatic looms at appropriate levels. They tried only to keep the manufacturers from using the new machines as an instrument to increase the work effort required for a given wage.[55] For the most part, it is probably true that the unions and the workers were principally concerned with work loads and wages and were not opposed to change on principle. In an important sense, however, this line of defense begs the question. Clearly, the work loads and wage rates agreed to were crucial in determining whether or not automatic looms were a good investment. The real question is thus whether the wage rates and work loads demanded by the British unions were indeed appropriate.

The British weavers, with their pre–World War I standard assignment of four plain looms per head, obviously had much lower work loads than did American weavers. What is perhaps more important, they demanded that their work loads be increased by a smaller percentage and their earnings increased by a larger percentage when moving to automatic looms than did the American weavers.

It is certainly possible to argue that the British weavers "should" have increased their work loads by the same percentage as the American weavers and with a similar change in weekly wages. In addition, short-time work can be regarded as an abuse. Because weaving labor per unit of output was somewhat higher in Great Britain than in the United States and machine costs were somewhat lower, such behavior by the workers would have made the automatic loom a somewhat better investment in Great Britain than it was in the United States.

How important would such a development have been for the health of the British cotton industry as a whole? The extent of this effect, of course, depends on what the rate of return on the investment in automatic looms would have been, as well as the rate of return on the rest of the equipment in the industry.

Table 9 shows estimates of the rate of return on the total investment in an integrated mill with automatic looms, assuming

---

[55] Turner, *Trade Union Growth, Structure, and Policy*, p. 259. For the workers' statement of their case, see the *Cotton Factory Times*, 24 July 1908.

TABLE 9

RATES OF RETURN OF INTEGRATED MILLS
WITH AND WITHOUT AUTOMATIC LOOMS
(% per annum)

Rate of return without automatic looms	4	6	8	10	12	14
Rate of return with automatic looms at 12%	5.33	7	8.66	10.33	12	13.66

TABLE 10

SAVINGS PER YARD OF CLOTH MADE POSSIBLE BY THE INTRODUCTION OF AUTOMATIC
LOOMS RETURNING 12%

Rate of return without automatic looms	4%	6%	8%	10%	12%	14%
Savings per yard of cloth in cents per yard	.053	.040	.027	.013	0	−.013

NOTE: Based on Uttley's example adjusted for British conditions.

that the extra capital invested in automatic looms returned 12% (this estimated rate includes an adjustment for the expected level of capacity utilization), at various rates of return on the rest of the equipment.

Perhaps a more illuminating exercise is to see what effect these 12% investments in automatic looms would have had on the prices at which the cloth could be sold while maintaining the rate of return previously earned without automatic looms. Table 10 contains estimates of these savings. Once again, a 12% rate of return is assumed on the extra capital put into automatic looms. These savings should be compared with a total conversion cost of about two cents per yard and a sales price in the vicinity of five cents per yard.

These cost-saving estimates should not be considered to be more than approximations, but there can be no doubt that the cost differences are small. A way to judge the importance of these cuts is to compare them with the effect of a 10% wage cut in weaving. This particular comparison is of interest because British cotton textile workers accepted such cuts in the interwar period.[56] A 10% wage cut would have permitted a price cut of about 0.04 cents per yard of cloth.[57] That is more or less equivalent to the saving resulting from the use of 12% automatics, if the overall rate of return was to be kept at 6%.[58]

It must also be kept in mind that the wage cuts applied to all weaving sheds. The automatic loom, on the other hand, would clearly not have been adopted by all British weaving sheds under the conditions posited above. Some types of cloth were not well suited to production on automatic looms, and such types of cloth made up an unusually large percentage of British production.[59] In addition, at a yield of 12% it would not have paid to throw out well-functioning plain looms. Considering these points, and that the American industry was expanding more rapidly than the British industry, it is almost certain that Britain would have had a smaller percentaage of automatics in 1914 than the 45% registered for the United States. Furthermore, some portion of these automatics would have been installed in weaving sheds originally designed for plain looms. The necessary conversion of the buildings would have required an extra investment and therefore a rate of return below that 12% posited above.[60]

These speculations are, of course, based on the conditions

[56] See Jewkes and Gray, *Wages and Labor in the Lancashire Cotton Spinning Industry.*

[57] Again, this refers to the type of cloth involved in Uttley's example.

[58] Six percent is clearly a conservative estimate of the rate of return on cotton textile investment in the pre-World War I period. In the period 1900–1914, British spinning companies paid annual dividends approximately equal to 7.25% of their capital (Robson, *The Cotton Industry in Britain,* p. 338). During roughly the same period, it is estimated that the average rate of return on all industrial investment in Great Britain was 14% per annum. This number, however, assumes a somewhat lower rate of depreciation than that which I have used (see E. H. Phelps Brown and B. Weber, "Accumulation, Productivity and Distribution in the British Economy, 1870–1938," pp. 266, 273). This data on average returns makes it difficult to believe that the failure to invest in 12% automatic looms was a major misallocation of resources in the British economy. It is, of course, still true that the money may have been put into some other very low rate of return investments instead of into automatic looms. In that case, however, the automatic looms were not so much a lost opportunity as the other low rate of return investments were mistakes.

[59] See, for example, Tyson, "The Cotton Industry," p. 122.

[60] See Frankel, "Obsolescence and Technical Change in a Maturing Economy," p. 313; and Salter, *Productivity and Technical Change,* p. 85.

TABLE 11

<small>Capacity Utilization in British Cotton Weaving in Selected Years</small>

1922	71%
1923	74
1924	84
1925	85
1930	54
1935	74
1936	80
1937	83
1938	66

<small>Sources: 1922–25: Daniels and Jewkes, "The Crisis in the Lancashire Cotton Industry," p. 45; 1930–38: Robson, *The Cotton Industry in Britain*, p. 344. Robson gives a lower figure than Daniels and Jewkes for the only overlapping year 1924. It should be noted that only one year from the depths of the depression is included.</small>

that existed before World War I, and implicitly assumed that a rational decision-maker at that time should have assumed that those conditions would continue. This is probably the best way to judge entrepreneurial and union behavior. Before accusing these groups of excessive conservatism when it came to sinking money into capital intensive equipment, however, I think it is useful to apply the advantages of hindsight to see what would have happened to less conservative investors. Thus, it is certainly reasonable to inquire into what would have happened to an entrepreneur who installed automatic looms just before World War I. In doing so, I shall once again assume that a 12% rate of return applied.

The periods just before and just after the war would have been very prosperous for this manufacturer. With capacity utilization at 100%, or even above, he would certainly have made his 12%. During the war itself, he may have been hindered somewhat by the cotton shortage, but this would probably not have been a really serious problem. During the decline that set in after these years of prosperity, however, his investment would not have looked so good. Table 11 contains estimates of capacity utilization in British weaving during these years.

An automatic weaving firm might have been able to operate at a slightly higher level of capacity utilization than the above averages, but the practice of short-time work would have made much higher rates of operation very unlikely. In addition, during this period, prices fell sufficiently low so that large numbers of plain looms were junked. At prices that failed to cover variable costs on plain looms, the automatic looms would not have returned their incremental 12%, even at 100% capacity utilization.

Thus, though it is undoubtedly true that a British industry equipped with automatic looms would have been more competitive on world markets in the 1920s and 1930s,[61] it is hardly likely that the extra capital involved would have earned a satisfactory rate of return. Having more capital invested in an industry with collapsing foreign markets may allow the industry to stay in business longer, but only because there is more equipment that has to be physically depreciated.

Although British cotton manufacturers were probably better off in the 1920s and 1930s without a lot of expensive automatic looms, however, the British workers *might* have been better off with those looms. If the lower price made possible by the automatic looms permitted an increase in output greater than the percentage decrease in labor input resulting from the automatic loom, then more work would have been available. There would undoubtedly have been less work in the weaving sheds, but this *might* have been more than offset by increases in employment in the spinning and finishing sections. It is also possible, of course, that there would have been no net increase in employment. Furthermore, any increase in the demand for labor would have been temporary. The adjustment of the economy away from cotton textiles would have had to come eventually and it is by no means clear that a short delay would have made the process any less painful.[62]

[61] It should be noted, however, that a Britsih industry with lower variable costs would probably have encountered even more protection and perhaps more Japanese devaluation. Most of Lancashire's competitors were in a position to call upon the assistance of their governments and would certainly have done so before handing over much of their markets to the British. See chapters 9 and 10.

[62] This argument is almost identical to one made with regard to the New England cotton textile industry. The New England textile manufacturers have been widely criticized for not having used the large profits they earned during World War I and the years immediately after the war to buy new equipment. It is claimed that had they done so they would have been able to meet southern competition more effectively and would have stayed in business longer. Although this is probably true, and although such a policy might have reduced short-run unemployment in New England, it would certainly not have helped the stockholders. Asking

Much stronger assumptions have to be made if it is to be demonstrated that the unions seriously hurt the Lancashire cotton textile industry by their opposition to automatic looms. Thus, for instance, it might conceivably be argued that the workers "should" have gone from 4 plain looms apiece to the American standard of about 20 automatic looms apiece. Furthermore, the argument might continue, there was no reason they should have gotten any increase in their weekly wages because of the shift from plain to automatic looms. Applying these assumptions to the data given by Uttley gives a rate of return on the extra capital investment in automatic looms of about 32% (assuming 100% capacity utilization and 7% for depreciation, depletion, and upkeep). This, in turn, implies the increases in the rate of return on the total investment in an integrated plant presented in Table 12. The saving per yard of cloth (Uttley type) at various rates of return on the rest of the equipment is shown in Table 13.

These savings are quite substantial. At an overall rate of return of 6%, it is now possible to cut the price of this type of cloth by about 5%. This, in turn, implies a cut in the markup over the cost of the raw cotton of approximately 12.5%. This is also the equivalent of an approximately 30% wage cut in the wages of the workers in a shed using plain looms. Clearly, such a price reduction would have made a substantial difference to the British position in the post–World War I period. From the point of view of being able to continue production in the face of low prices, it can also be noted that, under these circumstances, variable costs would have been about 0.2 cents per yard less with the automatic than with the plain looms.

Furthermore, had British workers really moved from 4 plain to 20 automatic looms without any increase in weekly earnings, a large majority of all British cotton looms would probably have been automatic by 1914. On the other hand, some of

them to put in equipment that would not bring an adequate rate of return is no different from asking them to continue to produce with the old equipment even at prices below variable cost (see A. Sweezy, "The Amoskeag Manufacturing Company," pp. 473–512). It is fascinating to note how much better, financially speaking, the technically "conservative" Amoskeag Company did than her more venturesome New England competitors.

TABLE 12

RATES OF RETURN ON INTEGRATED MILLS
WITH AND WITHOUT AUTOMATIC LOOMS
(% per annum)

Rate of return without automatic looms	4	6	8	10	12	14
Rate of return with automatic looms at 32%	8.66	10.33	12	13.66	15.33	17

TABLE 13

SAVINGS PER YARD OF CLOTH MADE POSSIBLE BY THE INTRODUCTION OF AUTOMATIC
LOOMS RETURNING 32%

Rate of return without automatic looms	4%	6%	8%	10%	12%	14%
Savings per yard of cloth in cents per yard	.133	.125	.116	.108	.100	.092

the new automatics would have had to be installed in ill-designed sheds and some well-functioning plain looms would have been junked, thus reducing somewhat the rate of return assumed in the above calculations.

Although the situation assumed above would undoubtedly have placed the British cotton textile industry in a stronger post–World War I position than that it actually experienced, and although the British manufacturers would probably have been able to make a reasonable rate of return on the extra capital invested even during the depression, it would probably not have saved the industry from a considerable contraction. More important, these calculations are based on very strange assumptions. Indeed, these calculations can best be viewed as an example of the extreme assumptions that have to be made in order to demonstrate that worker opposition, or any other kind of opposition for that matter, to the introduction of the automatic loom seriously harmed the Lancashire cotton textile industry.

Certainly, if the unions were responsible for the failure of British weavers to adopt the "American" standard of around 20 automatic looms per worker, they were also responsible for the British quota of 4, instead of 6 or 8, plain looms. If the unions were responsible for low work loads, then they hurt the British industry about equally badly with either the plain or the automatic loom. Of course, it could still be argued that unions hurt the industry because they prevented the attainment of workloads of 20 or so automatic looms by 1914. Even if this were so, however, in the absence of unions the automatic looms would not in themselves have earned anything like 32% because the workers would also be operating 6 or 8 plain looms. Under those circumstances, the automatic loom would once again have been about as good an investment in Great Britain as it was in the United States.

Indeed, even the assumption that the British unions were responsible for keeping British work loads below American levels is probably unsound. Although the unions may have had something to do with it, it should be noted that British work loads in general were lower than American work loads. Furthermore, these lower work loads in Great Britain were not limited to industries or crafts with strong unions. The argument about British unions and work loads thus easily deteriorates into the not-very-illuminating conclusion that the British cotton industry would have been better off had British weavers accepted American work loads in return for British earnings.

5

OVERALL EFFICIENCY
AND LABOR
PRODUCTIVITY IN
LANCASHIRE AND
MASSACHUSETTS BEFORE
WORLD WAR I

Easily the most important and influential work on productivity changes in the Lancashire cotton textile industry, as well as the Massachusetts cotton textile industry and a number of other industries, is that of G. T. Jones. This is particularly true of the period leading up to World War I because the later work of Marc Blaug ends in 1886.[1] Jones's calculations are included in *Increasing Returns,* published in 1933.

The most important conclusion reached by Jones, at least for the purposes of this study, is that there was "little, if any, net change in the efficiency of British cotton . . . manufacturing" between 1885 and 1910.[2] Indeed, his figures indicate that a similar conclusion holds up to 1914 as well as up to 1910.[3] Jones also concludes that during the same period efficiency in the Massachusetts cotton textile industry increased

---

[1] M. Blaug, "The Productivity of Capital in the Lancashire Cotton Industry during the Nineteenth Century."

[2] Jones, *Increasing Returns,* p. 51.

[3] Jones's figures indicate an efficiency improvement of between 0% and 2% between 1885 and 1914, depending on what type of moving average is used. I shall be conservative and use the 0% result. See Jones, *Increasing Returns,* p. 274.

by about 17%.[4] The conclusion concerning Lancashire is made
even more startling when Jones subdivides the period. He finds
that efficiency increased by about 1/2% per annum during
the 1890s but that this improvement was offset by a similar
rate of *decrease* in efficiency between 1900 and 1910, or 1914
for that matter.[5] Jones himself is somewhat perplexed by the
decrease in efficiency after 1900.

> Curiously [he states] this progressive fall in efficiency, at least
> so far as the consumer is concerned with the term, accompanied
> great expansion of plant and a rapid increase in the average
> size of firms operating.[6]

Despite Jones's own apparent surprise at his findings, they
have had a tremendous influence on subsequent views of the
Lancashire cotton industry in the pre–World War I period.
To take only one prominent example, J. H. Clapham states
that "the real costs of cotton manufacture, on the other hand,
fell a little in the nineties and then rose."[7] Clapham then
proceeds to quote, without any reservation, Jones's conclusion
that efficiency in the British cotton textile industry did not
improve between 1885 and 1910. He also notes the improvement
Jones found in the efficiency of the Massachusetts industry.[8]
Other prominent economic historians who agree that there
was no improvement in the efficiency of the Lancashire (or
British) cotton textile industry between 1885 and 1910 include
E. H. Phelps-Brown, S. J. Handfield-Jones,[9] Sidney Pollard,[10]
R. E. Tyson,[11] W. Ashworth,[12] and Colin Clark (Jones's editor).[13]

---

[4] Jones states that the improvement was 17% (Ibid., p. 51), but his tables indicate
that it was either about 15% or about 13% depending on whether 1910 or 1860
weights are used (pp. 289–90).

[5] Ibid., pp. 55, 117.

[6] Ibid., p. 117.

[7] Clapham, *The Economic History of Modern Britain,* p. 70.

[8] Ibid.

[9] E. H. Phelps-Brown and S. J. Handfield-Jones, "The Climacteric of the 1890's:
A Study in the Expanding Economy," p. 274.

[10] S. Pollard, *The Development of the British Economy, 1914–1950,* p. 4.

[11] Tyson, "The Cotton Industry," p. 123.

[12] W. Ashworth, *An Economic History of England, 1870 to 1939,* p. 106.

[13] C. Clark, *The Conditions of Economic Progress,* pp. 306–10.

A. E. Musson refers to "declining efficiency" in the British cotton industry and mentions the much better performance of the American industry.[14] C. P. Kindleberger also mentions Jones's findings on the British cotton industry, but his statements concerning the efficiency of the industry are more restrained than those of Jones himself and the authors listed above.[15]

There can be no doubt that these authors have been influenced in their general view of the British cotton textile industry by Jones's results. With the possible exception of Tyson, they are all highly critical of Lancashire for not adopting the automatic loom and for not going all out for ring spinning. What is more, Tyson, who apparently believes that the automatic loom and ring spindle were ill suited to Lancashire's needs, still concludes:

> The greater use of these two inventions [i.e., the automatic loom and the ring spindle] was a major factor in the much more rapid increase in efficiency in the American cotton industry.[16]

Tyson presents Jones's results to justify his statement that American (or at least Massachusetts) efficiency increased much faster than British (i.e., Lancashire) efficiency.[17] Kindleberger also links a drop in the rate of increase in efficiency with the failure to adopt ring spindles and automatic looms.[18]

Although Jones's results are generally accepted and widely used by economic historians, however, they nonetheless have some very peculiar aspects. In particular, it is very difficult to reconcile the lack of improvement in overall efficiency between 1884 and World War I, not to mention the decrease in efficiency recorded after 1900, with what was happening to output per unit of labor input.

A first estimate of output per unit of labor input in Lancashire is presented in Table 14. This table contains an index, and

---

[14] A. E. Musson, "The Great Depression in Britain," p. 207.
[15] Kindleberger, *Economic Growth in France and Britain*, pp. 137, 273.
[16] Tyson, "The Cotton Industry," p. 122.
[17] Ibid.
[18] Kindleberger, *Economic Growth in France and Britain*, p. 273.

TABLE 14

INDICES OF OUTPUT PER WORKER IN THE
LANCASHIRE COTTON TEXTILE INDUSTRY
(1890–1899 = 100)

Year	Index	Three-year Moving Average
1884	92	90
1885	83	89
1886	92	89
1887	92	93
1888	94	93
1889	93	96
1890	100	97
1891	98	97
1892	92	94
1893	91	93
1894	99	97
1895	100	100
1896	101	100
1897	100	103
1898	108	106
1899	111	108
1900	105	108
1901	107	106
1902	105	105
1903	98	100
1904	98	107
1905	114	109
1906	115	115
1907	117	110
1908	99	108
1909	108	100
1910	94	104
1911	111	108
1912	120	117
1913	119	120*

SOURCE: Phelps-Brown and Handfield-Jones, "The Climacteric of the 1890s," pp. 294, 295, 297.
*Based on two years only.

a three-year moving average of this index, relating the output of cotton goods to employment in the British cotton textile industry. The output part of this index was developed by none other than G. T. Jones himself.[19] This output part (i.e., the numerator) consists of the mean of the indices of cotton

[19] Jones, *Increasing Returns*, p. 275.

consumption (i.e., yarn produced) and yarn consumed. Yarn consumed is defined as yarn produced minus exports and increases in stocks. The employment series (i.e., the denominator of the index) consists of employment in British cotton mills and is based on the occupational classifications used by *The Census of England and Wales,* 1911, vol. 9, *Occupations and Industries,* Part 1.

The three-year moving average of this output-per-worker index indicates approximately a 38% increase in output per worker between 1885 and 1913. It is likely that this is a slight exaggeration, however, because the period 1912–14 was somewhat more prosperous for the cotton industry than was the period 1884–86. Good years tend to give higher output-per-worker figures because there is less unemployment than in bad years. Indeed, it can easily be seen from Table 14 that there is something of a cyclical movement in these indices and that this movement corresponds, at least roughly, to movements of prosperity and recession in the industry. In view of this fact, I would estimate that a 35% increase in output per worker is a more accurate figure than 38%.

This series, moreover, should be adjusted for several other factors. First of all, there is the 6% improvement in average wages resulting from changes in the composition of the work force to be considered. Because the principal purpose of this exercise is to measure the improvement in output per unit of labor due to such factors as improved machinery, organization, and management, it seems appropriate to subtract this 6% from the 35% increase in output per worker. On the other hand, the 3% decrease in the work week that occurred in 1901 should be added. The net effect of these two adjustments in the output-per-worker series is to reduce the 35% improvement in output per worker to a 32% improvement in output per unit of labor input.

So far, it has been assumed that the quality of the product remained constant between 1885 and 1913. In fact, however, it is perfectly clear that average quality was improving. My earlier study of changes in the quality of British cotton textile exports indicates a 7% to 8% improvement in the quality of the average piece of cotton cloth and pound of cotton yarn exported between 1885 and 1913.[20] Because exports amounted to almost 80% of British cotton output (by weight) in 1900, changes in export quality must have had a preponderant effect on overall quality. Moreover, observers of the industry are virtually unanimous in the opinion that this period witnessed considerable improvement in the average quality of output.[21] I believe that using the 7% to 8% estimate I calculated for exports as a measure of overall quality improvement will not result in much error.

After this final adjustment, my calculations indicate that output per unit of labor input increased by approximately 40% between 1885 and 1913. This represents a growth rate of almost exactly 1% per annum compounded. The cyclical nature of the series makes it very difficult to say much about the trend rate during various subperiods. I think the most reasonable preliminary conclusion is that the rate of increase was about the same over the entire period. Certainly, there is no evidence of an end to the growth of output per unit of labor input after 1900. This is especially true when it is considered that the work week was reduced by 3% in 1901 and that the period 1898–1900 was a prosperous one for the cotton industry.[22]

Thus, the problem arises of reconciling a 40% increase in output per unit of labor input between 1885 and 1914 with Jones's finding of *no* decrease in real cost. One possible way of reconciling such results would be to assume a constant technology combined with a very large increase in capital per head. In other words, a replacement of labor by capital without any improvement in the average productivity of the capital equipment despite its average later date of construction.[23] In fact, however, technology was improving,[24] and the standard

[20] Sandberg, "Movements in the Quality of British Cotton Textile Exports," p. 11.

[21] See, for example, S. Chapman, *A Reply to the Report of the Tariff Commission,* p. xv.

[22] Cotton consumption set new records in both 1898 and 1899, and consumption in 1900 was greater than in any year before 1898. See Chapter 3, Table 6.

[23] This is the approach taken by Phelps-Brown and Handfield-Jones, although they only try to explain "part" of the difference between the real cost and the output-per-head series (ibid., p. 274 n).

[24] Interestingly enough, this fact is clearly accepted by Clapham (at least in

criticism of the industry was that it was *not* adopting the new capital intensive methods. Furthermore, though capital deepening might explain the slow improvement in real cost up to 1900, it is difficult to see how it could reconcile continuing growth in output per unit of labor after 1900 with an *increase* in real cost.

Another approach to explaining the failure of real cost to decline in the 1885–1910 period is taken by Tyson. He accounts for the lack of improvement by accepting Jones's proposition that "the reasonable conclusion seems to be that a large proportion of the economies reaped from technical progress have been offset by the high cost of meeting the demands of the workers as regards hours and conditions of work."[25]

Although it may be true that the workers held back progress by such demands, this effect is already included in the index of output per unit of labor input. This explanation, originally offered by Jones and repeated by Tyson thus could not possibly reconcile a rapid increase in the output/labor ratio with a zero growth rate in overall efficiency.

The only reasonable conclusion possible to my mind is that all the writers who accepted Jones's figures, including Jones himself, did not bother to look at the readily available figures on output per unit of labor input. A glance at these figures, together with the generally accepted belief that the average quality of output was increasing during the period, should have been enough to convince anyone that there was something very strange about Jones's figures for the period after 1900 and that these results were in need of reexamination. I now intend to proceed with such a revision.

THE NATURE OF JONES'S "REAL COST" INDEX

Jones's conclusions are based on a series that he describes as being an index of "real cost." He uses changes in this series

---

spinning) on page 176 of *An Economic History of Modern Britain* despite the fact that he also accepts Jones's conclusions about no improvements in efficiency on page 70.

[25] Tyson, "The Cotton Industry," p. 123.

to measure changes in "efficiency." The index Jones computed for each given year is the following:

$$P'_a = P - \sum_{i=1}^{M} \frac{(\pi_i - A_i) Y_{ai}}{X_a} \qquad \text{where,}$$

P'_a =   the "real cost" per unit of the product,

P =   the current sales price of each unit,

π_i =   the supply prices of the various inputs i in the current year,

A_i =   the supply prices of the various inputs i in the base year,

Y_{ai} =   the amounts of the various factors i used in producing X_a units of the product in the base year,

X_a =   the amount of the product produced in the base year, and

M =   the number of inputs.

In other words, the real cost is the per unit *price* received in any year minus the weighted sum of the difference between the price per unit of each input in the given year and in some base year. "Normal profits" are, of course, included because they represent the costs of capital and entrepreneurship. This real cost thus represents what it would have cost to produce a unit of the goods in a given year had the prices and levels of relative factor inputs experienced in the base year also occurred during the given year.

The reader will note that P'_a is the exact inverse (or shadow) of the total productivity measure that has achieved such prominence in the last decade.[26] This, of course, means that the rate of decline in P'_a is exactly the same thing as the rate of increase in total factor productivity since measured by Solow and others. Ironically enough, though Jones's empirical results have been readily—in fact, too readily—accepted, he has never

[26] This equivalence is asserted by D. N. McCloskey in an article in the *Quarterly Journal of Economics,* and is proved in his Ph.D. thesis (see D. N. McCloskey, "Productivity Change in British Pig Iron, 1870–1939," p. 290; and "Economic Maturity and Entrepreneurial Decline: British Iron and Steel, 1870–1915", p. 114).

been given the recognition due his theoretical precociousness.

For his computations, Jones puts the Ps and π_is in index form, with the base year values set equal to 100. All of the A_is are thus equal to 100. Y_{ai}/X_a is simply the percentage of total costs in the base year represented by each input. This type of calculation will produce P_as in index form with the value for the base year being 100.

In the particular case of cotton textiles, only three inputs (π_is and A_is) are used. These are raw cotton, labor, and all other expenses. The least satisfactory element in this calculation is clearly the "all other expenses" item. This item includes fuel, lubricants, upkeep, rates (i.e., property taxes), the cost of capital, salaries, and so on. The arbitrary nature of this category is increased by the fact that the trend of its supply prices (i.e., its πs) is estimated by using Sauerbeck's wholesale price index,[27] which is really an index of raw material prices.

BIASES IN JONES'S CALCULATIONS FOR LANCASHIRE

It is absolutely clear that the final index of real cost in the Lancashire cotton industry in the 1885–1914 period contains a number of biases, the net result of which is to seriously overstate the industry's real cost at the end, relative to the beginning, of the period. I will discuss these biases one by one:

1. The first and most important problem concerns the Ps (i.e., the price index of cotton cloth). Jones uses the price quotations on a group of well-defined cotton gray cloths that were published throughout this period by the London *Economist.* (This is a fine series; in addition to Jones, both Marc Blaug and I have used it in our studies of the Lancashire cotton textile industry.[28])

A serious difficulty arises, however, at the turn of the century. In 1903, the *Economist* suddenly changed the collection of gray

[27] Mitchell, *Abstract of British Historical Statistics,* p. 474–75.

[28] See Blaug, "The Productivity of Capital in the Lancashire Cotton Industry during the Nineteenth Century"; and Sandberg, "Movements in the Quality of British Cotton Textile Exports."

cloths whose prices it published. The reason for this switch is clear. The old set of gray cloths had been selected in 1845, and by 1903 they were no longer representative of the industry's output. Indeed, around 1898 or 1899, the prices of this old set of gray cloths began to behave very strangely.[29] Fortunately, when the new set of cloths was introduced, their prices were quoted back through 12 February 1898. The problem, therefore, is how to join the two series.

Jones begins his discussion of this matter by reporting that both sets of prices were available for 1902, 1901, 1900, and 1899,[30] omitting 1898. He then argues cogently that an early transition should be used because "the business done in the constituents of the first series was already falling off in 1899."[31] On this basis, he links the series in 1899.[32] On his own assumptions and arguments, however, it would have been better to make the transition in 1898. The only reasonable explanation of the procedure used by Jones is that he was unaware that the 1898 data was available.[33]

The choice of year in which to link the two series turns out to be of utmost importance. The old set of prices increased by an average of 11% between 1898 and 1899 while the prices of the new set remained virtually constant. Thus, if the new series is used starting in 1898 instead of 1899, the whole real-cost index is pushed down by approximately seven points (and seven percent). This simple adjustment eliminates the very peculiar decline in efficiency after 1900 reported by Jones and replaces it with an increase in efficiency of about 0.25 percent per annum.[34]

[29] Sandberg, "Movements in the Quality of British Cotton Textile Exports," p. 23.

[30] Jones, *Increasing Returns*, p. 108.

[31] Ibid., p. 109.

[32] That is, he sets the value of the second series in 1899 equal to the index value of the first series in that year.

[33] I find it difficult to understand how Jones could have missed the 1898 data. My suspicion is that he only looked at issues of the *Economist* where the January 1898 data (which was not presented) would have appeared if the *Economist* had in fact published it.

[34] Additional evidence for the superiority of the 1898 linkage comes from the behavior of the indices that have been calculated on the basis of this data. My index of the quality of British cotton cloth exports increases by 1.9% between

2. The second difficulty with Jones's results concerns the wage series he uses. For the years up to 1906, he uses G. H. Wood's index of weekly wages in the British cotton textile industry. On the whole, this seems to be an appropriate series. For purposes of measuring productivity or efficiency, however, this series should be adjusted in two ways. First of all, it should be adjusted for changes in the composition of the work force. The period 1885–1906 saw a sharp drop in the number of children working half-time in the industry. On the other hand, the percentage of youths and women increased. After a very careful study of these changes, G. H. Wood concluded that changes in the composition of the work force resulted in an increase in the average wage by almost 6%.[35] Thus, for my purposes, this effect means that Jones overstates the increase in wages by almost 6%. On the other hand, the average work week was reduced by about 3% in 1901.[36] The net effect of these two factors is to overstate the wage change between 1885 and 1906 by almost 3%.

Because the Wood series ends in 1906, Jones was forced to use some other index of wages after that date. He chose to use a series of *piece* rates. This, however, amounts to assuming that there was *no* increase in output per worker after 1906. Jones clearly recognizes that he has made this implicit assumption and tries to justify it with the following statement:

> It seems to me that there has been little change either in personal application or in technical equipment, therefore changes in piece rates may fairly be used to continue Mr. G. H. Wood's index of time rates.[37]

1898 and 1899 if the 1898 connection is used. If the 1899 linkage is used, however, quality shoots up by a totally inexplicable 18% (Sandberg, "Movements in the Quality of British Cotton Textile Exports," p. 11). As for Jones's index of real cost, the 1898 connection results in a 2% reduction between 1898 and 1899, and the later transition causes a very strange 5% increase in real cost (Jones, *Increasing Returns*, p. 274).

[35] G. H. Wood, "The Statistics of Wages in the Nineteenth Century, Part XIX. The Cotton Industry, Section V. Changes in the Average Wage of All Employed with Some Account of the Forces Operating to Accelerate or Retard the Progress of the Industry," p. 608.

[36] Jones, *Increasing Returns*, p. 103.

[37] Ibid.

In fact, however, as was demonstrated above, it appears that output per operative was increasing at a rate of about 1% per annum during the period concerned. For the years 1906 through 1914, this is approximately the equivalent of an 8% understatement of the increase in wages.

The net effect of the three factors considered above is to give the wage series used by Jones an approximately 5% downward bias for the entire 1885–1914 period. Because wages have a weight of 22% in the real-cost index, this means that a downward adjustment in real cost at the end of the period of about 1% is called for.

3. Jones's real-cost index assumes that "normal profits" are earned at all times. Profits higher than "normal" resulting from an increase in the price of cotton cloth (i.e., a higher P), without any adjustment in factor cost (i.e., the π_is), will result in higher real cost. High profits resulting from input savings (i.e., lower π_is) without a decrease in P will also result in a higher level of measured real cost. In other words, high profits are associated with "inefficiency," and low profits are associated with "efficiency."

The close relationship between Jones's real cost and profits can be seen in Table 15, which contains his index on an annual basis together with an estimate of average profits and average dividends in British cotton *spinning*. Unfortunately, profit and dividend data are not available for weaving companies.

Although it is difficult to make any exact measurement of this effect, it is perfectly clear that bad years for business were good years for real cost and vice versa. It is also clear that the period after 1900 was a better period in terms of profits and dividends than were the 1890s. This means that the first decade of this century should be given credit for some extra improvement in efficiency when compared with the those years. More important, though 1909 and 1910 were bad years, 1912–14 was certainly a better period than was 1884–86.[38] Thus, if Jones's index is used for the 1885–1914 period, a couple of percentage points should probably be subtracted from the index of real cost in 1914.

[38] Any kind of longer moving average would also show the end of the period to have been more profitable than the beginning.

TABLE 15

Dividends and Profits in the British Cotton Spinning Industry Compared with Jones's Real-Cost Index

Year	Real Cost Index (1910 = 100)	Average Profits (per company in £)	% Dividend
1884	103	2,083	5.0
1885	104	−31	2.0
1886	106	−686	3.0
1887	105	986	4.75
1888	106	2,952	5.0
1889	106	2,565	5.0
1890	106	4,220	7.0
1891	112	384	5.25
1892	108	−957	1.25
1893	107	−614	1.0
1894	106	48	1.5
1895	104	678	1.625
1896	98	528	1.75
1897	99	1,676	3.0
1898	103	3,020	4.5
1899	108	4,432	6.125
1900	102	4,307	7.25
1901	104	3,494	7.5
1902	101	−16	4.66
1903	100	−503	3.0
1904	104	352	2.5
1905	113	7,701	7.0
1906	111	6,555	9.66
1907	107	13,211	15.875
1908	105	5,865	11.75
1909	90	−2,720	7.875
1910	100	−3,680	5.75
1911	115	288	4.75
1912	111	5,584	7.25
1913	108	5,366	7.25
1914	105	531	6.875
1915	96	−150	5.0
1916	96	4,004	7.5
1917	83	5,739	7.5
1918	216	14,403	16.25
1919	186	14,786	21.25
1920	327	n.a.	40.21
1921	158	n.a.	9.97
1922	115	n.a.	4.01
1923	111	n.a.	2.27
1924	141	n.a.	2.43
1925	140	n.a.	4.65

Sources: Jones Index, Jones, *Increasing Returns*, p. 274; profits and dividends, Robson, *The Cotton Industry in Britain*, p. 338.

4. The weighting of the various factor price series creates an "index" problem. In the case of British cotton textiles, it seems certain that the use of 1910 weights tends to increase the real cost at the end of the period. This is the case because labor costs were a smaller percentage of total costs in 1885 than in 1910, and wages increased more rapidly over the course of the period than did either cotton prices or "general prices."[39] Although the direction of this effect is clear, its importance is probably not great; and I shall make no explicit attempt to include it in my adjustment of Jones's "real cost" series for Lancashire.

5. The use of Sauerbeck's index of wholesale, raw material prices to estimate the price trend of "all other expenses" creates yet another bias in Jones's results. The Sauerbeck index increased less during this period than did the best available index of the cost of investment in manufacturing as well as the likely advance in salaries. In addition, the price of coal, which played a much more important role in "all other expenses" of British cotton mills than it did in the Sauerbeck index, increased considerably more rapidly than did the index as a whole.

In order to eliminate this bias, I have disaggregated the "all other expenses" category and applied separate price indices to the resulting components.

Jones estimates that of the 17% in the catch-all category, 7% "is normally absorbed by gross interest (including depreciation) upon capital engaged in the industry."[40] A perusal of the detailed production costs of British mills collected by the U.S. Tariff Board confirms that this is a reasonable estimate.[41] On the basis of the same data, I have concluded that a reasonable division of the remaining 10% of total costs is: salaries 2.5%, fuel 2%, other supplies 2%, and the residual (e.g., property taxes) 3 1/2%.

The standard index of the cost of physical capital in manufacturing during this period is that developed by Phelps-Brown and Handfield-Jones.[42] According to this index, the cost of

[39] See Jones, *Increasing Returns*, p. 274.
[40] Jones, *Increasing Returns*, p. 109.
[41] U.S. Tariff Board, p. 414.
[42] Phelps-Brown and Handfield-Jones, "The Climacteric of the 1890's," p. 305.

manufacturing equipment, including factory construction, increased by approximately 17% between 1885 and 1912. In view of the ongoing inflation, the increase was certainly somewhat greater between 1885 and 1914. This compares with an increase of 13% in the Sauerbeck index between 1885 and 1914. If we assume that there was constant interest, depreciation, and "normal" profit rates between 1885 and 1914 (changes, in any case, should have been accounted for in section 3 above), this difference implies that for 1914 Jones's index of "real cost" is too large by approximately 0.3%.

If the reasonable assumption is made that salaries in the British cotton industry increased at the same rate as wages, another overestimate of 0.5% is discovered.

British coal prices increased by approximately 28% between 1885 and 1914.[43] Applying this price increase, instead of the Sauerbeck index, to the 2% of total costs allocated for fuel yields yet another overestimate of 0.3%.

The sum of these biases is that real cost as estimated by Jones is about 1% too high at the end of the period. There remains, moreover, the two remaining categories of expenses (all other supplies and the residual). The most reasonable price index to apply to the "other supplies" category seems to be Sauerbeck's separate index for "sundry raw materials." The contents of the two categories are at least similar in that lubricants play an important role in both of them.[44] If this is done, another upward bias of 0.4% is discovered.

Finally, there is the matter of the remaining 3 1/2% of costs I classified as the residual. Wishing to avoid over-estimating British productivity increases, and for want of anything better, I have accepted the original Sauerbeck index for this category. Fortunately, the small weight of this category makes it highly unlikely that much error has been introduced by this decision.

When the various adjustments listed above have been made, the net effect is to reduce Jones's real-cost index for 1914 by about 1.5 percentage points. (It may be of some interest to note that in making these adjustments I have implicitly

[43] Mitchell, *Abstract of British Historical Statistics*, p. 482.
[44] Ibid., p. 475.

replaced the Sauerbeck index, with its 13% increase between 1885 and 1914, with a new price index for "all other costs" that increased by 22% over the same period.)

REVISED "EFFICIENCY" RESULTS FOR LANCASHIRE

The adjustments I have made above make a good deal of difference in the results derived concerning efficiency changes in the Lancashire cotton textile industry. Whereas Jones's original calculations showed *no* improvement in efficiency between 1885 and 1910 and very little or no improvement between 1885 and 1914, his calculations including my modifications indicate—conservatively—a reduction of real cost by 9% to 10% between 1885 and 1910 and of 11% to 12% between 1885 and 1914. Furthermore, the importance of the reduction in real cost is greatly understated by this type of numerical result. It must be remembered that raw cotton has a weight of 61% in the real-cost index. Since virtually no economies in cotton usage were achieved during this period, almost all the increase in efficiency (i.e., reduction in real cost) must have referred to the utilization of labor, fuel, capital, and a few other minor items.[45] This, in turn, implies an increase in the efficiency (or productivity) of these factor inputs by about 25% to 30% between 1885 and 1914. What is more, after my corrections have been made, this improvement is spread fairly evenly over the period. The peculiar deterioration Jones recorded for the post-1900 period has vanished. It has, roughly speaking, been replaced by a continuation of the trend he noted for the 1890s.

COMPARISONS BETWEEN "EFFICIENCY" CHANGES AND LABOR
PRODUCTIVITY GROWTH IN LANCASHIRE

The two indices calculated above thus indicate that there was approximately a 25% to 30% improvement in output per

[45] The evidence indicates that major improvements in cotton utilization were made during and just after the American Civil War. It is generally assumed that cotton wastage did not decrease markedly after that period (see Blaug, "The Productivity of Capital in the Lancashire Cotton Industry," p. 377).

unit of all inputs, other than raw cotton, and approximately a 40% increase in output per unit of labor input. The relative sizes of these two figures seem eminently reasonable, for the innovations of this period appear to have been more labor- than capital-saving.[46] It seems certain that there was at least some capital-deepening in the British cotton industry during this period.[47]

My revision of Jones's series also provides an answer to another mystery. Namely, if Jones's efficiency series was correct, how was it that Britain was able to increase her exports of cotton goods between 1885 and World War I? An even bigger mystery was how to explain the continued growth of British cotton textile exports after the alleged decline in efficiency set in about 1900. That these increases in exports were far from negligible can be seen from Table 16.

The only attempt to reconcile Lancashire's allegedly poor productivity performance with her excellent export perform- ance that I have seen was made by Kindleberger. While discussing the growth of British exports before World War I, Kindleberger makes the following statement concerning cotton textiles:

[46] These numbers seem to be compatible with the findings of Jewkes and Gray on wage increases for mule spinners. They found that between 1886 and 1914 the average mule spinner's wage increased by about 18 more percentage points than can be explained by changes in the wage lists (Jewkes and Gray, *Wages and Labor in the Lancashire Cotton Spinning Industry*, pp. 18–20, 197–98). This increase in wages was thus the result of increases in output per man. The structure of these wage lists was such, however, that an 18% increase in wages would have required more than an 18% increase in output per head, at least to the extent that faster or longer frames (i.e., spinning machines) had anything to do with the increase (as they undoubtedly did). Indeed, under the most important mule- spinning wage list, the Oldham list, an 18% increase in wages in all probability reflects more than a 36% increase in output per man. Although the other lists were less demanding, the 18% wage increase found by Jewkes and Gray in all probability reflects an increase of not less than 30% in output per man, and a 15 to 20% increase in overall productivity (excluding raw cotton) seems reasonable. In addition, these numbers would be somewhat larger if account were taken of the shortening of the work week. That they still remain smaller than the overall figures I calculated for the entire cotton industry should be no cause for alarm. The rapid growth of ring spinning makes it certain that the figures for the entire spinning section were greater than those for mule spinning alone and probably greater also than my industry wide figures.

[47] See Phelps-Brown and Handfield-Jones, "The Climacteric of the 1890's" p. 274.

TABLE 16

BRITISH EXPORTS OF COTTON PIECE GOODS IN VARIOUS YEARS
(in millions of yards)

Year	To All Countries	To India	To All Countries except India
1883	4,359	1,620	2,739
1890	5,125	2,183	2,932
1895	5,033	1,840	3,193
1900	5,032	2,016	3,016
1905	6,197	2,539	3,658
1910	6,017	2,356	3,661
1913	7,075	3,216	3,849

SOURCE: *British Parliamentary Papers,* Trade Returns for the above years.

Of the expansion from five to seven billion yards between 1900
and 1913, when Manchester had its last boom, fully half went
to India. The rate of technological advance had slowed down
after 1870, and the ring spindle and automatic loom were
virtually neglected. [At this point there is a reference to Jones.]
But the industry succeeded in achieving the removal of the
Indian 5 per cent revenue import [duty?] in 1882 and the
equalization of the excise tax on British and Indian output
in 1896.[48]

It is true that the complete abolition of cotton duties in 1882
probably helped Lancashire increase her exports to India in
the 1880s, but it is difficult to believe that the "equalization"
of taxes achieved in 1896 had much effect on the post-1900
period. What happened in 1896 was that the 5% duty on
imported yarns and goods, accompanied by a 5% excise on
Indian yarns "above 20's counts," that had been imposed in
December 1893 was replaced by a 3.5% duty on imported
piece goods (but not yarn) and a 3.5% excise on Indian piece
goods produced on power looms. Indian cotton cloth produced
on handlooms remained exempt from taxation.[49] These changes
meant that Lancashire was in a slightly better position after
1896 than she had been between December 1893 and 1896,
but not as well off, principally because of the exemption of

[48] Kindleberger, *Economic Growth in France and Great Britain,* p. 273.
[49] A. Redford, *Manchester Merchants and Foreign Trade, Vol. II, 1850–1939,* pp.
27–31, 40–41.

Indian handloom weaving from taxation, as she had been between 1882 and December 1893. In view of these facts, the "equalization" of 1896 seems to be a very thin reed on which to rest an explanation of the rapid increase in British cotton textile exports, even to India, between 1900 and World War I. The only other possible explanation for the export boom combined with constant, or decreasing, overall efficiency would be a compression of profits. In fact, however, available data do not indicate any great squeeze on profits during the period 1900–1913.[50] Apparently, the improvement in efficiency was great enough to permit a growth in exports with customary profit.

"EFFICIENCY" GROWTH IN THE
MASSACHUSETTS COTTON TEXTILE INDUSTRY

Because the standard approach has been to compare slow, or nonexistent, growth in British productivity with rapid improvement in America, I intend to compare the series I have calculated for Lancashire with their American (or rather, Massachusetts) counterparts. These comparisons will help to put the British figures in perspective as well as to shed some further light on the role of the automatic loom and the ring spindle in the two countries.

The Jones index of real cost for the Massachusetts cotton textile industry indicates a drop in real cost between 1885 and 1910 of 15%, if end-period weights are used, and 13% if 1860 weights are used.[51] The results for the period up through 1913 are virtually identical to those for 1910, but their reliability is reduced by the fact that some World War I years enter into the moving average. Jones used a weight of 55% for raw cotton both in 1860 and the end of the period.[52] A 45% weight on inputs other than raw cotton implies an increase in the efficiency with which labor, capital, fuel, and the like were used of between 29% and 33%.

[50] Robson, *The Cotton Industry in Britain*, p. 338.
[51] Based on a seven-year moving average (Jones, *Increasing Returns*, pp. 298–90).
[52] Ibid., p. 192.

Jones's series for Massachusetts seems to be largely exempt from the problems that plague his Lancashire series. For the product prices (the *P*s), Jones uses a continuous series for the period 1847–1920.[53] This, of course, eliminates the problem of splicing series that was so crucial in the British case. In addition, Jones has apparently accounted for changes in the composition of the labor force in the process of calculating his wage series.[54] On the other hand, he takes no account of the 10% reduction in the work week in Massachusetts that occurred during this period.[55] This implicit increase in weekly wages raises the 29% to 34% range calculated above to 34% to 39%. This latter range is similar in nature to the 25% to 30% figure calculated for improvements in British productivity.

I have decided not to try to explicitly disaggregate the "all other expenses" category as I did in the case of England. The principal reason for this decision is that Jones used a much more satisfactory index for estimating what happened to prices in this category for Massachusetts than he did for England. The considerable deficiencies of the subseries of prices that are available are such that I would place no greater confidence in the results of a disaggregation in this particular case than I place in Jones's results.[56] The components of this index are: wholesale prices, 20%; wage payments, 35%; "elements of the cost of living," 35%; and rents, 10%. In view of the very heavy weight placed on wages, by far the most rapidly growing component of the index, it is my judgement that the Snyder index is more likely to overestimate than to underestimate the true price increase for the "all other expenses" category. Thus, if anything, the rate of productivity growth in the Massachusetts cotton industry is slightly exaggerated as a result of the use of this index.

[53] Ibid., p. 156.

[54] Ibid., p. 165.

[55] Ibid., p. 161.

[56] For the price of the "all other expenses" category in Massachusetts, Jones used the price index developed in 1924 by Carl Snyder (see C. Snyder, "A New Index of the General Price Level from 1875," pp. 189–95).

TABLE 17

INDICES OF OUTPUT PER WORKER IN THE
UNITED STATES COTTON TEXTILE INDUSTRY
(1890–1899 = 100)

Year	Index	Three-year Moving Average
1884	70	77
1885	86	80
1886	84	87
1887	90	89
1888	94	96
1889	103	101
1890	106	107
1891	111	103
1892	91	95
1893	83	93
1894	104	90
1895	84	93
1896	92	95
1897	109	104
1898	112	110
1899	109	108
1900	103	108
1901	113	110
1902	113	110
1903	105	112
1904	116	114
1905	122	120
1906	121	117
1907	107	116
1908	121	112
1909	108	111
1910	104	110
1911	117	115
1912	124	121
1913	123	124

SOURCE: B. Weber and S. J. Handfield-Jones, "Variations in the Rate of Economic Growth in the USA, 1869–1939," p. 127.

LABOR PRODUCTIVITY GROWTH IN MASSACHUSETTS

Once again, it is of considerable interest to see what happened to output per unit of labor input. Table 17 contains information for the United States comparable to the information for Britain contained in Table 14.

These numbers—in particular, the three-year moving

average—indicate approximately a 55% increase in output per person employed in the cotton industry between 1885 and 1913.[57] To make this figure comparable to the British one, however, some adjustments are necessary. The British figure is based on output *per hour* of labor input. During this period, there was a 10% reduction in the work week in Massachusetts. This reduction was certainly somewhat greater than the average work week reduction in the United States as a whole. Because the efficiency (Jones) series is based on the Massachusetts industry alone and because my problem is to explain an unusually high increase in output per unit of labor in the United States, I have decided to be conservative and assume a 10% reduction in the work week. Such a reduction, combined with the series in Table 17, indicates that there was approximately a 71% increase in output per hour of labor.

Adjustments should also be made for changes in the composition of the work force and for changes in the average quality of output. Unfortunately, very little is known in detail about these factors. It seems clear that the quality of output in Massachusetts increased because of the movement of low-quality production to the South. The series in Table 17, however, refers to output per worker in the whole United States, and it is difficult to say much about the quality of production for the whole United States.[58] A problem also occurs with regard to the composition of the work force. It is generally believed that the quality both of the Massachusetts work force and the national cotton textile work force improved during this period.[59]

[57] Since the efficiency figures are really based on a period ending in 1910, the figure for increases in output per worker between 1885 and 1910 is also of interest. This figure turns out to be only 38%. It must be noticed, however, that the three-year average of the output/labor index is in the bottom of a slump in 1910. Its value for 1910 was the lowest since 1899. It seems clear that the 38% figure is an aberration on the low side. In view of this, and since my problem is to explain a very high, not low, rate of increase in the output/labor ratio for the United States, I shall take the conservative route and use the 55% increase for the period up to 1913.

[58] Reasonable arguments can be made both for and against improved quality. On the one hand, increased per capita income would probably tend to raise the average quality demanded. On the other hand, most of the labor- and cost-saving innovations of the period (i.e., the automatic loom) were particularly well suited to the production of relatively low quality goods.

[59] See Jones, *Increasing Returns*, p. 164; and Copeland, *The Cotton Manufacturing Industry of the United States*, pp. 112–14.

The percentage of women in the cotton industry labor force continually declined starting at least in 1870, and the number of children actually declined sharply in absolute numbers in New England between 1880 and 1905.[60] It is, however, difficult to estimate an exact value for this improvement. In view of these problems, and in order to make a conservative (i.e., large) estimate of labor productivity growth, I have assumed that the improvement in the labor force that almost certainly occurred was offset by an equal improvement in the average quality of output.

One further problem deserves to be mentioned. As was noted above, the real-cost index computed by Jones refers only to the Massachusetts industry, but the output-per-worker series refers to the entire United States. For my purposes, however, I doubt whether that makes much difference. For one thing, in 1914, New England still had a considerably larger cotton textile industry than did the South.[61] More important, there was relatively little difference in the equipment used in the two regions. As was noted in chapter 3, there were almost no mules at all used in American cotton spinning, except possibly for the very highest qualities. As for weaving, the slightly higher percentage of automatic looms in the South (50% versus 40%) can be explained by the type of cloth produced in the two regions.

This judgment is supported by the fragmentary data available on the Massachusetts cotton textile industry taken separately. Census data indicate that between 1889 and 1914, cotton consumption per worker in Massachusetts increased by about 11 percentage points less than it did in the country as a whole.[62] Part, but certainly not all, of this difference can be explained by a more rapid improvement in the average quality of output in Massachusetts than elsewhere.[63] Thus, the 71% figure I have computed for the increase in output per unit of labor

[60] Copeland, *The Cotton Manufacturing Industry of the United States*, pp. 112–14.

[61] In 1914, there were 263,683 cotton looms in the South and 380,177 in the North (Feller, "The Draper Loom in New England Textiles," p. 326).

[62] Jones, *Increasing Returns*, p. 291.

[63] Part of the difference is also due to the large decreases in the Massachusetts work week that were introduced in 1909 and 1910. This particular effect, however, has already been included in my 71% figure.

input in Massachusetts is probably a reasonable upper limit and can usefully be compared to the 34% to 39% range I estimated for overall "efficiency" growth.

COMPARISONS BETWEEN THE RESULTS FOR MASSACHUSETTS
AND THOSE FOR LANCASHIRE

The first point of interest about the American figures is that the difference between the increase in output per unit of labor input and the increase in efficiency was greater than the corresponding difference I obtained for Great Britain. On the other hand, the American difference is *smaller* than the difference in Britain that would result from accepting Jones's conclusion of zero improvement in British efficiency. In fact, of course, the reasonable expectation is that the difference would be *considerably greater* in America. This follows from the fact that America went much further than Great Britain in adopting capital intensive, labor-saving machinery, particularly in weaving. There can be no doubt that there was much more capital-deepening in the American than in the British cotton industry.

This observation naturally leads to the question of how to explain the differing rates of growth in output per unit of labor input and in "efficiency" that occurred in the United States and Great Britain.

First, what factors can be used to explain the fact that output per unit of labor input increased by about 71% in the United States and by only 40% in Great Britain?

1. The first and most obvious factor that comes to mind is automatic weaving. Fortunately, it is possible to estimate the reduction in American labor input per unit of output that can be explained by the introduction of automatic weaving. Weaving labor accounted for almost 60% of the total labor costs involved in converting raw cotton into gray cloth with plain looms,[64] and automatic looms reduced the amount of weaving labor needed by between 35% (Uttley) and 40% (United States Tariff Board). Combining this information with the fact

[64] U.S. Tariff Board, p. 472.

that by 1914 about 45% of all United States cotton looms were automatic implies that the use of automatic looms in the United States reduced the labor input of American cotton mills by at least 10%. Because the proportion of cloth produced on automatic looms is the true determinant of the saving and because automatic looms generally had higher unit outputs, this estimate is extremely conservative. A more realistic figure would be that the automatic looms (45% of total) produced close to 60% of all cloth output. In that case, the resulting labor-saving would be 13.5%. Considering that 40% of all New England cotton looms were automatic, the labor-saving in Massachusetts was probably only slightly less than for the country as a whole. Thus, the automatic loom can be credited with at least one-third of the difference in labor productivity growth between Massachusetts and Great Britain. In addition, some allowance should be made for the substantial number of warp stop motions (particularly popular in New England) that were in use in 1914.

2. Another factor was the greater use of ring spindles in Massachusetts. Ring spinning of counts above 40 saved labor at some cost in capital and, more important, higher quality raw cotton.[65] Spinning of such high counts on rings was, of course, the rule in all of the United States by 1914, whereas it was practically unheard of in Great Britain. Ring spinning

[65] The use of higher-quality cotton would not affect the cost of inputs, according to Jones's formula. Thus, if a new method required more expensive cotton to produce a given quality of cloth by a new method, the Jones index would tend to exaggerate the decrease in real costs due to the new method. Similarly, if more expensive cotton permitted easier spinning and weaving with a given technology, then the introduction of this more expensive cotton would reduce "real costs" (as measured by Jones) without there being any real increase in efficiency. This fact implies that just as I have tried to adjust Jones's productivity indexes and the output per unit of labor input indices for changes in the average quality of the labor used and the cloth produced, so I should have included an adjustment for changes in the average quality of the raw cotton used.

Unfortunately, however, the quality of the raw cotton has at least as much to do with the quality of the product as with the cost of producing it. Thus, if I were to include an estimate of the quality of raw cotton consumed in my revision of Jones's indices, I would also have to estimate the changes in the quality of the output. In view of the poor data available on these questions, I do not feel that these elaborate calculations would improve on my results. Nevertheless, I expect that the undoubted improvement in the average quality of output both in Lancashire and Massachusetts means that even my revisions of Jones have a slight downward bias.

of counts below 40 saved both labor and capital. The saving of labor was clearly much more important than the saving of capital, however. The spinning of sub-40 counts was common in Great Britain by 1914, but in the United States it was the only method used. It might also be noted that in many cases in the United States, including Massachusetts, rings were put in to replace well-functioning mules. In these cases, even low-count ring spinning must be considered capital intensive. In terms of Jones's index, producers who threw out well-functioning mules and replaced them with new rings were increasing their investment (not reducing it as they did when they chose to put in new low-count rings rather than low-count mules), and they could only receive "normal profits" if the labor-saving was sufficiently large to provide a return on this increase in invested capital. For the purposes of this particular problem, however, the effect of ring spinning is somewhat reduced by the fact that, at least at low counts, it had already made a good deal of progress in Massachusetts by 1885.

3. All accounts indicate that the United States as a whole was behind Great Britain in preparatory machinery and methods in the middle 1880s and was catching up in this field during the period up to World War I.[66]

4. Reductions in the hours of work usually result in a proportionately smaller decrease in output.[67] Since the Massachusetts work week fell by more than the British work week during this period, some of the difference in output per hour of labor can probably be credited to this factor.

Whether these four points are enough to explain the British-Massachusetts divergence in labor productivity growth, or whether additional considerations such as managerial inefficiency or union obstruction in Great Britain have to be considered, is difficult to say. It seems extremely unlikely, however, that such factors can have accounted for more than a very small portion of the British lag.

[66] See, for example, Copeland, "Technical Developments in Cotton Manufacturing Since 1860," pp. 114–21.

[67] For a recent discussion of the evidence available on this point, see F. Leveson, "Reductions in Hours of Work as a Source of Productivity Growth," pp. 199–204. See also P. S. Florence, *Economics of Fatigue and Unrest*.

Finally, there is the British lag in efficiency improvement as measured by the (revised) Jones index. The gap here, appropriately enough, is less than half the labor productivity gap. Basically, however, I believe it can be explained by the same factors used to explain the labor productivity gap. Surely, the automatic loom and the ring spindle helped improve Massachusetts "efficiency," although this improvement in efficiency was certainly much smaller than the improvement in labor productivity resulting from the introduction of these machines. Furthermore, since they were better suited to American than to British conditions, it is by no means certain that British efficiency would have benefited from a more rapid rate of adoption. In any case, these innovations were bound to improve Massachusetts efficiency more than British efficiency even if adoption rates had been the same in both countries.

In addition, the above points about American catching-up in the preparatory processes and the larger decrease in the work week also apply to the efficiency index. In regard to the preparatory processes, there is certainly no sign of British irrationality or technical lag. Once again, however, it cannot be proved conclusively that the factors listed can explain all of the British lag in efficiency growth.

6

INVESTMENT IN
LANCASHIRE BETWEEN
THE WORLD WARS

Before this discussion of investment policy and productivity is concluded, something has to be said about investment policies in Lancashire during the interwar period. This period was basically one of depressed demand and low, or nonexistant, profits, at least after 1921. The seriousness of this depression can be seen from the profit and dividend data in Table 18. Equally impressive is the fact that in 1930 average capacity utilization in the British cotton textile industry was down to 58% in spinning and 54% in weaving.[1]

Thus, for most of the interwar period, there was little reason to invest in the British cotton textile industry. Not only was net investment generally negative but there was very little gross investment. The problem of choice of machinery and technique principally took the form of which types of equipment to keep and which to throw out.

A good idea of what happened in the spinning sector can be obtained from Table 19.

The only period of expansion shown in these tables is the 1913–24 period. Even then, capacity did not increase by more

[1] Robson, *The Cotton Industry in Britain*, p. 144.

TABLE 18

DIVIDENDS AND PROFITS IN THE BRITISH COTTON SPINNING INDUSTRY

Year	Average Profits (per company in £)	% Dividend
1919	14,786	21.25
1920	n.a.	40.21
1921	n.a.	9.97
1922	n.a.	4.01
1923	n.a.	2.27
1924	n.a.	2.43
1925	n.a.	4.65
1926	3,553	4.08
1927	−5,953	2.73
1928	−2,383	2.19
1929	−3,391	2.07
1930	−6,548	1.91
1931	−7,727	1.46
1932	−3,550	1.55
1933	−3,273	1.50
1934	−356	1.57
1935	196	1.75
1936	1,658	1.91
1937	8,857	4.28
1938	10,742	5.53
1939	5,596	5.39

SOURCE: Robson, *The Cotton Industry in Britain*, p. 338.

NOTE: This table must be treated with some degree of caution. The very bad results recorded for the twenties and early thirties were no doubt made worse by the overcapitalization (mostly with fixed-interest securities) that occurred in the years immediatly following World War I. Similarly, the improvement in the late 1930s was undoubtedly exaggerated by the bankruptcy of the most inefficient and most heavily debt-burdened companies in the industry.

than 4% (even with each ring counted as 1 1/3 mule). It seems clear, however, that there was no lack of interest in ring spinning during these years of relative prosperity.[2]

[2] The figures below represent the distribution of spindles by type of product in 1939.

Count of Yarn	Mules (millions)	Rings (millions)	Mule Equivalent Rings (ring = 1 1/3 mule, millions)	% Ring Capacity
0–16	3.9	1.5	2.0	33.9
17–26	2.3	3.6	4.8	67.6
27–48	6.6	3.3	4.4	40.0
49–80	7.6	1.6	2.1	21.6
81–	2.9	0.1	0.1	3.3

SOURCE: Board of Trade, Working Party on Cotton, *Report*, p. 39.

TABLE 19

CAPACITY AND INVESTMENT IN THE BRITISH COTTON SPINNING INDUSTRY

	EQUIPMENT AVAILABLE IN VARIOUS YEARS (MILLIONS OF SPINDLES)				
Year	Mules	Rings	Waste	Total	Rings as % of Mule Equivalents (1 Ring = 1.33 Mule)
1913	45.2	10.4	0.7	56.3	22.7
1924	43.7	13.1	0.8	57.6	28.2
1927	43.8	13.5*	0.8	58.1	28.4
1930	42.1	13.1	0.8	54.0	28.5
1937	27.0	10.7	0.9	38.6	34.0
1939	24.1	10.3	0.9	35.3	35.4

	INVESTMENT AND SCRAPPING (ANNUAL RATES IN THOUSANDS OF SPINDLES)				
Period	New Spindles Installed (Both Kinds)	Spindles Scrapped Mule	Ring	Net Increase Mule	Ring
1924–29	160	340	...	−180	...
1930–34	15	2,000	300	−2,000	−300
1935–38	50	1,330	170	−1,330	−120

SOURCES: Robson, *The Cotton Industry in Britain*, pp. 339, 349, 355. Figures for 1927 are from J. Ryan, "Machinery Replacement in the Cotton Industry," p. 577.

*The highest number of rings recorded in any year.

Between 1924 and 1930, there was very little change in spinning capacity. Gross investment during the period 1924–29 was only about 800,000 spindles. The rate of scrapping exceeded new installations slightly, at least for mule spindles. In view of the low profits earned during these years, it is surprising that the decline in capacity was not greater than it was. In fact, capacity only started to decline with any speed after the onset of the Great Depression. At the same time, gross investment declined almost to the vanishing point.

A number of reasons can be suggested for this rather precipitous drop in capacity after a period of almost no change. For one thing, the depression that had been plaguing Lancashire

The most surprising aspect of these figures is the relatively small role reported for rings in the sub-16 category. I believe this phenomena can principally be explained by a very low, or even negative, rate of growth of production of the very low counts starting well back in the nineteenth century. The undoubted improvement in the average quality of British cotton cloth after 1890 lends credence to this explanation. It also points out the extraordinary long physical life of mule frames.

ever since 1921 or 1922 plunged even deeper in 1930. This further decline not only worsened the objective condition of the industry, it also destroyed any lingering hopes of a recovery from the depression of the 1920s. The industry could no longer question the necessity of adjusting to a drastically reduced level of demand. Many manufacturers who had held on to their factories and equipment during the 1920s, despite losses, must have given up when they were faced with even worse market conditions. In addition, the bankruptcy rate increased while the number of people prepared to outbid the junkman (or sometimes foreign cotton manufacturers) in order to keep a bankrupt cotton mill in operation (or even in condition to operate in case business conditions should improve) was very small.[3]

As important as these market effects was the fact that for the first time organized steps were taken to reduce capacity.[4] Thus, for example, the Lancashire Cotton Corporation Ltd., which was formed in 1929 under the "auspices" of the Bank of England, had by 1939 absorbed 9 million spindles and had junked 4 1/2 million of them.[5]

The relevant question to ask about this process of disinvestment is whether the types of spindles taken out of operation seem reasonable. To give some idea of the kind of capacity needed in view of the composition of demand, I have included Table 20, which contains information on the counts of yarn spun in Great Britain in various years.

In chapter 2, I estimated that this information for 1924 implied that about 35% of all demand for British spinning capacity was for the spinning of sub-40 yarn. It seems likely from Table 19 that this percentage increased during the 1930s. Indeed, by 1937 it appears that over half the demand for

---

[3] As early as 1927, it was extremely difficult to sell a cotton mill to anyone who wanted to do anything but junk or cannibalize it (see B. Bowker, *Lancashire under the Hammer*, pp. 78–79).

[4] For a discussion of these capacity-reducing activities, see Robson, *The Cotton Industry in Britain,* chap. 7; A. F. Lucas, *Industrial Reconstruction and the Control of Competition: The British Experiment,* chap. 7; and Allen, *British Industries and Their Organization,* pp. 236–39.

[5] Robson, *The Cotton Industry in Britain,* p. 158; and Allen, *British Industries and Their Organization,* p. 238.

TABLE 20

COUNTS OF YARN SPUN IN GREAT BRITAIN
IN VARIOUS YEARS
(in millions of pounds)

Year	Up to 40s	41s–80s	81s–120s	121s–	Total
1912	n.a.	n.a.	n.a.	n.a.	1,982.8
1924	1,022.0	313.7	55.9	3.6	1,395.2
1930	821.6	185.2	36.8	3.5	1,047.1
1935	1,010.9	176.8	37.0	3.1	1,227.8
1937	1,135.1	181.2	37.1	4.4	1,357.8

SOURCE: Robson, *The Cotton Industry in Britain*, p. 343.

spindle capacity in Lancashire must have been for the production of sub-40 yarn. In absolute terms, however, the demand for sub-40 spinning capacity in 1937 was probably about the same as it had been in 1924. What is more important, since there was excess capacity in the industry even in 1924, it seems likely that the 13.1 million rings available in 1924 were probably just about enough to meet the entire demand for sub-40 yarn in that year. It is clear, however, that a great deal of sub-40 yarn must have been produced on mules.[6] Even in 1930, when there were probably *more* than enough rings to produce all the required sub-40 yarn, there were mules producing this kind of yarn. By 1937, however, the number of available rings had decreased, and there were probably no longer enough to meet the entire demand for sub-40 yarn. What is more, even then it seems that these rings were not working at full capacity.

Clearly, some explanation is needed for this phenomenon. Why were the rings not able to put the less efficient mules out of the sub-40 business when there were probably enough rings to meet the demand for this kind of yarn, and why did the number of rings decline? The problem is not eliminated even by the likelihood that the available mules were operated less than the available rings.

Some part of the continued ability of mules to produce sub-40 yarn can be explained by the special qualities of mule-spun yarn. An example of such a situation is the very cheapest type

[6] Robson, *The Cotton Industry in Britain*, p. 65; Board of Trade, *Report*, p. 39.

of cloth being sent to India. This cloth was designed to contain as much sizing and as little cotton as possible. Because the softer mule-spun yarn absorbed more sizing than did ring yarn, there must have been some weavers who were prepared to pay a premium for mule-spun low-count yarn.[7] In my judgment, however, this factor can by no means account for all the low-count mule spinning.

The most important reason for the continued survival of low-count mules, and the failure of the rings to work at full capacity on sub-40 yarn, however, was probably the agreements reached within the industry to spread the work through organized short-time and to maintain prices. These practices made it much more difficult for the ring-spinning firms to use their lower marginal costs to take business away from their mule-spinning competitors. This does not necessarily mean that these more efficient firms were made worse off by these regulations. All firms may have benefited. That is, the ring-spinning firms may have been better off spinning lower quantities at higher prices. The more efficient firms, however, obviously gained less from these agreements than did their competitors.

Between 1920 and the end of 1926, organized short-time became "the general rule" in the spinning of American cotton.[8] This system was organized by the Federation of Master Spinner's Associations. During most of this period, activity did not exceed two-thirds of a full single shift.[9]

This type of regulation did not permit the selling of output quotas, or even the concentration of a firm's output on its most efficient machines. Not only did this situation help keep low-count mule firms in operation, it also prevented firms with both types of equipment from concentrating their low-count output on their rings. As long as the cartel price covered variable cost on the mules, and the mules could only be sold for junk if they were to be removed, firms would keep and use their mules.

The rationale for this remarkably inefficient arrangement

---

[7] See U.S. Tariff Board, p. 494.
[8] Robson, *The Cotton Industry in Britain*, p. 222.
[9] Ibid.

naturally came from the trade unions, whose paramount interest was to spread the available work among all their members.

When this system of short-time work was abandoned, it was replaced by an agreement that took the form of a joint stock enterprise, the American Cotton Yarn Association Ltd. This company, or association, also attempted to provide output quotas. It did, however, have the desirable feature of permitting firms to sell their quotas.

In principle, this means that it was a joint profit-maximizing cartel. As Salter has shown, such a cartel should utilize the same scrapping and replacement rules as a firm operating in a competitive market.[10] A problem arose, however, because the share of each firm in the cartel depended on the number of spindles it had.[11] A firm's share of the monopoly profits thus depended on its spindlage. Clearly, this was an inducement to maintain, although not to use, sub-40 mules. By November 1927, however, this attempt at collective regulation had collapsed under the pressure of falling demand and price-cutting by nonmembers.[12]

After the collapse of the American Cotton Yarn Association, no organized attempt at output or price control achieved any success until 1933. In that year a price-fixing—or rather, a minimum price—agreement was reached. When this agreement threatened to collapse in 1934, a new agreement, which was legally binding on the signatories, was negotiated. These price-fixing agreements, of course, reduced the ability of the more efficient firms to take business away from their competitors.

It is, of course, true that a good deal of price-cutting was practiced throughout this period, and short-time quotas were exceeded even during periods when agreements were supposed to be in effect.[13] The worst years of the period, which were the years when no agreements were in effect, must have witnessed a fierce competition for orders. Furthermore, because the ring spinners had relatively low variable costs, they were probably among the leaders in cutting prices. There were forces

[10] Salter, *Productivity and Technical Change*, pp. 91–92.
[11] Robson, *The Cotton Industry in Britain*, p. 222.
[12] Ibid., p. 223.
[13] See Bowker, *Lancashire under the Hammer*, chaps. 4, 5.

working in the other direction, however. For one thing, the unions supported the short-time agreements. This could make violations dangerous regardless of variable costs. Second, though there was a good deal of price competition in the British cotton industry, there were also many imperfections in the market. In fact, complaints about the lack of standardization among processors and an excessive number of middlemen and exporters are among the standard complaints made about the industry. Under these circumstances, it seems certain that spinning firms with good connections would have had to be underbid by much more than an infinitesimally small amount before they lost all their customers.

Finally, before the ring-spinning firms could completely monopolize sub-40 spinning, they would have had to drive prices below the marginal costs of all the mule spinners for some period of time. It seems unlikely that they would have been able to do this, however. During the prosperous years right after World War I, many if not most British spinning firms were refinanced in such a way as to burden them with extremely heavy loads of fixed debt. Clearly, those ring-spinning firms who had accepted heavy debt loads were in no position to bankrupt those sub-40 mule-spinning firms that avoided this dangerous temptation. In any case, these heavy debt loads must have been a restraint on price-cutting; and this, in turn, must have been a great help to those relatively inefficient firms who had been financially prudent. It may have been possible to survive with either a heavy debt load or inefficient equipment but not with both.

Under these circumstances, it seems understandable that a substantial number of low-count mules survived during the depression.[14] Similarly, it seems reasonable that these low-count mules were not replaced by new rings. Although the relative advantage of rings over mules at sub-40 yarn well may have increased as compared with the pre–World War I situation,[15] the low level of capacity utilization and the bleak prospects for the industry clearly militated against such an investment.

[14] The percentage of rings, of course, increased continuously during the whole period (see Table 19).

[15] See chaps. 2, 3, above.

The failure to install any large number of rings for high counts is also easy to explain. Even if, as is quite likely, rings became a better new investment than mules even for high counts sometime after World War I, they were certainly not so much better that the mules in operation should have been thrown out. Furthermore, conditions in the industry were so bad that replacements were seldom made even for mules that wore out. During the whole decade of the 1930s, less than 300,000 spindles of any kind were installed in Great Britain.

The only problem that remains is how to explain the decline in the number of ring spindles in Great Britain from 13.1 million in 1930 (and 1924) to 10.3 million in 1939, while many sub-40 mules remained operable. It would seem that all, or almost all, of the sub-40 mules should have been junked before any of the more efficient rings were removed. It must be remembered, however, that though the British cotton textile industry was not the only cotton textile industry in the world, it was the most depressed. Throughout most of this period, there were protected cotton industries in countries other than Great Britain that were making money and expanding their capacity.[16] Thus, whereas no type of equipment could make much of a profit in Great Britain, modern equipment was of value elsewhere. Thus, British ring spindles could be dismantled and sold abroad at prices above the scrap value, although well below the prices of new rings.[17] It seems highly unlikely that anyone would have been willing to pay anything but scrap value for low-count mules. In other words, at least part of the superior efficiency of rings over mules at low counts was capitalized into the resale value of the equipment. Thus, if little or no money could be made with either type of equipment in Great Britain (because of low prices and low rates of capacity utilization), then the opportunity cost of keeping idle or almost-idle rings was much greater than the cost of keeping idle low-count mules.

The likelihood of exporting used equipment increased tremendously when a firm went bankrupt. As noted above, the

[16] See Robson, The Cotton Industry in Britain, p. 335. World spinning capacity outside Great Britain expanded between 1927 and 1937.

[17] For some comments on the early aspects of this trade, see Bowker, Lancashire under the Hammer, pp. 78–79.

financial manipulations engaged in right after World War I meant that the financial stability of a firm was not necessarily related to its technical efficiency. Thus, a lot of firms having at least some rings must have been vulnerable to bankruptcy. Once bankruptcy did occur, export of the rings was quite likely to follow even though other British firms, who had at least some equipment that was less modern than the equipment of the bankrupt firm, continued in business. In view of the problems of moving and reinstalling equipment, and the natural reluctance of British cotton-spinning firms to spend *any* money on their equipment during this period, it seems reasonable that the surviving firms permitted the modern equipment of bankrupt firms to go abroad, even at quite low prices.

One final reason for the decline in the number of ring spindles after 1930 is that the best policy for a firm to follow when it is covering variable but not average costs is usually to cannibalize some of its machines to provide spare parts and replacements. This was the policy that was practiced with great determination, and a good deal of financial success, by the Amoskeag Manufacturing Company of Manchester, New Hampshire, during this same period.[18] At least some part of the reduction of ring-spinning capacity in Great Britain probably resulted from such actions.

The problem of looms is much more straightforward than that of spindles. There were very few automatic looms in Great Britain in 1913 and this number had increased very little by 1939. Out of 495,000 looms in the industry in 1939, only 19,000, or less than 4%, were automatics.

The interwar period was one of almost no gross investment in British cotton weaving. All that happened was that a large number of plain looms were junked. Thus, the total number of looms shrank from 792,000 in 1924 to 495,000 in 1939.[19] In view of the low level of demand for weaving capacity throughout this period (see Table 11) and the very doubtful future of the industry, it is not surprising that almost no one was willing to put any money into the very expensive automatic looms.

[18] See Sweezy, "The Amoskeag Manufacturing Company."

[19] Robson, *The Cotton Industry in Britain*, p. 339.

7

SOME FINAL REMARKS ABOUT TECHNOLOGICAL PROGRESS IN LANCASHIRE

By any reasonable standard, the years leading up to World War I witnessed at least a creditable performance by the British cotton textile industry. This is certainly true for the years 1900–1913. It is also true, however, for periods such as 1890–1913 and even 1870–1913. All these periods witnessed considerable advancements in production, exports, and technological performance.[1]

The idea that the industry performed badly during these years is largely the result of unfavorable comparisons with its performance during earlier periods of truly spectacular advance. It is, however, utterly unreasonable to have expected that such progress would continue up to World War I, especially with regard to the growth output and exports. This becomes readily apparent when the implications of a continuation of these earlier rates of growth are considered. The classic example of such an extrapolation is John Meyer's input-output study of what would have happened to the British economy had the rates of increase in exports achieved by various industries

---

[1] For production and export figures, see chaps. 1 and 7.

during the period 1854–72 continued up to 1907.[2] If the rate of increase in British textile exports achieved in the 1854–72 period had continued, by 1907 the value of British textile exports would have been about four times as large as the actual level reached in that year.[3] Furthermore, British textile production would have been over three times as large as its actual level had *all* British exports maintained their 1854–72 rates of growth and somewhat less than three times the actual level had all exports *except* textiles grown at their actual rates up to 1907.[4] These growth rates would have resulted in a rapidly growing British share of total world textile production. Indeed, by 1913, the value added in the British cotton textile industry would have been close to the actual total worldwide value added in cotton textiles for that year.[5] In view of the ease with which textile production by factory methods spread throughout the world, and the extent to which the industry was given tariff and other types of support in many countries, it is not surprising that Great Britain failed to increase, or even maintain, her share of world cotton textile production.

The view that the technological performance of the British cotton textile industry in the pre–World War I period was poor is primarily based on the Jones index of real cost in the industry together with the observed fact that Great Britain was much slower than most other countries, especially the United States, in adopting ring spinning and automatic weaving. Although Jones is no doubt right about the decline in the rate of productivity increase after 1870, such a decrease does not seem to be sufficient grounds for calling the industry's performance bad. More important, according to Jones, real cost did not decline between 1885 and 1910 and actually increased between 1900 and 1910. These results, however, are incorrect. As noted in chapter 5, the corrections I have made in Jones's series indicate that for the whole period 1885 through 1913 real cost declined almost as fast in Lancashire as it did in

[2] J. Meyer, "An Input-Output Approach to Evaluating the Influence of Exports on British Industrial Production in the Late 19th Century."

[3] Ibid., p. 16.

[4] Ibid., p. 17.

[5] See Robson, *The Cotton Industry in Britain*, p. 355.

Massachusetts. Furthermore, at least some of the remaining difference in real-cost savings between the two industries can be attributed to the unquestionable fact that the principle innovations of the period, especially ring spinning, were better suited to American than to British conditions. Indeed, the analyses presented in earlier chapters make it seem quite likely that the British industry would not, in fact, have been any better off had ring spinning and automatic weaving been introduced more rapidly. If this is true, then the British lag in these techniques did not represent any technological lag, at least not from an economic point of view.

THE ROLE OF ENTREPRENEURSHIP AND MANAGEMENT

Because I am giving the whole Lancashire cotton textile industry a relatively clean bill of health for the pre–World War I period, it seems logical that I must also give the entrepreneurs and managers in the industry a relatively good rating. Indeed, I have already reported that I felt that those responsible for choosing technology for the industry—at least spinning and weaving technology—did a fairly good job. The worst charge that can be made against them is that they *may* have displayed somewhat excessive caution when the new technology involved an increase in fixed capital. Any charge of technological blindness or total irrationality, however, is, in my opinion, without foundation.

What does this conclusion do to the theory that Britain's relative decline as an industrial power after 1870 was primarily due to entrepreneurial failure? For the more extreme adherents to this point of view, such as Derek Aldcroft[6] and A. L. Levine, it invalidates some of their most spectacular examples of supposed entrepreneurial failure. Although I can only speak about the cotton textile industry, the fact that examples of alleged entrepreneurial failure in this industry appear at first glance to be at least as gross as those reported for other industries

[6] As was noted in footnote 1 of chapter 4, however, Aldcroft has recently moderated the position he took in "The Entrepreneur and the British Economy," published in 1964.

raises the suspicion that the other supposed failures will also evaporate under more careful scrutiny.[7] Some confirmation of this thesis comes from the recent studies of the British iron and steel industry by Peter Temin and Donald McCloskey.[8] Although not completely exonerating British iron and steel managers and entrepreneurs, they certainly credit the industry with a much better performance than had previously been the fashion among economic historians.[9]

This defense of the British entrepreneur in general, and the cotton textile entrepreneur in particular, however, should not be carried too far. Thus, it in no way touches on the larger economic failure of Britain. That is the failure to shift resources out of the production of staples such as textiles, steel, coal, and shipbuilding.[10] Moreover, I have by no means shown that the British cotton entrepreneurs did all they could have done to advance themselves and their industry. It is quite possible that they could have done more in the way of minor machinery improvement or improvements in the organization of production.

Perhaps more important, the British cotton entrepreneurs can be accused of not directing sufficient effort to the development of new techniques and new machinery fitted to their needs. They apparently adopted the new techniques available in a rational manner, but the major technical developments of this period were achieved in the United States. Under these circumstances, it seems natural that they were better suited to American than to British conditions. What is more surprising, and perhaps largely a result of bad luck, is that some of these new methods, especially ring spinning, were also better suited to conditions in the world at large. The reason for this is that

[7] On the other hand, it must be noted that the cotton textile industry was relatively unconcentrated and had relatively low barriers to entry (see Bowker, *Lancashire under the Hammer*, chap. 1). Thus, to the extent that the failure of British entrepreneurship is connected with monopoly and conservative established firms, the cotton textile industry should not in any case have been a leader in technological mistakes.

[8] P. Temin, "The Relative Decline of the British Steel Industry, 1880–1913"; and McCloskey, "Productivity Change in British Pig Iron."

[9] See, for example, D. L. Burn, *The Economic History of Steelmaking, 1867–1939.*

[10] It is by no means clear to me, however, that this failure should be shouldered primarily by the managers in these particular industries.

these new methods economized on the factor that the British textile industry had in greatest relative abundance—labor skill. Thus, ring spinning seriously undermined the great advantage that Lancashire had enjoyed as a result of its large corps of skilled mule spinners.

It is possible, of course, that no reasonable efforts on the part of British entrepreneurs could have prevented this development. On the other hand, technical developments favorable to Britain may have been feasible. In any case, little or no effort was devoted to looking for such possibilities. Any blame for this somewhat hypothetical failure must, however, be shared with the British machine-building industry. After all, most American developments in cotton technology were contributed by the machine-builders, particularly the Draper Company.

Finally, there is the question of commercial, as opposed to technological, performance. Were the British cotton firms good at selling their product? Did they strive through service and product design to meet the desires of potential buyers? Such questions are certainly worthy of study, although they fall outside areas I have choosen to examine directly. Part Two of this work, however, details Lancashire's experience in world markets. Hopefully it will clarify what actually happened to British cotton textile exports and throw some light on the role of commercial behavior in Lancashire's rise and fall.

PART II

INTERNATIONAL TRADE

8

LANCASHIRE'S EXPORT EXPERIENCE PRIOR TO WORLD WAR I

This portion of the book will consider whether the collapse of British cotton textile exports after World War I, and the subsequent collapse of the entire British industry, can be explained in terms of factors outside the control of the industry. That is, do the commercial policies of foreign nations and the growth of foreign cotton industries provide an adequate explanation of what happened; or did British entrepreneurial failure, technological backwardness, or worker obstructionism also play non-negligible roles in the tragedy? Clearly, this question can only be answered in terms of what happened after World War I. To give some perspective to these events, however, I feel that it is extremely important to study Britain's experience with cotton textile exports during the century of expansion between 1815 and 1914.

OVERALL BRITISH EXPORT EXPERIENCE, 1815–1914

Table 21 contains summary information on the growth of British cotton textile exports in the century before World War I. In order to avoid making the computations hopelessly

TABLE 21

AVERAGE ANNUAL BRITISH COTTON CLOTH EXPORTS TO ALL PARTS OF THE WORLD
COMBINED BY DECADES

Years	Thousands of Yards	% Increase	Average Quality (1815 = 100)	% Increase, Quality Included
1815–24	260,128		98.9	
1825–34	411,104	58.0	101.0	61.4
1835–44	738,926	79.7	84.4	50.2
1845–54	1,324,593	79.3	78.0	65.7
1855–64	2,158,530	63.0	68.9	43.9
1865–74	3,058,053	41.2	66.6	36.9
1875–84	4,099,148	34.0	70.2	41.3
1885–94	4,904,342	19.6	65.0	10.8
1895–1904	5,217,510	6.4	73.1	19.6
1905–13	6,296,415	20.1	72.1	19.0

SOURCE: Quantity figures are from various issues of the *British Parliamentary Papers*. For information on the calculation of the quality index, see Appendix C below.

complicated, the figures are limited to cloth. Thus, no account is taken of such items as yarn, sewing thread, hosiery, and lace. Cloth was by far the most important item, however, amounting to about 75% of all British cotton textile exports by value (and probably somewhat more in terms of value added in Britain) by the end of the period. If anything, the exclusion of items other than cloth somewhat understates the growth of British exports, since the exports of these other items increased faster than did cloth exports.

The one major adjustment I have made in the raw export data is to take account of fluctuations in the average quality of the cloth exported. This gives a more realistic picture of what happened to exports than do the basic yardage figures. Indeed, because the value added in Great Britain as a percentage of the price of a yard of cloth was generally directly related to the quality of the cloth, the adjustments I have made are not large enough. At least, if exports are viewed as the selling of British services (that is, excluding the re-export of the raw material), then even column 4 of Table 21 reflects too high a rate of growth for periods of decreasing average quality. In specific terms, this principally means that the rates of growth of exports shown in column 4 for the decades 1835–44 and 1855–64 are somewhat exaggerated.

The record of export growth shown in Table 21 is remarkable. It is true that the growth rates at the bottom of the table are lower than those at the top of the table. This, however, should not in itself be taken as a sign of a declining competitive position or as a danger signal for the future. Indeed, the record could easily have been read so as to encourage optimism during the years just before World War I. Using the numbers adjusted for quality changes, the main break in the rate of export growth occurred in 1885–94, when the rate of growth dropped from its previous level in the vicinity of 40% per decade to something like 10%. By 1913, however, two decades of growth at approximately 20% per decade had followed. This good recovery must have looked even more gratifying in 1913, for that year witnessed an all-time, all-country record of almost 7.1 billion yards of cotton cloth exported.[1]

Despite the growth of British cotton goods exports over this period as a whole, however, Britain's *share* of world exports of cotton goods was declining toward the end of the period. On the basis of weight, Britain's share rose from about 70% in 1829–31 to a high point of about 82% in 1882–84. It then declined to 58% in 1910–13.[2] On the basis of value, all of these numbers, but especially the last one, would certainly be larger. This trend would be further accentuated if the percentages referred to the trade in value added to raw cotton. Regardless of the index used, however, there was a considerable decline in Great Britain's hold on world trade in cotton goods between 1882–84 and 1910–13.

BRITISH COTTON EXPORTS BEFORE WORLD WAR I
ON A REGIONAL BASIS

Disaggregation is of considerable help in giving insight into the meaning of the numbers in Table 21. The first disaggrega-

---

[1] Indeed, in each of the years 1905, 1906, 1907, and 1910–13, Great Britain exported over 6 billion yards of cotton cloth. Britain had never reached that figure before nor has she since. As for other countries, none has ever approached six billion yards.

[2] Robson, *The Cotton Industry in Britain*, p. 2.

TABLE 22

BRITISH COTTON CLOTH EXPORTS TO INDIA AND TO THE
REST OF THE WORLD IN VARIOUS YEARS

(in thousands of yards)

Year	India*	% Increase	Rest of World	% Increase
1815	1,356		253,147	
1824	24,470	1,704.0	314,416	24.1
1835	51,777	111.6	505,047	60.8
1845	229,261	342.8	862,426	70.8
1855	467,374	103.9	1,470,362	70.5
1865	561,089	20.1	1,454,067	−1.3
1874	1,026,926	83.0	2,332,189	60.4
1887	1,964,450	91.3	2,932,560	25.7
1895†	1,839,878	−6.3	3,192,683	8.9
1905	2,538,704	38.0	3,658,007	14.6
1913	3,216,450	26.7	3,848,603	5.2

SOURCES: Various issues of the *British Parliamentary Papers.*

*India includes Pakistan, Burma, Ceylon, and the Straits Settlement (Malaya). Before 1835, it includes all shipments east of Iran.

†The year 1895 was a very bad one for British cotton cloth exports to India.

tion I have performed is to separate India[3] from the rest of the world. The results are shown in Table 22. This table is rather simpler than Table 21. It includes only exports in particular single years, and it takes no account of quality changes.

The reason for singling out India should be obvious at a glance. By 1913, India accounted for 45% of the total yardage of cotton cloth exported from Great Britain. What is perhaps even more important, the percentage of increase in exports to India between any given year and 1913 is greater than the corresponding increase for the rest of the world. Although the introduction of quality consideration would somewhat reduce the importance of India, it would not substantially change the figures noted above.

The picture presented in Table 22 seems less encouraging for Britain's cotton industry than that seen in Table 21. Clearly, there was a drop in the rate of growth of exports to India after 1887. Because exports to India were extraordinarily bad in 1895, the loss recorded between 1887 and 1895 cannot

[3] India is here defined to include Pakistan, Burma, Ceylon, and the Straits Settlement (Malaya). Before 1835, it includes all of East Asia.

be taken as representing a trend. This, however, means that the 38% increase recorded between 1895 and 1905 is too large. Furthermore, the 26.7% increase between 1905 and 1913 can best be viewed as the result of a short spurt culminating in the record year of 1913. Clearly, the year 1913 represented the peak of an export boom as far as the Indian market was concerned.

Even more serious for Britain's prospects as a cotton exporter was the low rate of growth of exports to the rest of the world after 1887. This is especially true of the mere 5.2% increase between 1905 and 1913. A pessimist could well have taken this as a sign of future stagnation or even decline outside of India. The low rate of growth outside of India, in fact, meant that about three-fourths of the yardage increase between 1887 and 1913 went to India, with the rest of world accounting for only one-fourth of the total increase. Thus, Britain was becoming increasingly dependent on India for a continued growth of cotton cloth exports at a time when the rate of increase in exports to India was almost certainly on a long-term downward trend.

For purposes of this analysis, a further disaggregation of the "rest of the world" is called for. I have done this by dividing the world outside India into nine different areas. These are: (1) the United States; (2) Northern Europe (Scandinavia, the Benelux countries, Germany, and France); (3) Canada, Australia, and New Zealand; (4) Other Europe (i.e., Europe other than Northern Europe); (5) the Middle East (including Turkey, North Africa, and Iran); (6) Africa (i.e., Sub-Saharan Africa); (7) Latin America; (8) China; and (9) Other Asia (i.e., Asia east of Iran but excluding India and China; this category thus principally consists of Japan, the Netherlands East Indies, Thailand, and the Philippines). Information on British cotton cloth exports to these various areas is presented in Table 23. As in Table 22, the data refer only to individual years, and no account has been taken of quality fluctuations.

These more disaggregated data present quite a different picture from the overall data included in Tables 21 and 22. Table 23 makes it clear that British experience varied considerably from area to area. Excepting the almost universal decline between 1855 and 1865, which can be credited to the dislocations and the shortage of raw cotton associated with the American Civil War, there are two areas included in Table 23 which display a persistent and rapid growth in their cotton cloth imports from Great Britain. These are Canada, Australia, and New Zealand (3) and Africa (6). Africa in this case refers almost entirely to British colonies, so this means that the best market areas—the two mentioned above plus India—were all part of the British Empire.

Outside the British Empire, performance was much more mixed. In the case of the United States, except for a few years right after the end of the Napoleonic Wars, Great Britain was never able to establish a real hold on the cotton cloth market. Indeed, by far the largest share of the American cotton cloth market ever held by British suppliers was during 1815 and 1816.[4] What is even more startling in view of the rapid growth of the American ecomomy is that the absolute yardage for 1815 was not surpassed until 1835. After that year, it was not again exceeded until 1847. After reaching this higher absolute level (representing, however, only a very small share of the total American market), British exports to the United States declined rapidly and were in fact on a pronounced downward course just before World War I. The very high quality of the cloth still exported to the United States was simply a reflection of the fact that Britain had no chance in low and medium qualities; only at the very highest qualities was she able to sell at all in the United States.

The data on Northern Europe (2), also indicate a failure on Britain's part to capture a really substantial share of the market. Between 1815 and the middle 1850s, there was only a doubling of the yardage exported to that area. In all probability, this represented a considerable decline in what had never been more than a modest market share. There was something of a boom in British cotton cloth exports to Northern Europe in the 1870s and early 1880s. The relatively high yardage figures

---

[4] Compare the output estimates given by Robert Zevin (see R. B. Zevin, "The Growth of Textile Production after 1815," in R. Fogel and S. Engerman, eds., *The Reinterpretation of American Economic History*) with the import figures in Appendix D.

TABLE 23

British Cotton Cloth Exports to Various Markets in Various Years
(in thousands of Yards)

YEAR	United States (1)		Northern Europe (2)		Canada, Australia, and New Zealand (3)		Other Europe (4)		Middle East (5)	
	Quantity	% Change	Quantity	% Change	Quantity	% Change	Quantity	% Change	Quantity	% Change
1815	70,813	...	57,125	...	9,013	...	45,934	...	1,056	...
1824	41,380	−41.6	50,818	−11.0	7,762	−13.9	83,225	81.2	13,674	1,194.9
1835	74,963	81.1	72,218	42.1	20,134	159.4	94,418	13.4	38,371	180.6
1845	31,237	−58.3	78,350	8.5	44,853	122.8	139,963	48.2	132,452	245.2
1855	184,588	490.9	115,881	47.9	30,877	−31.2	208,287	48.8	365,367	175.8
1865	122,384	−33.6	118,090	1.9	57,015	84.7	166,334	−20.1	315,393	−13.7
1874	105,340	−13.9	278,437	135.8	93,186	63.4	274,531	65.0	439,548	39.4
1887	44,029	−58.2	184,258	−33.8	125,135	34.3	265,843	−3.2	509,460	15.9
1895	64,996	47.6	167,744	−9.0	188,119	50.3	107,081	−59.7	598,487	17.5
1905	65,563	0.9	204,855	22.1	214,034	13.8	76,631	−28.4	732,451	22.4
1913	44,415	−32.3	330,724	61.4	325,085	51.9	123,922	61.7	760,417	3.8

TABLE 23 (continued)

YEAR	AFRICA (6) Quantity	% Change	LATIN AMERICA (7) Quantity	% Change	CHINA (8) Quantity	% Change	OTHER ASIA (9) Quantity	% Change
1815	893	...	68,583	...	...	...	...	...
1824	2,295	157.0	114,562	67.0	...	...	...	...
1835	8,161	255.6	171,614	49.8	11,213	867.2	13,951	...
1845	21,222	160.0	272,034	58.5	108,449	-31.7	33,866	142.7
1855	39,968	88.3	396,681	45.8	74,032	69.9	50,442	48.9
1865	30,129	-24.6	397,750	0.3	125,801	212.6	94,437	87.2
1874	73,608	144.3	579,372	45.7	393,263	40.6	80,018	-15.3
1887	117,410	59.5	809,831	39.8	552,743	-4.5	210,222	162.7
1895	166,052	41.4	919,617	13.6	528,145	51.4	274,066	30.4
1905	194,046	16.9	741,107	-20.4	799,735	-10.4	398,094	45.3
1913	341,224	75.8	749,439	1.1	716,533		420,396	5.6

SOURCES: Various issues of the *British Parliamentary Papers.*

for those years, however, were followed by a decline. Only after 1905 was there some recovery, and in the 1905–13 period, yardage figures for Northern Europe were finally exceeding the records established several decades earlier. In fact, however, these new record figures still constituted only a very small market share. As in the case of the United States, Northern Europe was a market where Great Britain was only able to compete in the high-quality sector.

British experience in the Other Europe market (4) was quite similar to that in the Northern European market. In both cases, an absolute peak was reached in the 1870s and early 1880s. The main difference between the two was that in Other Europe there was little or no recovery in the post-1905 period. The yardage of British cotton cloth exported to Other Europe in the last decade before World War I was far below the levels reached thirty-five years earlier.

The Latin American market (7) must have been highly pleasing to British cotton manufacturers and traders throughout most of the nineteenth century. The rate of growth of British exports was rapid, and the absolute level was high. In 1887, for example, the yardage exported to Latin America was about twice as great as that exported to *all* of Europe. It was about that year, however, that something approaching stagnation set in. This development can be seen in Table 23, although the start of the stagnation period is somewhat obscured by the fact that 1895 was an extraordinarily good year. If any of the years around 1895 is substituted for that year in Table 23, then the 1887–95 increase and the 1895–1905 decline both vanish. Between the late 1880s and 1913, exports of cotton cloth from Britain to Latin America show no trend at all.

The Middle East (5) was generally a very gratifying market for the British cotton industry. Growth throughout the period was not only quite rapid but it was also relatively stable. The very small size of the increase between 1905 and 1913 results mainly from the fact that exports to the Middle East in 1913 were at their lowest level since 1906. Furthermore, an all-time record had been set in 1911 (18% above the 1905 level).

In Asia, China (8) was an important and generally growing

market. It was also, however, a volatile market.[5] This condition makes it very difficult to interpret the decline that occurred between 1905 and 1913. The problem is made worse by the fact that both years were relatively good ones compared with surrounding years. It would be very difficult, however, to find any trend in these years more favorable than stagnation. Still, it is virtually impossible to tell what the appropriate reaction to this should have been at the time. Was it a harbinger of absolute decline, or was it merely another temporary setback to be followed by a renewed rapid growth? In any case, a reasonable observer at the time should have tempered any optimism he may have felt about developments in Northern Europe with concern over the future of the Chinese market.

The remaining area to be discussed is Other Asia (9). On the whole, this must also have been a gratifying market. The only cause for concern that can be detected in Table 23 is the small increase between 1905 and 1913. In fact, however, 1905 was an extraordinarily good year. If there was a period of stagnation in this market, it occurred between 1890 and 1904. The decade between 1904 and 1913, on the other hand, shows approximately a two-thirds increase.

This division of the world into subareas has greatly increased the information obtainable from the British export figures. It is now apparent that though some areas or markets grew at a rapid and even a fairly stable rate throughout this period, other markets did not. What is particularly striking is that in some markets stagnation and decline had set in well before World War I. Thus, the Latin American market had stopped growing in absolute terms sometime around 1890, and both the European areas declined, and declined sharply, sometime in the late 1880s. As for the United States, a very steep decline set in as early as 1816 or 1817, and even the very modest records achieved in the late 1850s were not reached after the Civil War.

---

[5] This volatility was at least to some extent the result of cotton crop fluctuations in China.

BRITISH COTTON EXPORTS BEFORE WORLD WAR I
ON A NATIONAL BASIS

The next step in disaggregating British cotton export data is naturally to go to the level of individual countries. This step is particularly important because it is only at a national level that it makes much sense to talk about tariff and other governmental policies or about the growth and development of local cotton industries. Indeed, it will be noted that when I discussed British experience in those of my areas (i.e., the United States, India, and China) that consist solely of a single political entity, I avoided all mention of government policies or domestic industries. For organizational purposes, I postponed such discussion to this section where all the markets dealt with will be individual countries.

One major problem arises when the data are disaggregated to a national level. There are obviously too many countries in the world for all to be discussed in any kind of detail. Some rational standards for deciding which countries to consider must therefore be established. Roughly speaking, my selection criteria are as follows: (1) the importance of a given market to the British industry, (2) the importance of a given local cotton industry, (3) the extent of a government's efforts at developing a domestic cotton industry, and (4) the availability of useful information. On the basis of these criteria, I have selected the following countries for more intensive study: the United States, France, Germany, Italy, Brazil, India, China, and Japan. Summary data for India are contained in Table 22 and for the United States in Table 23. Data on the other countries are contained in Table 24. Further data on all these countries are available in Appendix D.

The United States

The modern American cotton textile industry originated in New England during the turbulent years of the Napoleonic Wars.[6] During these years, embargo and war gave the American

[6] For a comprehensive history of the New England cotton textile industry up

TABLE 24

British Cotton Cloth Exports to Selected Countries in Various Years

(in thousands of yards)

YEAR	FRANCE Quantity	FRANCE % Change	GERMANY Quantity	GERMANY % Change	ITALY Quantity	ITALY % Change	BRAZIL Quantity	BRAZIL % Change	JAPAN Quantity	JAPAN % Change
1815	193	...	29,561	...	11,734	...	15,823	...	...	...
1826	408	111.4	38,672	30.8	28,085	139.3	24,928	57.5	...	...
1835	2,432	495.8	43,572	12.7	34,682	23.5	58,831	136.0	...	...
1845	2,506	3.0	43,621	0.1	54,424*	56.9	87,076	48.0	...	...
1855	7,028	180.4	71,179	63.2	54,175*	-0.5	124,962	43.5	...	...
1865	21,405	204.6	54,034	-24.1	52,133	-3.8	114,779	-8.1	26,367	...
1875	87,748	309.9	58,660	8.6	90,301	73.2	197,522	72.1	39,622	50.3
1885	45,052	-48.7	44,693	-23.8	85,567	-5.4	190,096*	-3.8	45,412	14.6
1895	21,297	-52.3	49,604	9.8	26,498	-69.0	194,485	2.3	96,033	111.5
1905	14,875	-30.2	65,842	32.7	8,746	-67.0	131,504	-32.4	128,724	34.0
1913	12,764	-14.2	76,732	16.0	10,243	17.1	96,538	-26.6	50,187	-61.0

SOURCES: Various issues of the *British Parliamentary Papers.*

*These figures are unusually low relative to surrounding years.

industry protection and, by the same token, excluded Great Britain from the American market. With the restoration of peace, however, British manufacturers flooded the American market with cotton cloth. American (or at least New England) production appears to have held up in 1815, but there was something akin to a collapse in 1816.[7]

Not surprisingly, the American cotton manufacturers reponded to this situation with a call for protection. Their plea was answered in 1816 when a duty of 25% was imposed on cotton cloth.[8] As important as the rate of the tariff was the fact that no cotton cloth could be valued at less than 25 cents per yard. As cotton cloth prices fell rapidly after 1816, this minimum valuation clause resulted in higher and higher real rates on low-quality cloth.[9] Taussig claims that this minimum tariff quickly became "prohibitive of the importation of the coarse kinds of cotton cloths."[10] Zevin quotes a source that calculates the minimum rate to have implied (probably in 1816) a rate of 83.5% on the actual value of "coarse Indian goods."[11] This tariff policy was reinforced by the acts of 1824 and 1828, which increased both the formal rate and the minimum valuation.

The results of these tariffs are clear. New England's production of cotton textiles boomed, and imports from Great Britain sagged. From an 1815 level of 70.8 million yards, cotton cloth imports from Great Britain declined to an annual average level

---

to the American Civil War, see C. F. Ware, *The Early New England Cotton Manufacture;* and Zevin, "The Growth of Textile Production after 1815."

[7] Zevin, "The Growth of Textile Production after 1815," p. 123.

[8] A comprehensive account of American tariff policy with regard to cotton textiles during the nineteenth century can be found in F. W. Taussig's book, *The Tariff History of the United States.*

[9] Even a tariff involving an equal rate for all types of cloth would probably have rested most heavily on low qualities. This is because the higher the quality of a yard of cloth, the higher was the percentage of value added in Great Britain as a percentage of the price. Thus, a 25% tariff on all goods would have implied a higher tariff on British value added (i.e., a higher effective tariff rate on British services) on low- than on high-quality cloth. It might also be noted that low-quality cloth is particularly well suited to new industries because it requires much less skill on the part of the work force than does the production of high-quality cloth.

[10] Taussig, *The Tariff History of the United States*, p. 30.

[11] See Zevin, "The Growth of Textile Production after 1815," p. 127.

of around 40 million yards throughout the 1820s. In the meantime, New England's cotton cloth production grew from 2.4 million yards in 1815 to 141.6 million yards in 1830, and 231.5 million yards in 1833. This increase represents an annual average compounded rate of growth of cotton cloth production of approximately 29% between 1815 and 1833.[12] As might be expected under these circumstances, the average quality of British exports to the United States increased considerably during this period. American manufacturers were taking over the low-quality market, leaving the British only a share of the much smaller, although still growing, high-quality market.

The frequent changes in American tariffs after 1828 are reflected in the British export performance. In particular, the especially high tariffs during the 1842–46 period were accompanied by a sharp drop in quantity (imports averaged less than 30 million yards per year over the period) and a distinct increase in quality. These trends were reversed after the elimination of the minimum valuation system and the reduction of the rate on cotton cloth to 25% in 1846. Imports reached a level of 104.2 million yards in 1850, 184.6 million yards in 1855, and 225.1 million yards in 1859. At the same time, there was a pronounced decline in average quality.[13]

These tariff changes also appear to have had at least some effect on American production trends. The average annual compounded rate of growth of cotton cloth production in New England was reduced to 5.1% between 1833 and 1860. Even more important is the fact that imports from Britain spurted up in the early 1850s, but New England cloth production only grew at an annual rate of 1.2% between 1850 and 1855. Even in 1855, however, the yardage produced in New England was over three times as great as the yardage imported into the United States from Great Britain.[14]

During the Civil War, there was a sharp drop in both the quality and the quantity of the cloth imported. The decrease in quality was probably due to the reintroduction of high cotton

[12] Ibid., pp. 123–24.

[13] See Sandberg, "Movements in the Quality of British Cotton Cloth Exports," pp. 16–17.

[14] See Zevin, "The Growth of Textile Production after 1815," pp. 123–24.

textile tariffs. Because these new tariffs were specific, falling prices in the post–Civil War period resulted in higher and higher real *ad valorem* rates. Consequently, cotton cloth imports from Great Britain decreased sharply in volume during this period of rapid economic growth in the United States. In the late eighties and in the nineties, they averaged about 50 million yards per year. At the same time, average quality rose rapidly. With 1845 = 100, my index of the quality of British cotton cloth imported into the United States stood at 73.1 in 1855, 93.3 in 1880, 96.0 in 1890, and 140.9 in 1895. This last increase can, at least in part, be attributed to the further tariff increase of 1890. A drop in quantity after 1909 and a sharp increase in quality during 1912 and 1913 may perhaps be connected with the tariff of 1909.[15]

A further indication of the effects of tariff changes on British cotton textile exports to the United States can be obtained from the behavior of yarn exports after 1890. The rate structure of the McKinley Tariff of that year favored the importation of fine British yarn to be woven in the United States.[16] The effect on yarn imports was considerable. From a level consistently well below 1 million pounds per year, American imports of British cotton yarn advanced to 2.5 million pounds in 1895, 4.4 million pounds in 1905, and 5.4 million pounds in 1913. As noted above, during these years cloth imports were stagnating if not declining.[17]

As interesting as the effects of American tariffs, and perhaps even more indicative of the long-run position of the British cotton textile industry in the early part of the twentieth century, is the remarkable rise of the southern states as cotton textile

---

[15] Sandberg, "Movements in the Quality of British Cotton Textile Exports," pp. 16–17.

[16] See Aldcroft, "Introduction," p. 3.

[17] The good performance of British yarn presumably took some of the sting out of the poor performance of British cloth on the American market. 5.4 million pounds of yarn, however, was probably only enough to produce about 30 million yards of cloth. More important, the value of a pound of yarn is much less than the value of a pound of cloth, but the raw cotton content is about the same. Thus, adding the value of yarn and cloth imports tends to exaggerate the amount of value added being imported from Great Britain when the proportion of yarn in the total is increasing.

producers.[18] In 1880, the South had less than 5% of all American cotton spindles. In 1890, the figure was approximately 12%; in 1900, it was 24%; and in 1910, it was almost 40%.[19] Southern competition began with low counts. By 1890, the South was producing almost as much sub-20 yarn as was New England. By 1914, the South was producing 2 1/2 times as much sub-20 yarn and slightly more 21 to 40 yarn than was New England. Between 1890 and 1914, the South also increased her share of yarn above 40 from 0% to 16% of the national total.[20]

This remarkable growth occurred in a previously unindustrialized region in open competition with the well-established New England industry. Virtually all observers agree that the South's great advantage that allowed her to make such remarkable progress was a cheap and docile supply of labor.[21] The opportunity inherent in the possibility of using this labor force for the production of cotton textiles now seems so obvious that the principal task of economic historians is to explain why it did not happen sooner.[22]

It has been argued by some that the New England cotton manufacturers were handicapped by a failure to recognize and rapidly adopt the machinery improvements that were becoming available. The most recent study of this question, however, argues persuasively that the New England manufacturers reacted in an economically rational manner when they were faced with technological choices.[23] There has also been available for some time evidence indicating that when the New England industry ran into really serious trouble after World War I, the most rational policy was to either get out of New England or out of cotton manufacturing altogether. This, at least, was

---

[18] For a description of the rise of the South, see Copeland, *The Cotton Manufacturing Industry of the United States*, chaps. 2, 3; B. Mitchell, *The Rise of Cotton Mills in the South*, and *The Industrial Revolution in the South*.

[19] Copeland, *The Cotton Textile Industry of the United States*, p. 34.

[20] Feller, "The Draper Loom in New England Textiles," p. 330.

[21] See, for example, Copeland, *The Cotton Textile Industry of the United States*, pp. 39–40.

[22] The dispute seems to lie between sociological explanations bearing on the unfavorable legacy of slavery versus more technological explanations that emphasize the advantages resulting from the development of artificial humidifiers and highly automatic (i.e., presumably low skill intensive) machinery.

[23] See Feller, "The Draper Loom in New England Textiles."

the case if profit maximization for the firm is taken as the appropriate criteria of economic rationality.[24]

Before concluding these remarks about the United States, something must be said about American cotton cloth exports. The first point to be made is that they were never large, at least not as a percentage of total output. Thus, in the period 1910–13, American cotton cloth exports averaged less than 7% of total output. This contrasts with a figure of over 80% for Great Britain during these same years. In absolute terms, these figures represent American exports of about 400 million yards of cloth per year as compared with 6,650 million yards for Great Britain.[25]

The second major point about American exports is their great instability.[26] This instability, in turn, was largely caused by the extreme instability of American exports to China.[27] China was easily America's best customer, but she was not very reliable. Interestingly enough, the best years for American exports to China, 1905 and 1906, were also very good years for Great Britain, both in the Chinese market and overall. This, combined with the much greater stability of British over American exports to China,[28] gives the impression that American exports were largely of a marginal nature in the Chinese market. That is, only a shortage of British cloth caused Chinese buyers to turn in large numbers to American suppliers. It is true, however, that America had a special niche in the Chinese market, at least until Japanese cloth took over. This speciality consisted of heavy and coarse, but not heavily sized, gray cloth sent to northern China and Manchuria. This cloth was used to make the familiar padded winter outfits of northern China.[29] It is at least suggestive that the United States should specialize in an item using so much cotton relative to other inputs.

It is clear, in any case, that America was not a major threat to British cotton textile exports and that exports were not a

---

[24] See Sweezy, "The Amoskeag Manufacturing Company."

[25] Robson, *The Cotton Industry in Britain*, p. 358.

[26] Copeland, *The Cotton Manufacturing Industry of the United States*, pp. 220–24.

[27] Ibid., p. 224.

[28] Ibid.

[29] Ibid., pp. 224–25.

major force sustaining the prosperity of the American industry. The export trade can best be described as a combination of a few specialized products together with a possible outlet for overproduction in America or a source for alleviating a shortage in the rest of the world. This, in turn, reflects the fact that the American cotton textile industry was not in a sufficiently strong competitive position to be able to permanently devote a major share of its capacity to production for export.

France

British cotton cloth exports to France throughout the period 1815–1913 were seriously affected by French commercial policy. Although somewhat modified in 1836, the basis of French policy until 1860 was prohibition of British textile goods.[30] It will be noted that this prohibition did not mean that no British cotton cloth was imported into France. It simply meant that smuggling was required. In fact, given the circumstances, fairly substantial quantities of British cotton cloth were declared for export to France,[31] at least in the years just prior to 1861 when the Cobden-Chevalier Treaty went into effect with regard to cotton cloth. The quantity of British cotton cloth declared for export to France increased from 193,000 yards in 1815 and 139,000 yards in 1830 to 2.4 million yards in 1835, 5 million yards in 1850, 7 million yards in 1855 and 10.8 million yards in 1860. As might be expected, these amounts consisted largely of high-quality cloth. In 1815, the average-per-yard declared price of the cloth going to France was 151.7% of the average price per yard of all cotton cloth being exported from Great Britain.[32] Although average quality remained high, it did fall somewhat once the quantities exported to France increased after 1830.

[30] A. L. Dunham, *The Anglo-French Treaty of Commerce of 1860 and the Progress of the Industrial Revolution in France*, p. 186.

[31] Some of this cloth, however, was probably shipped to a French free port and then reexported (see A. L. Dunham, *The Industrial Revolution in France, 1815–1848*, p. 19).

[32] See Sandberg, "Movements in the Quality of British Cotton Textile Exports," p. 14, for more complete information on relative export prices to various areas of the world.

This period of prohibition witnessed a rapid growth in French cotton textile production. Between 1816 and 1848, French consumption of raw cotton increased from 12 to 65 million kilograms. Before 1860, annual cotton consumption exceeded 100 million kilograms; in addition, there was some net importation of yarn. These yarn imports probably did not exceed 1 million kilograms, however.[33] As a comparison with the 10.8 million yards of British cloth imported in 1860, it might be noted that 100 million kilograms of raw cotton was enough to produce approximately 1,100 million yards of cloth.[34]

The position of British cotton cloth exports improved markedly after the Cobden-Chevalier Treaty went into effect. This treaty allowed British cotton cloth to enter France on payment of a 15% duty. As a result, despite the difficult supply situation with regard to raw cotton, British cotton cloth exports rose to 21.4 million yards in 1865. In 1869, they reached 41.6 million yards. At least partly as a result of the loss of the Alsatian industry after the Franco-Prussian War, British exports to France jumped to 86.5 million yards in 1871 and 87.7 million yards in 1875. Not surprisingly, average quality declined somewhat as the volume increased.

It is extremely difficult to tell what effect the tariff change had on the development of the French industry because its introduction coincided with the outbreak of the American Civil War.[35]

[33] See Dunham, *The Industrial Revolution in France*, p. 164; and *Anglo-French Treaty of Commerce of 1860*, p. 193. The 100 million kilogram figure is based on the assumption that the bales involved weighed the usual 478 pounds apiece.

[34] This calculation assumes a 10% waste rate in spinning and that 5 1/2 yards of cloth weighed one pound.

[35] It might be noted, however, that during the last year before the disastrous war with Prussia, French raw cotton consumption set a new record of 124 million kilograms (see, J. H. Clapham, *The Economic Development of France and Germany, 1815–1914*, p. 246). This volume of raw cotton should have been enough to produce approximately 1,350 million yards of cloth. David Landes presents consistently lower estimates of French raw cotton consumption. He sets consumption at 44.8 million kilograms in 1848 (but 63.9 million in 1849), 59.3 million in 1850, 93.7 million in 1869 and 80.3 million in 1872 (see D. S. Landes, "Technological Change and Development in Western Europe, 1750–1914," pp. 394, 423). For my purposes, however, it does not matter very much whether Clapham or Landes is right. The important point is that British cotton cloth exports to France were, with the possible exception of the years right after 1870, very small compared with the level of French production.

The loss of Alsace naturally reduced output for a while. As early as 1874, however, the raw cotton consumption record set in 1869 had been exceeded.[36] This impressive performance was the result of rapid growth in the Nord and the partial reconstruction of the Alsatian industry in the Vosges. In 1876, consumption reached a high point of 158 million kilograms. This, however, was a level not reached again until 1891. There was thus a fifteen-year period of stagnation. After 1890, however, there was renewed and relatively steady growth. The all-time pre–World War I peak was reached in 1909 when 319 million kilograms of raw cotton were consumed in France.[37]

British exports were not able to sustain the level of 1871 once France started to recover from the loss of Alsace. They fell from 86.8 million yards in 1871 to 56.3 million yards in 1880. The decline did not stop at that point, however. By 1885, exports to France were down to 45.0 million yards, and in 1890 they amounted to only 30.4 million yards. This further drop was undoubtedly accelerated by the French conversion to specific tariffs in 1881. Because cotton cloth prices generally fell after 1880, this change resulted in a rising level of real protection.

In 1892, the Méline Tariff dealt a further blow to British cotton textile exports to France. By 1899, British cotton cloth exports had fallen to a mere 16.4 million yards, and in 1913 they were only 12.8 million yards. The average quality of British exports to France rose as the quantity declined after 1871.

The positive effect of these two tariff changes on the growth of the French industry is clear. Certainly the Méline Tariff must be connected with the renewed upsurge in production after 1890. The failure of the gradual tariff increase after 1881 to have an appreciable effect on the French cotton industry can probably be explained by the generally very poor performance of the whole French economy during the 1880s.

France, as might be expected from the above description,

---

[36] Alsace had over one-third of all French spindles before 1870. The area concentrated on the production of relatively fine textiles, however, and no doubt accounted for considerably less than one-third of French raw cotton consumption (ibid.).

[37] Clapham, *The Economic Development of France and Germany,* p. 247.

was not a major exporter of cotton cloth. In the years just before World War I, French cotton cloth exports were at a level (in value terms) equal to approximately 7% to 8% of total British cotton cloth exports.[38] These French cloth exports accounted for about 25% of all the raw cotton consumed in France. Of this amount, however, approximately one-half by value, and over one-half by weight, went to the French colonies, where foreign (especially British) competition was prohibited. The rest of the exports were mostly specialty items of particularly high quality. In fact, Great Britain was the single most important customer for these items.[39]

Germany

British experience in the German market was not quite as variable as in the French market, largely because German tariffs did not fluctuate as much as French tariffs (and prohibitions). The quantity of British cotton goods imported into Germany right after the end of the Napoleonic Wars was large relative to the size of the German market for these goods,[40] and did serious damage to the German industry that had grown up during the wars.[41] After 1815, there was some growth in the quantity, and decline in the quality, of British cotton cloth shipped to Germany until approximately 1830. At that point, stagnation in both quality and quantity set in at least through 1850.

This was generally a period of rising tariffs. The founding of the Zollverein tended, like any customs union, to divert trade from outside to inside the union. Furthermore, tariffs tended to become heavier during these years, both because of falling prices (the tariffs were specific in form) and because of increased rates.[42] It was also a period of growth for the

[38] U.S. Tariff Board, p. 218.

[39] Clapham, *The Economic Development of France and Germany*, pp. 248–49.

[40] In this period, linen was the principal cloth used by the bulk of the German population.

[41] As far as factory production was concerned, this industry was limited to spinning.

[42] Clapham, *The Economic Development of France and Germany*, p. 101.

German cotton textile industry. By the middle of the nineteenth century, Germany was consuming about 15,000 tons of raw cotton per annum.[43] This was enough cotton to produce approximately 150 million yards of cloth. This figure may be compared with imports of 47.4 million yards of cloth from Great Britain in 1850.

Immediately after 1850, there was a considerable increase in cotton goods imports. To some extent, however, this increase may have been a statistical peculiarity resulting from the Crimean War.[44] The succeeding period up to 1870 is difficult to interpret because of the American Civil War and the Franco-Prussian War. It is interesting to note, however, that German raw cotton consumption increased by about four and one-half times between 1846–50 and 1866–70.[45] During the same period, British cotton cloth exports fell somewhat short of doubling. It seems extremely unlikely that any change in re-exporting patterns could have been so important as to have kept the British share of the German cotton cloth market from decreasing during this period. What is more, these trends continued unabated after the German conquest of Alsace. In fact, British cotton cloth exports to Germany declined quite sharply between 1871 and 1880. At the same time, German raw cotton consumption increased by about 70% between 1866–70 and 1871–75.[46]

After 1880, British cotton cloth exports to Germany stagnated until almost the end of the nineteenth century. This stagnation was accompanied by rising German tariffs. In particular, the tariffs on high-quality goods were raised. This action was very undesirable from Britain's point of view because she had a comparative advantage in high qualities. The stagnation in the quantity of British exports to Germany resulted in a sharp

[43] Ibid., p. 295.

[44] During the Crimean War, Britain attempted to place an embargo on exports to Russia. Because my data is based on the destination declared by the exporter at shipment from Great Britain, no goods were listed as being headed for Russia during the period of the embargo. In fact, however, substantial amounts of British cotton cloth did reach Russia, much, if not most, of it via Germany.

[45] Clapham, *The Economic Development of France and Germany*, pp. 295–96. Unlike the French case, Landes's figures agree well with Clapham's numbers on Germany (see Landes, "Technological Change and Economic Development in Western Europe," p. 423).

[46] Ibid., pp. 296–97.

decline in Britain's share of the German market. In 1871–75, Germany consumed enough cotton to produce about 1.2 billion yards of cloth per annum; and in 1871, she imported 78 million yards of cotton cloth from Great Britain. In 1895, Germany consumed cotton at a rate equivalent to a production of about 2.5 billion yards of cloth but imported only 50 million yards of cotton cloth from Great Britain.[47] After the turn of the century, British cotton cloth exports to Germany started to increase once again. This can probably be credited to rapidly rising incomes in Germany together with a relatively high income elasticity of demand for high-quality cloth. At the same time, however, German raw cotton consumption was growing at least as fast as imports from Great Britain. By 1910, Germany consumed enough raw cotton to produce about 4.5 to 5 billion yards of cloth, and imports from Great Britain amounted to 86 million yards.[48]

Germany was a more serious threat to Britain in third markets than was France. Before the outbreak of World War I, Germany was exporting somewhat more cotton cloth by value and weight than was France. More important, Germany did not have any large colonial market. Almost all of the German exports had to withstand the cold blast of international competition. Of course, Germany was still a minor cotton cloth exporter by British standards. In 1910, the value of German cotton cloth exported was less than 10% of the value of British cotton cloth exported.[49] Interestingly enough, the single largest buyer of German cotton goods was Great Britain.[50]

Italy

Starting after the end of the Napoleonic Wars and going all the way up to at least 1880, Italy was a large and growing

[47] Ibid.

[48] Ibid.

[49] U.S. Tariff Board, p. 215.

[50] Clapham, *The Economic Development of France and Germany,* p. 298. As in the case of France, it should be noted that Germany did relatively much better in the export of speciality items such as cotton hosiery, lace, embroideries, clothing, and so on, than in the export of cloth. In 1910, *total* German cotton goods exports had a value of about 25% as great as the value of *total* British cotton goods exports (U.S. Tariff Board, p. 219).

market for British cotton cloth. British exports of cotton cloth to Italy increased from 11.7 million yards in 1815 to 79 million yards in 1860. The rapidity of this growth is readily apparent if Italy is compared with Germany. In 1815, Italian cotton cloth imports from Great Britain were about 35% as great as were German imports. By 1840, Italian imports exceeded German imports, and that situation continued through 1860. Some of this rapid growth in volume, however, was offset by a decline in the average quality of the British cotton cloth going to Italy.

In the meantime, there was some growth of the domestic Italian *factory* cotton textile industry. This development was far from spectacular, however.[51] In 1861, Italy imported 12,400 tons of raw cotton.[52] Roughly speaking, this amount was enough to produce 125 million yards of cloth. This figure may be compared with 1860 imports of 79 million yards of cotton cloth from Great Britain alone.

It was after Italian unity was achieved, and especially after the enactment of the tariffs of 1878 and 1887, that the domestic Italian industry really started to mushroom. Over the whole period, 1861–1913, Italian raw cotton imports increased from 12,400 tons to 201,900 tons.[53] In the meantime imports of cotton cloth from Great Britain declined sharply. This decline is especially noticeable after 1887. In 1885, Italy imported 85.6 million yards of British cotton cloth. By 1890, this figure had fallen to 56 million yards. As the Italian industry continued to prosper, British exports to Italy continued to fall. They reached a level of 26.5 million yards in 1895, 8.7 million yards in 1905, and increased very slightly to 10.2 million yards in 1913. By comparison, the 201,900 tons of raw cotton imported into Italy in 1913 should have been enough to produce approximately 2 billion yards of cloth.

As expected, the quality of British cotton cloth imported into Italy increased rather sharply as the quantity fell. Indeed, by 1913, the average quality of British cotton cloth entering

---

[51] See S. B. Clough, *The Economic History of Modern Italy*, pp. 20–21.

[52] Ibid., p. 63.

[53] Ibid.

Italy was higher than that sent to any other market with the single exception of the United States. In that year, the price of the average yard of cotton cloth going from Britain to Italy was over twice as high as the price of the average yard of cotton cloth exported to all markets from Britain.[54]

Italy's complete control of her domestic low- and medium-quality markets eventually spilled over into a considerable export trade. By weight, Italy in 1910 exported about as much cotton cloth as did France or Germany. The average quality of this cloth, however, was lower than the quality of French and German exports.[55] This in turn means that the average quality of Italian cotton cloth exports was far below average British quality, despite the low quality of British cloth bound for India. Italian exports were concentrated on the Middle East and Latin America. As a supplier of low-quality cotton cloth to these areas, Italy was rapidly becoming a real threat to Britain during the years just before World War I.[56]

Brazil

For at least the first half of the period under review, Brazil must have been a very satisfying market for British cloth exporters. As can be seen in Table 25, the quantity of British cotton cloth taken by Brazil grew steadily from 15.8 million yards in 1815 to 156 million yards in 1860. After a period of slack associated with the American Civil War, exports to Brazil reached 233 million yards in 1880. After 1830, this rapid growth of cloth exports to Brazil was accompanied by a decline in average quality. This seems normal enough in view of the rapid growth of the market. What is more, at least part of this growth in demand resulted from the "tremendous expansion of the slave trade" that occurred between 1830 and 1850.[57]

[54] See Sandberg, "Movements in the Quality of British Cotton Textile Exports," p. 14.

[55] U.S. Tariff Board, p. 215.

[56] See G. W. Daniels and J. Jewkes, "The Post-War Depression in the Lancashire Cotton Industry," p. 164.

[57] See S. J. Stein, *The Brazilian Cotton Manufacture*, p. 4.

This great growth of British exports took place despite the mildly protective tariff of 1844. This tariff levied a tax of 30% *ad valorem* on cotton goods.[58] This may have reduced the level of British exports somewhat below the levels they would otherwise have reached, but it did not do much to accelerate the growth of domestic Brazilian production. It was only after a long period displaying a "steady protectionistic trend" after 1879 that the local cotton industry entered into a period of rapid growth. After 1879, real tariff rates increased almost continuously because of three different developments: (1) nominal rates were increased, (2) the percentage of the tariff to be paid in gold (instead of depreciated milreis) was raised, and (3) official valuation of imports was combined with falling actual values.[59] This protectionistic trend received an especially big boost from the "remarkably protective" tariff of 1900.[60]

During this period, the growth of Brazilian cotton cloth output was nothing short of sensational. From an estimated level of 22.7 million yards (20.6 million meters) in 1885, output increased to 290.4 million yards in 1911.[61] Naturally enough, imports were not faring well. With the exception of the years 1892 and 1893, when cotton cloth imports from Great Britain reached an all-time high, the general trend after 1880 was downward in quantity and upward in quality. By 1905, British cotton cloth exports to Brazil had fallen to 131.5 million yards, and in 1913 they were all the way down to 96.5 million yards. This drop occurred despite the fact that Britain continued to be the dominant supplier of imports.[62] At the same time, Britain's share of the whole Brazilian cotton cloth market (in yardage terms) dropped from about 90% in 1880 to about 20% in 1913. Under these circumstances, the fact that Brazil did not amount to anything as a cotton goods exporter must have seemed small consolation indeed to British producers and traders.

[58] Ibid., p. 10.
[59] Ibid., pp. 84–85.
[60] Ibid., p. 85.
[61] Ibid., p. 100.
[62] Compare the figures for total Brazilian imports on page 193 of Stein, *The Brazilian Cotton Manufacture,* with the figures for British exports to Brazil presented in Table 24.

India

India was easily Britain's most important, and most rapidly growing, cotton goods market during most of the nineteenth century. Indeed, in 1913 India imported no less than 3.2 billion yards of British cotton cloth. This impressive figure can be contrasted with the mere 1.4 *million* yards of British cotton cloth taken by India in 1815. Interestingly enough, in 1815 India imported very-high-quality cloth, the average price per yard being 132.9% of the overall average price per yard of British cotton cloth exports in that year.[63] By 1913, India was Britain's low-quality market *par excellence,* the average price per yard being only 84.4% of the overall average price.[64] By my estimate, the average quality of British cotton cloth exported to India declined by almost exactly 50% between 1815 and 1913.[65]

The decline in quality was almost continuous until around 1890 and was accompanied by a virtually uninterrupted, and usually very rapid, increase in quantity. It is perfectly clear that India could not remain the highest-quality importer once British sales spread beyond colonial officials and local notables. In the years following 1815, Lancashire greatly expanded her Indian sales by appealing to groups who could afford only relatively cheap cloth. Not only did Lancashire ship out her regular assortment of cheap cloth but she deliberately developed special types of cheap cloth for India and other low-income markets. A leading example of this policy was the introduction of very cheap, heavily sized goods during and after the American Civil War.[66]

The net effect of British competition on the domestic Indian handloom industry is a matter of some dispute. The traditional view is well expressed in Karl Marx's famous quotation from

[63] Sandberg, "Movements in the Quality of British Cotton Textile Exports," p. 14.

[64] So heavy was India's weight in the calculation of the overall average price that, of the ten regions separated out, only "Other Asia," in addition to India, had an average price below the overall average. The other eight regions all had average prices above the overall average (ibid.).

[65] Ibid., p. 18.

[66] Copeland, *The Cotton Manufacturing Industry of the United States,* p. 79.

the governor-general's report of 1834–35: "The bones of the cotton weavers are bleaching the plains of India."[67] Other evidence, however, indicates that very substantial numbers of handloom weavers must have continued to function throughout the nineteenth century.[68] There can be little doubt that more cotton cloth would have been produced in India had British cloth not been available. It is not, however, clear whether the level of Indian handloom production actually declined after 1815. The total Indian market for cotton cloth must have been growing rapidly given the population explosion of this period. In addition, although British cotton cloth imports no doubt hurt the Indian handloom weavers, cheap British yarn probably helped them. Indian imports of British yarn increased fairly steadily until around 1880.[69] In that year, these imports amounted to some 46.9 million pounds. This amount of yarn was probably enough for close to 250 million yards of handwoven cloth. In addition, there must have been some domestic handspun yarn (made out of Indian raw cotton) available.

Between 1890 and 1913, the average quality of British cotton cloth imported by India increased somewhat despite a continued increase in the quantity imported. The principal reason for this development was clearly the establishment of a domestic factory industry. By the end of the period, this new factory industry had become a factor to be reckoned with on the Indian market. In the 1909–10 to 1913–14 period, Indian mill production of cotton cloth averaged 1.1 billion yards per annum compared with average annual imports of 2.6 billion yards.[70] In the single year 1913, Indian factory cotton cloth production amounted to about 35% of the yardage imported.[71] This high

[67] K. Marx, *Capital*, p. 471. A perplexing feature of this quotation is that Marx's reference is extremely vague. Morris Morris, who attempted to find the original, has informed me that he was unable to do so.

[68] I have this information directly from Professor Morris. See also M. Morris, "Towards a Reinterpretation of Nineteenth Century Indian Economic History," pp. 612–13.

[69] This alone, of course, does not mean that handweaving was necessarily increasing; domestic hand spinning may have been decreasing.

[70] See A. R. Burnett-Hurst, "Lancashire and the Indian Market," p. 404.

[71] The fact that this percentage appears to be slightly less than that achieved for the period 1909–10 to 1913–14 can probably be credited to the boom in

level of output was the result of rapid recent growth. It is estimated that between 1900 and 1913 the number of factory spindles in India increased by one-third and that the number of power looms more than doubled.[72] In addition to mill production, it seems apparent that there was an increase in handloom production during these years.[73] The growth of handloom weaving was aided by the spread of the fly shuttle as well as the growth of a domestic factory spinning industry.[74]

This early development of an Indian factory cotton textile industry, and the growth of the handloom industry, occurred with little or no protection. After 1896, the mill industry had no protection, and the handloom industry had virtually none. In addition, it should be remembered that the continual decline in freight rates during the nineteenth century had an effect similar to a *decline* in tariffs. Even more important, at least with regard to inland markets, was the building of the Indian railways and the general improvement in internal transportation and communication facilities.

Given these circumstances, it seems that the Indian situation just before World War I was not as favorable as the figures alone on yards of cloth imported from Great Britain might have indicated. The country had a rapidly growing, modern mill industry that was flourishing without benefit of tariffs. The ability of this domestic industry to take advantage of the cheap labor available in India had already permitted it to make serious inroads in the low-quality market.[75] Even without considering the possibility that Britain might be unable to maintain her overwhelmingly dominant position among foreign suppliers of cotton cloth to India,[76] the rise of the domestic

---

Indian cotton cloth sales experienced in 1913 (see A. S. Pearse, *The Cotton Industry in India*, p. 209).

[72] Daniels and Jewkes, "The Post-War Depression in the Lancashire Cotton Industry," p. 165.

[73] Arno Pearse refers to the "resuscitation" of the handloom industry (*The Cotton Industry in India*, p. 27).

[74] Ibid.

[75] For an excellent discussion of the growth of the Indian cotton textile work force, see M. D. Morris, *The Emergence of an Industrial Labor Force in India.*

[76] In 1913, Britain supplied 97%, by weight, of all cotton cloth imported into India (Daniels and Jewkes, "The Post-War Depression in the Lancashire Cotton Industry," p. 164).

Indian industry must have cast a shadow over Britain's long-term future in this all-important market.

China

Throughout most of the 1815–1913 period, China was a large and growing market for British cotton cloth. This is particularly true after the "Opium War" had effectively "opened" China to Western commercial penetration. British exports rose from 13 million yards in 1840 to 73 million yards in 1850, 194 million yards in 1859, and 469 million yards in 1871. After this point, the rate of growth slowed down considerably. Thus, only 448 million yards of British cotton cloth were imported into China in 1880. This quantity subsequently grew to 570 million yards in 1890, an amount not equaled until 1902. After 1902, the quantity fluctuated between a high of 800 million yards in 1905 and low of 471 million yards in 1910. The figure for 1913 was 717 million yards.

As expected, average quality decreased rapidly during the period of rapid expansion. Until after 1890, Britain was competing, on the Chinese market, almost exclusively with local handloom weavers. Thus, the rapid growth in British sales up to that date must have consisted almost exclusively of a capture of part of the handloom weavers' market.[77] After 1890, however, there was a resurgence in the average quality of British cloth going to China. With 1845 = 100, the average quality of British cotton cloth exports to China increased from 81.9 in 1890 to 118.9 in 1913.[78] During that same period, the average Chinese import price rose from 100% of the worldwide average

[77] This, of course, does not necessarily mean that the output of the handloom weavers was decreasing. Indeed, the study of Chi-Ming Hou concludes that handloom weaving in China generally was increasing in absolute amounts at least through 1930 (Chi-Ming Hou, "Economic Dualism: The Case of China," pp. 284, 286, 287). It seems highly probable, however, that during most of the period up to 1890, the British were slowly expanding their percentage share of the Chinese market at the expense of handloom weavers.

[78] These particular figures may somewhat exaggerate the real change. Taking the average of slightly longer periods, we find the results are 83.1 for 1889–91 and 112.4 for 1911–13.

price for British cotton cloth exports to 119.1% of the average price.[79]

This means that, in 1913, the British cotton cloth going to China was of a considerably higher average quality than that going to India and of a quality similar to that going to Sub-Saharan Africa and Other Europe.[80]

The reason for this turnabout, as well as the lack of significant growth in the quantity of British exports, can be traced to two developments. The first of these was the growth of a domestic factory industry. The number of spindles in Chinese factories grew from 65,000 in 1894 to 430,000 in 1902 and 964,000 in 1913. In the meantime, the number of power looms grew from 2,100 in 1896 to 4,564 in 1913.[81] By 1913, this factory industry was able to produce roughly 10% as much cloth as was being imported.[82] This, however, was still only a tiny fraction of total Chinese output. Little reliable information is available on Chinese handloom production, so only a rough estimate of total Chinese production can be made. It seems likely, however, that total Chinese cotton cloth production in 1913 was about 5 or 6 times as great as total imports.[83]

At the same time as a domestic Chinese factory industry was beginning to emerge, Britain was starting to encounter serious competition on the Chinese market from other export- ers. The first source of such competition was the United States, especially the South. By 1910, however, the United States had been overtaken in the Chinese market by Japan.[84] This competition from the United States and Japan was felt almost exclusively in the market for cheap gray cloth in northern China and Manchuria.[85] These countries did not seriously threaten Britain's hold on the higher-quality South China

[79] Sandberg, "Movements in the Quality of British Cotton Textile Exports," p. 14.

[80] Ibid.

[81] F. Utley, *Lancashire and the Far East*, pp. 239–40.

[82] Compare pp. 236, 233, 240, in Utley, *Lancashire and the Far East*.

[83] See ibid., p. 236, for some evidence on this question.

[84] U.S. Tariff Commission, *The Japanese Cotton Industry and Trade*, p. 149.

[85] For a discussion of the various Chinese submarkets, see R. H. Myers, "Cotton Textile Handicraft and the Development of the Cotton Textile Industry in Modern China," pp. 618–20.

market.[86] By the 1910–13 period, the domestic Chinese industry and competitive imports had reduced Britain's share of the Chinese market for *factory*-produced cotton cloth to approximately 55% by value and 50% by volume.[87]

Japan

In many ways, Japan is the most interesting of the British markets examined in this chapter. This is principally because Japanese competition in third markets played such an important role in Lancashire's decline after World War I. Indeed, even before World War I, Japan was the only really serious threat to Britain in third markets.

Japan, of course, entered the international economy at a relatively late stage. Almost from the beginning, however, she was a good customer for cotton goods. As early as 1868, total Japanese cotton cloth imports totaled over 32 million square yards.[88] Of that total, about 23 million yards originated in Great Britain. Following a generally upward path, Japanese cotton cloth imports reached a high of 97 million square yards in 1879 (62 million of these yards were British). This quantity was not exceeded until 1896. The peak in Japanese cotton cloth imports, however, was reached during the period 1905–10. Total imports exceeded 100 million yards in each of those years with Britain supplying almost all of it. After 1908, the trend was steadily downward. In 1913, Japan imported a total of only 52 million square yards and only 50 million yards from Great Britain.[89]

This decline in imports was, of course, the result of a rapid

[86] Ibid., p. 148; and Copeland, *The Cotton Manufacturing Industry of the United States*, p. 225–26.

[87] Utley, *Lancashire and the Far East*, pp. 230–31. Miss Utley quotes Bernard Ellinger's assertion that, in the (for Britain) very good year of 1913, Great Britain had 68% of the Chinese *import* market for cotton cloth by weight and 72% by value, and Japan had 23% by value and 19% by weight. The quality of domestic factory production was no doubt considerably lower than even the Japanese product (see Chi-Ming Hou, *Foreign Investment and Economic Development in China, 1840–1937*, p. 153).

[88] K. Seki, *The Cotton Industry of Japan*, p. 306.

[89] Ibid., p. 307.

growth in domestic factory output. Substantial growth came first in the spinning section, but even there it did not really amount to much before the 1880s. The 1880s, however, witnessed a veritable explosion in Japanese cotton textile production. Cotton-spinning capacity increased from 12,800 spindles in 1880 to 358,200 spindles in 1890. By 1900, the number of spindles had reached 1,361,100, and in 1913 it was 2,287,000.[90] The lead in spinning over weaving is reflected in the fact that Japanese yarn imports began to decline decisively as early as 1888. In both quantity and value terms, Japan had become a net exporter of cotton cloth by 1897.[91] Cotton cloth exports did not exceed cotton cloth imports, even in terms of quantity, until about 1901. In value terms, Japan did not become a net exporter of cotton cloth until after 1909. In 1913, however, Japanese cotton cloth exports were about five times as great as imports in yardage terms and over four times as large in value terms.[92] The single most important example of the force behind Japan's move onto world markets before World War I is unquestionably the way she pushed aside the United States in the North China and Manchurian markets.

The remarkable growth of the Japanese cotton textile industry in the decades after 1880 was accomplished largely without the aid of tariffs or any other kind of government assistance. Indeed, for most of this period the Japanese government was bound by treaties forbidding her to establish anything except extremely low tariffs.[93] It is true that a few mills were given government assistance, mainly in the form of easy credit, in the years around 1880. These government-supported mills did very badly, however, and played no important role in the development of the Japanese cotton textile industry as a whole.

---

[90] Ibid., p. 311.

[91] Ibid., p. 304.

[92] Ibid., p. 306–307.

[93] Under an agreement of 1866, Japan was obligated to limit her tariffs to 5% *ad valorem*. This restriction was not escaped until after Japan's victory in the Sino-Japanese War of 1894–95. Other treaties, however, continued to limit the amount of tariff protection that could be given and tariffs remained very low until 1911 (W. W. Lockwood, *The Economic Development of Japan: Growth and Structural Change, 1868–1938*, pp. 19, 539).

Rather, the industry was built by a vigorous private sector that operated without government support.[94]

Even in 1913, Lancashire must reasonably have been apprehensive of this booming Japanese industry. In only a few decades and without much government assistance, it had come from virtually nothing to both capture its domestic market and become a major force in all other Asian markets.

CONCLUSION

After this review of various British cotton textile markets, it is now appropriate that we try to distill some more general conclusions. I believe that the following are supported by the facts presented above:

1. Throughout the nineteenth century, the performance of British cotton textile exports was heavily dependent on the commercial policies followed by importing countries. Even in the early part of the century, British exports were adversely affected by the French prohibition and the American tariffs of 1816, 1824, and 1828. Later, British exports were hurt by increased tariffs in the United States, Germany, France, Italy, and Brazil among the countries examined in this chapter. On the other hand, British exports were assisted by tariff reductions such as those that were enacted in the United States in 1846 and in France in 1861 (the Cobden-Chevalier Treaty).

2. Throughout the century, domestic cotton textile industries developed outside Great Britain behind tariff barriers. The earliest and most obvious case of this was in the United States. Of the countries discussed above, it was also true of Italy and Brazil as well as France and Germany. Among countries not discussed above, it was true of Russia.[95]

3. These infant industries had their greatest initial success at low counts and qualities. This was partly because protection was usually greatest at low counts and partly because low counts and qualities required relatively less skill than did high counts

---

[94] Seki, *The Cotton Industry of Japan*, p. 15.

[95] See W. L. Blackwell, *The Beginnings of Russian Industrialization*, pp. 43–44, 47.

and qualities. It is also true that these industries usually advanced more rapidly in spinning than in weaving. As time progressed, however, there was a clear tendency to produce higher-and-higher-quality goods and for weaving to catch up with spinning.

4. The cotton textile industries that grew up behind tariff walls were usually the first, or one of the first, industries to adopt modern methods in each particular country. This happened even when other industries were given equal, or even greater, protection. In other words, because cotton textiles were a relatively easy industry to establish on a modern factory basis, the industry responded unusually well to tariff protection.

5. As the nineteenth century wore on, a number of cotton textile industries began to develop without the aid of tariffs. This was true of the southern states of the United States (unprotected against the established industry of New England), India, China, and, perhaps most important, Japan. This tendency was undoubtedly assisted by the development of low-skill-intensive methods, particularly in spinning. In all these cases of unprotected development,[96] cotton textiles, when not the first, was an early industry to be mechanized. In all four cases listed above, factory production began with very low counts and qualities and then slowly spread to higher counts and qualities. Furthermore, in all these cases, with the possible exception of the United States South, where no handloom weavers were available, spinning was mechanized earlier and faster than was weaving.

6. Before the outbreak of World War I, several of these new industries, protected and unprotected, were beginning to compete with Great Britain on world markets. This is true despite the fact that Great Britain remained easily the predominant exporter of cotton goods and that no other national industry was primarily dependent on exports. Part of the decline in Britain's share of world trade in cotton goods between 1882–84 and 1910–13 was due to the very rapid growth of markets in which Britain did not participate to any large extent. This is particularly true with regard to the French colonies and, to a lesser extent, eastern Europe. Much of the decline,

[96] There were a few unimportant subsidies paid in Japan (see p. 171 above).

however, was due to direct competition. This is certainly the case with American and Japanese penetration of the Chinese market and Italian gains in Latin America and the Near East. In addition, Britain herself imported rapidly growing amounts of high-quality goods and specialty items from western Europe.

9

LANCASHIRE'S EXPORT EXPERIENCE BETWEEN THE WORLD WARS

Starting in 1914, British exports of cotton goods went into a steep and almost continuous decline that has persisted into the post–World War II period. A record of this decline and the decline in British raw cotton consumption, together with a record of the rise of Japanese competition, up to 1938 is presented in Table 25. The severity of the drop in British exports can be appreciated from the fact that in 1938 and 1939 Britain exported only about 1,450 million yards of cotton cloth per year. This was a smaller amount than that recorded for any year since 1850, and it compares very unfavorably with the 7,075 million yards exported in 1913. The current position of the British cotton textile industry is apparent when it is noted that even the extremely low export levels of 1938 and 1939 have not subsequently been equaled. Thus, the period since 1913 has witnessed the virtual elimination of Britain as an important exporter of cotton textiles. This, in turn, has caused the British cotton textile industry to shrink to a small fraction of its pre–World War I size and importance. This is true with regard to total output, employment, invested capital,

TABLE 25

BRITISH AND JAPANESE COTTON CLOTH EXPORTS AND
BRITISH RAW COTTON CONSUMPTION, 1913–38

Year	British Raw Cotton Consumption (Millions of Pounds)	British Cotton Cloth Exports (Millions of Linear Yards)*	Japanese Cotton Cloth Exports (Millions of Square Yards)*
1913	2,178	7,075	235
1914	2,077	5,736	337
1915	1,931	4,749	403
1916	1,972	5,254	535
1917	1,800	4,978	794
1918	1,499	3,699	1,006
1919	1,526	3,524	883
1920	1,726	4,435†	827
1921	1,066	3,038	689
1922	1,409	4,313	781
1923	1,362	4,329	812
1924	1,369	4,585	1,009
1925	1,609	4,637	1,298
1926	1,509	3,923	1,425
1927	1,557	4,189	1,483
1928	1,520	3,968	1,419
1929	1,498	3,765	1,791
1930	1,272	2,491	1,572
1931	985	1,790	1,414
1932	1,257	2,303	2,032
1933	1,177	2,117	2,090
1934	1,322	2,060	2,577
1935	1,261	2,013	2,725
1936	1,366	1,993	2,710
1937	1,431	2,023	2,644
1938	1,109	1,448	2,181

SOURCES: Robson, *The Cotton Industry in Britain*, p. 333, and Seki, *The Cotton Industry of Japan*, p. 307.

*Because cotton cloth varied considerably in width, it is not possible to convert accurately linear yards into square yards, or vice versa. In general, however, a square yard of cotton cloth was more than a linear yard. The difference for a whole country's imports could amount to as much as 20% (see R. A. Kraus, "Cotton and Cotton Goods in China, 1918-1936: The Impact of Mechanization on the Traditional Sector," Appendix J).

†Square yards

value added, or any other meaningful measure of economic activity.

This disastrous decline in exports began in a relatively innocent way during World War I. During these years, the problem faced by the industry was principally one of raw cotton supply or, more exactly, a shortage of shipping capacity. This problem got worse as the war progressed and reached a peak in 1918. Since it was the weight and volume of the raw cotton and the goods produced from it, together with the distance the goods were to be shipped, that determined the amount of shipping capacity required, low-quality cotton goods to be sent to Asia (especially India and China) was the category most constrained by the war. During the period of cotton shortage, the industry had excess capacity with regard to both equipment and manpower. The usual results to be expected from a shortage of raw cotton and an excess supply of equipment and workers (i.e., high cotton prices, high unemployment, low wages, and low profits) were avoided thanks to a system of price controls on raw cotton (but not cotton goods) together with legal restrictions on the rate of capacity utilization by each firm.[1] Despite low levels of output, labor did not suffer severely, and the manufacturers did very well.[2]

The end of World War I was followed by a brief boom. Despite the fact that output never reached prewar levels[3] there was pressure on capacity. To some extent, this was the result of a lack of investment in the industry during the war. A more serious problem, however, was the shortage of workers, especially skilled workers. This shortage was the result of a reduction in the work week,[4] together with the dislocations caused by the war. The high profits "earned" in 1920[5] were in large part due to a failure of wages to adjust rapidly to the labor shortage.

This recovery, however, was very short-lived. It had been in any case largely a domestic boom. Exports reached only 4,435 million yards in 1920 (versus 7,075 million yards in 1913), and yarn exports were only a third of their 1913 level. Domestic cotton consumption, on the other hand, increased by about

---

[1] For a description of this policy, see Henderson, *The Cotton Control Board.*

[2] See the profit rates presented in Table 18.

[3] In 1920, cotton consumption in Great Britain amounted to 1,726 million pounds compared with 2,178 million pounds in 1913 (see Table 25).

[4] The standard work week was reduced from 57 1/2 hours to 48 hours in July 1919 (Robson, *The Cotton Industry in Britain,* p. 7).

[5] See Table 18.

14% between 1913 and 1920.[6] Perhaps the best thing that can be said about this brief spurt is that it did not last long enough to result in any major investments in new capacity.

As can be seen in Table 25, 1921 was a complete disaster by any standard. Although there was some recovery in exports during the 1922–25 period (never, of course, approaching the levels of 1913) and in total cotton consumption during 1925–28 (not, however, reaching the level of 1920), the overall downward trend is unmistakable. The coming of the worldwide depression of the early 1930s made this clear beyond the slightest doubt. After 1928, there was nothing that can seriously be called a recovery, either in exports or in total cotton consumption.

It should be added parenthetically, but only parenthetically, that the average quality of British cotton textile exports improved somewhat as the quantity fell. Available data indicates that between 1913 and 1924 the average quality of British cotton cloth exports improved by approximately 12%.[7] Furthermore, it is unlikely that this trend was reversed, and it may well have continued, after 1924. It is clear, however, that this increase in quality could have done no more than offset a small percentage of the drop in the quantity of exports. Indeed, the principal reason for the increase in average quality was not an increase in the demand for high quality products. Rather, it occurred because the low-quality markets were being lost at a somewhat faster rate than the high-quality markets.

In order to place Lancashire's experience into a worldwide perspective, data on the evolution of world production and world trade in cotton goods, as well as Britain's share of this trade, are presented in Table 26. In some sense, it can be argued that these data make the post–World War I performance look better than it actually was. This is principally because the boom of 1912 and 1913 is played down by being averaged in with 1910 and 1911. On the whole, however, the data give a fair picture of the trends involved.

This table illustrates the fall in Britain's share of world trade

[6] Of course, if domestic demand had been lower, exports might have been somewhat higher.

[7] See G. W. Daniels and J. Jewkes, *The Comparative Position of the Lancashire Cotton Industry and Trade*, pp. 64–72.

TABLE 26

WORLDWIDE TRADE AND PRODUCTION OF COTTON TEXTILES IN SELECTED YEARS
(Annual Averages)

Years	Worldwide Mill Consumption of Cotton (Millions of Pounds)	Percentage of Production Entering World Trade	Percentage of Cloth Production Entering World Trade	Index of World Trade (1910-13 = 100)	Britain's Percentage of World Production	Britain's Percentage of World Trade
1829-31	420	55	—	7.9	57	70
1882-84	4,000	38	45	51.7	37	82
1910-13	10,500	28	31	100.0	20	58
1926-28	12,200	23	23	95.4	12	39
1936-38	14,000	16	18	76.2	9	28
1953-55	16,800	10	12	57.1	5	12

SOURCE: Robson, *The Cotton Industry in Britain*, pp. 2, 359.

in cotton textiles in the post–World War I period. It should also be noted, however, that the share of total world trade as a percentage of world production was falling. Clearly, if the share of world trade in world production had been maintained at the 1910–13 level and Britain had gotten her share of this trade,[8] then the decline in British cotton textile production would have been much moderated. Of greater interest is the fact that both Britain's share of world trade and the share of total world trade in total world production had also declined between 1882–84 and 1910–13. Although the rates of decline in these shares were somewhat greater after than before World War I, the principal difference between the two periods lay in the rate of growth of total world mill production of cotton goods. Had world production continued to increase at its earlier rate and had Britain been able to hold on to the share of trade she actually had in each year, despite the posited increase in output, then Lancashire would have prospered mightily during the interwar years.

In fact, of course, it simply was not possible for world production to keep growing at its earlier rate. This earlier growth had been based principally on the opening-up of new markets. By the beginning of World War I, however, there were very few unexploited markets available, and the rates of growth of population and income were not large enough to prevent a fall in the rate of growth of output.[9] The inevitable nature of the slowdown in growth is perhaps best demonstrated by the fact that the rate of growth of world production of cotton textiles has been slower since 1936–38 than it was in the period between 1910–13 and 1936–38.

The problem thus becomes one of explaining why world trade fell sharply as percentage of world production, and even declined somewhat in absolute terms, and why Great Britain was unable to hold on to her previous share of trade. The fact that both the percentage of trade in world production and Britain's percentage share of world trade declined in an

[8] This share presumably would have been the percentage of total trade actually achieved in the post-World War I years.

[9] The effect of income growth was in any case limited by the relatively low income elasticity of demand for cotton goods.

earlier period of rapid growth in total output is a pertinent observation, but it is clearly not a satisfactory answer to these questions.

BRITISH EXPORT EXPERIENCE IN SEPARATE AREAS AND COUNTRIES

The search for satisfactory answers must begin with a study of the particular markets in which these developments occurred. Indeed, even a casual glance at some individual markets leads to a modification of the data in Table 26. For instance, world trade in cotton goods after World War I was affected by the territorial changes resulting from the war. This particularly applies to the breakup of Austria-Hungary. Suddenly, after 1919, Czechoslovakia emerges as an important exporter of cotton cloth, accounting for 4% of total world exports in 1923–25.[10] Most of this trade, however, was simply a continuation of commerce that had been considered internal before the break-up of Austria-Hungary. It represented little more than the facts that Austria had most of the empire's spinning mills, and Bohemia had most of the weaving installations.[11] This political change in Central Europe thus tends to make the figures in Table 26 exaggerate the post–World War I level of international trade in cotton textiles and underestimate Britain's position as a trader.

Two other points also deserve to be mentioned, particularly with reference to Britain's declining share of world trade. First of all, a look at particular markets makes it obvious that some of the post–World War I exports from Japan consisted of extremely cheap, low-quality goods for which Japan was creating a new market. That is, if Japan had not exported these goods, Great Britain still would not have played much of a role in supplying them. The absence of these Japanese goods would probably have resulted in a slightly higher level of production by third-country domestic industries and somewhat lower levels of consumption in these countries.

[10] G. W. Daniels and J. Jewkes, "The Post-War Depression in the Lancashire Cotton Industry," p. 155.

[11] See L. Pasvolsky, *Economic Nationalism of the Danubian States*, pp. 157–58.

Second, some import markets contracted much more rapidly than others after World War I. Clearly, it makes a big difference to any evaluation of Britain's performance if she was traditionally a heavy exporter to the markets that contracted relatively rapidly or in those where developments were more favorable. In fact, Britain's problems were largely related to her concentration on markets that contracted very rapidly between the World Wars. Three markets were particularly costly to Britain: India, China, and the Middle East. Of these, India was by far the most important. Before World War I, India accounted for about 36% of all the cotton cloth produced in Great Britain.[12] This amount constituted no less than 97% of the cotton cloth imported into India from all sources.[13] In view of this crucial role, I shall begin my survey of particular areas and countries with a review of post–World War I developments in India.

India

As can be seen from the data on India contained in Table 27, the post–World War I Indian cotton textile market was a disaster for Lancashire. In fact, it was a disaster for world trade in cotton textiles in general. Because Great Britain at least started the postwar period as the completely dominant supplier of the Indian market, however, she bore the brunt of what happened.

The drop in total Indian imports of cotton piece goods was truly remarkable. Between 1910–13 and 1926–28, Indian imports of piece goods fell by approximately 30%. If Indian imports had stayed instead at their prewar level, total world trade in cotton goods would have increased, not decreased, during this time period. By 1936–38, Indian imports of piece goods were down by 73% from their prewar level. Although the cotton trade was sufficiently depressed on a worldwide scale by that time, so that India alone was not responsible for the decline in world trade since before World War I, it

[12] Robson, *The Cotton Industry in Britain*, p. 10.
[13] The 97% figure refers to 1912 and 1913 (ibid., p. 164).

TABLE 27

IMPORTS OF COTTON PIECE GOODS AND FACTORY PRODUCTION IN INDIA, 1913–38

(in millions of square yards)

Year	Total Imports	Imports from Great Britain	Factory Production
1913	...	3,216*	...
1913–14	3,207*	...	1,164*
1919	...	828.9	...
1919–20	1,081	...	1,640
1920	...	1,498	...
1920–21	1,510	...	1,581
1921	...	1,182	...
1921–22	1,090	...	1,732
1922	...	1,507	...
1922–23	1,593	...	1,725
1923	...	1,519	...
1923–24	1,486	...	1,702
1924	...	1,726	...
1924–25	1,823	...	1,970
1925	...	1,546	...
1925–26	1,564	...	1,954
1926	...	1,668	...
1926–27	1,788	...	2,317†
1927	...	1,766	...
1927–28	1,973	...	2,442†
1928	...	1,631	...
1928–29	1,937	...	1,916†
1929	...	1,489	...
1929–30	1,919	...	2,418†
1930	...	829.4	...
1930–31	890	...	2,538†
1931	...	428	...
1931–32	776	...	2,891†
1932	...	653	...
1932–33	1,255	...	2,988†
1933	...	522	...
1933–34	796	...	2,777†
1934	...	624	...
1934–35	944	...	3,168†
1935	...	602	...
1935–36	947	...	3,275†
1937	688*	323*	3,951*
1938	724*	258*	4,250*

SOURCES: 1913–36, *Statistical Yearbook for British India*, various years, and *British Parliamentary Papers*, various years; 1937–38, Robson, *The Cotton Industry in Britain*, p.10.

*Millions of linear yards.

†Assuming 4.3 yards per pound. This is the conversion rate recommended by the source.

is nevertheless true that had Indian imports been maintained at the 1910–13 level, about two-thirds of the decrease in world trade that occurred between 1910–13 and 1936–38 would have been eliminated.

The burden falling on Great Britain as a result of the decline in the Indian market was very heavy. At least one-third of the drop in total British exports of cotton goods between 1910–13 and 1926–28 can be directly credited to the shrinkage of the Indian market. That is, if Indian imports had remained at their prewar level in 1926–28 and Great Britain had obtained its actual 1926–28 share of these hypothetical imports, then the fall in total British cotton cloth exports over the period would have been reduced by approximately one-third. If it is hypothesized that Britain exported as much cotton cloth to India in 1926–28 as she did in 1910–13, then something like one-half of the actual drop in total British exports would not have occurred. The same things, more or less, can be said if 1910–13 is compared with 1936–38. A more startling observation can be made with regard to the later date, however. In 1938, India imported cotton cloth from Great Britain equal to 3% of the cotton cloth Britain produced in 1912–13. In 1912–13, India had imported 36% of all the cotton cloth produced in Great Britain. The shrinkage of Indian demand alone thus equaled one-third of the British industry's total demand from all sources in 1912–13.[14]

Contrary to widely held beliefs, the principal immediate reason for the drop in British exports to India was the development of the domestic cotton industry and the tariffs designed to aid it, not Japanese competition. It was not until the 1930s that Japan first drew close to, and then overtook, Great Britain as a supplier of the Indian market. By then, however, British exports to India, and indeed the whole Indian import market, had already collapsed. Even if Great Britain had had the entire Indian import market to herself during the 1930s, it would not have helped Lancashire very much. Table 28 provides a very brief, but accurate, summary of the situation.

As was noted in the previous chapter, the output of cotton

---

[14] Robson, *The Cotton Industry in Britain*, p. 10.

TABLE 28

THE INDIAN COTTON TEXTILE MARKET

(in millions of linear yards)

	Prewar Average	1930–31
Indian mill production	1,105	2,561
Indian handloom production	1,000*	1,400*
Imports from Great Britain	2,549	526
Imports from Japan	3	321

SOURCES: Mill production and imports from Burnett-Hurst, "Lancashire and the Indian Market"; handloom production figures from H. A. F. Lindsay's discussion of Burnett-Hurst's paper, p.451.

*Estimated

goods in India was growing rapidly before World War I. This was particularly true of factory production, but even handloom production appears to have been on the increase. This production was given a fillip by World War I. The curtailment of British production, particularly of coarse goods, and the shortage of shipping capacity to take cotton goods to the Far East cut sharply into British exports to India. Average annual Indian imports fell from a prewar (i.e., the average for 1909–13) level of 2,549 million yards to 1,841 million yards during the war. These figures probably underestimate the impact of the drop because exports were at their highest in 1913 and their lowest in 1918. The results for 1919–20 may be more indicative of the situation. In that year, Indian mill production reached 1,640 million yards, and imports were down to 1,081 million yards. In addition, handloom production had at least maintained its prewar output level of approximately 1,000 million yards per year.

The very substantial increase in domestic production was partly a continuation of earlier trends and partly a reaction to the protection that the war provided for domestic producers. Protection was an unaccustomed, but certainly not an unwelcome, luxury for the Indian cotton textile industry. As early as 1917, moreover, the "natural" protection of the war was reinforced by the beginnings of protective tariff legislation. In that year, the 3.5% *ad valorem* duty on cotton piece goods, matched by a 3.5% excise on domestic mill production, was replaced by a 7.5% duty on imports without any offsetting change in the domestic excise. In 1921, the rate of the duty was raised to 11%.[15]

With the restoration of "normal" postwar conditions in 1920–21, cotton textile imports rose, and domestic Indian production fell. This can presumably be taken as evidence for the contention that the wartime conditions had indeed aided the domestic industry. The recovery of 1920–21 was followed by a sharp drop in imports in 1921–22.[16] After that year, however, there was a recovery in imports that lasted through 1929–30. During the late 1920s, total Indian imports averaged about 1,900 million yards per year, as compared with a prewar average of over 2,600 million yards and lows in 1919–20 and 1921–22 of slightly less than 1,100 million yards.

The decline in total Indian imports was aggravated as far as Lancashire was concerned by a slow but steady decline in her market share. The principal beneficiary of these losses in market share was Japan. The shift in market shares during the 1920s is shown in Table 29. Part of this Japanese gain can probably be credited to the appreciation of sterling by about 12% in relation to the yen in 1924.[17] In the same year, the rupee increased in value from approximately 1s. 4d. to approximately 1s. 6d.[18] The appreciation of the rupee with respect to the yen was thus about twice what it was to sterling.

The political tension between Great Britain and the people of India also played some role in Britain's declining market share.[19] Nevertheless, there can be no doubt that Japan was strengthening her competitive position through improved relative prices during the 1920s.

Although the 1920s were bad for Lancashire as far as the Indian market was concerned, they were nothing compared with what happened with the coming of the world wide

[15] Burnett-Hurst, "Lancashire and the Indian Market," p. 409.

[16] The import fluctuations of these years were no doubt related to the sharp fluctuations that also occurred in silver prices and the foreign exchange value of the rupee (see Burnett-Hurst, "Lancashire and the Indian Market," p. 427). In addition, there was a boycott of British goods in 1921–22.

[17] Seki, *The Cotton Industry of Japan,* p. 408.

[18] Burnett-Hurst, "Lancashire and the Indian Market," p. 438.

[19] It must be noted, however, that no large-scale organized boycott of British cottons occurred between 1922 and 1930.

TABLE 29

PERCENTAGE DISTRIBUTION OF INDIAN IMPORT MARKET FOR COTTON PIECE GOODS BETWEEN
UNITED KINGDOM AND JAPAN THROUGH 1931–32

Year	United Kingdom	Japan
Prewar average	97.4	0.1
1913–14	97.1	0.3
1919–20	90.3	7.0
1920–21	85.6	11.3
1921–22	87.6	8.3
1922–23	91.2	6.8
1923–24	88.8	8.2
1924–25	88.5	8.5
1925–26	82.3	13.9
1926–27	82.0	13.6
1927–28	78.2	16.4
1928–29	75.2	18.4
1929–30	65.0	29.3
1930–31	58.8	36.1
1931–32	50.1	45.2

SOURCE: Burnett-Hurst, "Lancashire and the Indian Market," p. 422.

depression of the early 1930s. In March 1930, the Indian tariff was raised to 15% on British cotton cloth and to 20% on cotton cloth from other countries (principally Japan). In March 1931, these rates were increased by 5 percentage points; and in October 1931, a 25% surcharge was added. Thus, after October 1931, the tariff on British cloth was 25% *ad valorem,* and the tariff on Japanese cloth was 31.25% *ad valorem.* To make things worse for the British, and perhaps somewhat better for the Japanese, a nationwide boycott of British cloth was launched by the Congress Party in April 1930. Although a truce was declared in March 1931, the campaign was resumed on a full scale at the end of 1931.

As far as exchange rate movements are concerned, the rupee followed the pound when it was devalued in September 1931 (at 1s. 6d. per rupee). Japan, however, did not immediately respond, and there was some improvement in British cotton textile exports, both to India and overall.[20] By December 1931, however, the Japanese had reestablished the old parity with

[20] Sayers, *A History of Economic Change in England,* p. 54.

TABLE 30

INDIAN IMPORTS OF COTTON CLOTH ON MONTHLY BASIS, 1929–30 TO 1931–32
(in millions of yards)

Month	1929–30	1930–31	1931–32
April	213	164	71
May	155	134	54
June	100	91	69
July	141	72	68
August	171	73	62
September	160	49	65
October	132	43	63
November	148	36	48
December	134	46	45
January	194	62	71
February	157	46	63
March	179	67	73

SOURCE: Burnett-Hurst, "*Lancashire and the Indian Market,*" p.410.

sterling. Between that date and 1933, the yen was devalued relative to both sterling and the rupee. The stable exchange rate that developed in the middle and late 1930s was 1s. 2d. per yen.[21]

The disastrous effects of the measures taken by the Indian government to restrict trade can be seen in Table 30. Both British and Japanese exports were seriously affected. At the same time, domestic Indian production was aided by the added protection. Indian mill production rose from 2,359 million square yards in 1929 to 2,900 million square yards in 1931. By 1935, Indian mill production had climbed to 3,555 million square yards; and in 1938, it was approximately 4,250 million square yards.[22] Part of this growth may have been at the expense of domestic handloom production, but most of the increase represented import substitution.

The relatively minor discrimination in favor of British goods that had been enacted in March 1930 was considerably increased as the 1930s progressed. The tariff on Japanese goods was increased to 50% in 1935, and the tariff on British goods was reduced to 20% in 1937. More important, quotas were imposed

[21] Seki, *The Cotton Industry of Japan,* p. 408.
[22] Board of Trade, *Report,* p. 119.

on Japanese goods starting in January 1934. This quota system was clearly a response to the growth in imports from Japan that occurred starting in 1932. The increase was aided by the depreciation of the yen, and this alleged Japanese policy of "exchange dumping" was taken as an excuse for imposing discriminatory quotas. Japan objected strenuously to these quotas and used the threat of reduced imports of Indian raw cotton as a lever to obtain a more favorable agreement. The result was an Indo-Japanese treaty that tied Japanese exports of cotton goods to India to Japanese imports of Indian raw cotton.[23]

It is evident that these discriminatory actions in favor of Great Britain were not based on any particular affection for Lancashire. The tariff on British cloth was not reduced until 1937, and then it was only cut to 20% *ad valorem*. Rather, the discrimination in favor of Great Britain was the more or less coincidental result of the very real threat that the Japanese were posing for the domestic Indian cotton textile industry. The 25% *ad valorem* tariff in effect on British goods between 1931 and 1937 and the 20% tariff in effect after 1937 were apparently enough to protect the Indian industry from serious competition from Great Britain. Much of the remaining British imports were of high quality and did not really compete with Indian products. This was clearly not the case with Japanese exports. They continued to compete effectively at tariffs of 30% or even 50%. Under these circumstances, the quota system was a natural expedient. Indeed, if it had not been for the possibility of retaliation, the Japanese would have been allowed little or no part of the Indian market.

Given these circumstances, it seems certain that the Indian authorities would have acted with similar vigor against Great Britain if she had posed a serious threat to the Indian industry. The implication of this conclusion, in turn, is that the Indian authorities in the late 1930s were willing to admit a maximum of substantially less than a billion yards of cotton cloth per year, regardless of the source.

In retrospect, developments in India during the quarter-cen-

[23] T. Uyeda, *The Recent Development of Japanese Foreign Trade*, pp. 94–98.

tury between 1913 and 1938 reflect two trends. The first of these was the continued growth of the domestic industry. Like all growing cotton textile industries, it expanded into higher and higher qualities as it gained more experience and its work force became more skilled. This process had already started before World War I. During and after the war, it gained in speed and force from the protection that was provided, first by the wartime shipping shortage and later by tariffs and quotas. Indeed, by the late 1930s, India's position had improved to the point where she was able to export over 100 million yards of low-quality cloth a year.[24] This can be taken as a sign that India as the low-wage producer was beginning to undercut Japan at very low qualities. Since World War II, of course, India has become a major supplier of low-quality goods. This process was helped by India's membership in the Commonwealth, with its preferential tariffs.[25]

In its development of a protected domestic cotton textile industry after World War I, India was only repeating the process that had previously occurred in countries such as the United States, France, Germany, Russia, Italy, and Brazil. As far as Britain was concerned, the previous loss of these markets had not been a disaster because other markets, notably India, had been expanding rapidly enough to more than take up the slack. When the Indian market for British goods began to shrink, however, there was nowhere else to turn.

The other trend in India was the growth of Japanese competition. Before World War I, none of the domestic (i.e., non-British) cotton textile industries had yet had time to develop into a serious threat in third markets. There had been signs, however, that Italy and Japan were, in the future, going to cause serious trouble for Britain, especially in low-quality goods. Not surprisingly, the post–World War I period witnessed a fight between Italy and Japan as to who was going to succeed to Britain's position as the world's leading cotton textile exporter. This struggle, of course, resulted in a clear Japanese victory.

Despite the seriousness of Japanese competition in India,

---

[24] Robson, *The Cotton Industry in Britain*, p. 10.
[25] Ibid., pp. 18–19.

however, Lancashire's fall would have occurred without Japan's assistance. Even if Great Britain had supplied all of India's cotton cloth imports in 1938, this would only have amounted to 724 million yards as compared with the 3,216 million yards of British cloth India had taken in 1913. Indeed, even if all non-British imports into India had been brought to a complete halt, it is unlikely that British exports to India would have been in excess of 500 million yards in 1938.

China (including Hong Kong)

India was Lancashire's number one disaster area, but China did not lag far behind. The sad story of British cotton textile exports to China in the interwar period is eloquently told in Table 31. As was the case with India, Britain had a falling share of a declining total. The British experience in China differed from that in India because in China serious Japanese competition preceded a sharp drop in total Chinese imports. Indeed, as late as 1929 total Chinese imports of cotton cloth were at a level approaching the pre–World War I peak. After that year, however, a very sharp drop occurred. The figures for China alone exaggerate this drop because of the loss of Manchuria to Japan. If Manchuria is reintegrated with China, as is done in Table 31, then the drop becomes much smaller. From the British point of view, however, the trade with occupied Manchuria might just as well not have existed. That was certainly one market where Britain had no chance of competing with Japan.

The British share of the Chinese import market for cotton cloth began to shrink immediately after World War I. From a prewar level of about 60% (this in itself being a sharp drop from the pre-1890 period) the British share, by weight, was down to 30% in the early 1920s. By the late 1930s, her percentage share, even excluding the Manchurian trade, was down to the teens.

The post–World War I period witnessed a rapid expansion of the domestic Chinese factory cotton textile industry. Data on Chinese factory production together with estimates of

TABLE 31

CHINESE IMPORTS OF COTTON CLOTH, 1912–36

Year	Total Imports (Millions of Yards)		Total Imports Adjusted for Manchuria (Millions of Square Yards)	Imports from Britain (Millions of linear Yards to 1918, Square Yards After)
	Linear	Square		
1912	823	764	...	528
1913	1,109	1,017	...	717
1914	1,065	975	...	578
1915	815	724	...	375
1916	726	641	...	377
1917	859	749	...	310
1918	676	586	...	216
1919	906	816	...	304
1920	917	802	...	453
1921	689	603	...	211
1922	832	746	...	309
1923	702	612	...	235
1924	818	722	...	293
1925	844	725	...	173
1926	942	806	...	178
1927	734	618	...	103
1928	944	809	...	187
1929	938	793	...	188
1930	713	589	...	61
1931	459	390	...	81
1932	420	356	477	126
1933	220	187	391	52
1934	107	91	291	20
1935	101	86	375	14
1936	48	41	330	8

SOURCES: Total import figures from Kraus, *Cotton and Cotton Goods in China*, Appendix J. British figures are from various issues of the Trade and Navigation Accounts of the *British Parliamentary Papers*.

handloom production are contained in Table 32. Up until 1929, the rapid growth of the domestic industry was achieved with the assistance of little tariff protection. This was not because the Chinese government lacked the will to protect her cotton textile industry—quite the contrary. Until 1929, however, China was by treaty limited to a 5% *ad valorem* tariff. In fact, even this 5% rate was not maintained, despite occasional upward revision of specific duties, in the face of falling commodity prices.[26] Some increased protection did, however, result from

[26]Y. K. Chang, *Foreign Trade and Industrial Development of China*, p. 53.

TABLE 32

COTTON CLOTH PRODUCTION IN CHINA, 1918–36
(in millions of square yards)

Year	Power Loom Production	Handloom Production
1918	127	...
1919	147	...
1920	161	...
1921	212	...
1922	247	...
1923	303	...
1924	322	3,129
1925	381	4,445
1926	435	3,947
1927	496	2,489
1928	606	2,560
1929	740	3,521
1930	759	3,094
1931	872	3,272
1932	911	2,880
1933	1,108	2,525
1934	1,178	3,023
1935	1,280	3,378
1936	1,309	2,240

SOURCE: Kraus, *Cotton and Cotton Goods in China*, Table V-1.

the decline in the price of silver on the world market. Because China was on a silver standard until 1935, a fall in the price of silver was effectively a depreciation of the Chinese currency.[27]

When China did obtain tariff autonomy, the first independent tariffs were relatively low. The new tariffs that were applied as of 1 February 1929 placed a duty of only 12.5% *ad valorem* on most cotton goods.[28] In 1932, however, stiffer rates on cotton textiles were introduced. These rates ranged up to 30% *ad valorem*.[29] Finally, in July of 1934, tariff rates on cotton textiles were once again increased.[30]

These measures, together with the difficulties associated with the Japanese seizure of Manchuria, were sufficient to limit the importation of cotton textiles into the territory controlled

[27] Ibid., pp. 67–71. This fall in the price of silver, of course, affected all Chinese exports and imports in a similar way.

[28] S. F. Wright, *China's Struggle for Tariff Autonomy*, pp. 640, 707, 708.

[29] G. E. Hubbard, *Eastern Industrialization and its Effect on the West*, pp. 201–2.

[30] Chang, *Foreign Trade and Industrial Development of China*, p. 54.

by the Chinese Nationalist government to negligible levels.[31] At the same time, the reduction in imports did much to encourage the domestic Chinese cotton industry. It is difficult to establish any quantitative estimate of this effect, however, because the Chinese factory cotton industry had been growing rapidly before the tariffs were introduced and because this industry was also competing with the very large Chinese hand-loom industry. The data in Tables 31 and 32 indicate that Chinese factory production grew somewhat more rapidly than imports declined. On the other hand, it also seems likely that total Chinese cotton cloth consumption declined between the mid–1920s and the late 1930s. In any case, both the Chinese handloom and the Chinese factory industries were undoubtedly helped by the policy of protection.

The Chinese government shared at least one feature with the Indian government: a determination to protect her cotton industry from serious foreign competition. The tariffs of 1929 and 1933 were both imposed as soon as treaty obligations permitted it. Indeed, the modest rates imposed in 1929 were very much in the nature of a compromise between China and the countries (especially the United States, Great Britain, and Japan) that were the principal beneficiaries of China's low tariffs.[32] The Chinese government would have been delighted to impose higher rates and, indeed, soon did so; but her chief concern in 1929 had to be the *principle* of tariff autonomy.

Japan was clearly the chief target of China's cotton textile tariffs. This is especially true of the rate increases imposed in 1933 and 1934. By that time, Britain had been reduced to a minor factor in the Chinese market. Most of the small amount of British cloth still going into China was probably noncompetitive with Chinese and Japanese products. Thus, the Chinese industry had little to gain from further imposts on British textiles. From Britain's point of view, therefore, the final tariff increases, which left Britain with Chinese sales of less than 8 million yards in 1936 (approximately 1% of the

---

[31] Chinese imports would undoubtedly have declined even without the tariffs, but not by nearly as much.

[32] Wright, *China's Struggle for Tariff Autonomy*, p. 640.

1913 level), were an unfortunate accident. The virtual destruction of Britain's already depleted trade occurred as a by-product of China's determination to resist serious Japanese competition.

The Middle East

The third area where Lancashire encountered really serious market losses during the interwar period was the Middle East. As was noted in the previous chapter, the Middle East was a generally satisfactory market up to World War I. Nothing was said about any specific countries or any specific national policies. This was largely because not much of interest can be said along these lines concerning the prewar period. The situation changed radically, however, with the disintegration of the Ottoman Empire and the introduction of national policies of industrial protection after World War I.

Table 33 contains data on British cotton cloth exports to the Middle East as a whole and separately to Egypt and Turkey. These two countries were the dominant British markets in the Middle East, and the collapse of British cotton textile exports to the area as a whole principally reflects developments in these two countries.

As in the cases of India and China, British cotton textile exports to the Middle East were hurt both by third-party competition and by the growth of domestic production. In all these cases, the domestic industries were encouraged by protective tariffs. In the Middle East, however, Italy, not Japan, was Britain's first serious rival. For example, between 1913 and 1925, the British share of the Egyptian market fell from 86% to 61%, whereas the Italian share rose from 7% to 23%.[33] A similar trend was occurring in Turkey at the same time.[34] By the early 1930s, however, Japan was rapidly overtaking Italy and, in the process, cutting further into Britain's market share.[35]

[33] Daniels and Jewkes, "The Post-War Depression in the Lancashire Cotton Industry," p. 164.

[34] British Foreign Office, Department of Overseas Trade, *Economic Conditions in Turkey to April 1930*, pp. 35–38.

[35] British Foreign Office, *Economic Conditions in Turkey, 1932*, pp. 32–36.

TABLE 33

BRITISH COTTON TEXTILE EXPORTS TO THE MIDDLE EAST, TURKEY, AND EGYPT
(in millions of linear yards through 1918, square yards thereafter)

Year	Middle East	Turkey	Egypt
1913	760	...	...
1914	594	271	202
1915	394	10	243
1916	412	12	290
1917	434	...	320
1918	471	...	362
1919	590	333	183
1920	613	263	294
1921	464	56	215
1922	462	67	206
1923	499	85	207
1924	479	89	199
1925	553	96	237
1926	322	56	124
1927	403	62	160
1928	331	55	129
1929	337	53	152
1930	244	30	118
1931	207	36	72
1932	252	26	82
1933	193	35	64
1934	108	14	44
1935	91	15	36
1936	110	12	64
1937	94	15	52
1938	68	12	39

SOURCE: Various issues of *British Parliamentary Papers.*

Starting about 1930, moreover, both Turkey and Egypt began
to take steps to encourage the domestic production of cotton
textiles. Without protection, the Egyptian cotton textile industry
had been able to expand only at a relatively slow rate. Between
the beginning of the 1920s and 1930, Egyptian production
of cotton cloth (including handloom production) grew by
somewhat less than 100%, leaving total production at an annual
level of only about 25 million square yards.[36] When tariffs
were increased after 1930,[37] however, the rate of growth of

[36] Z. Y. Hershlag, *Introduction to the Modern Economic History of the Middle East,*
p. 219; and C. Issawi, *Egypt: An Economic and Social Analysis,* p. 86.

[37] Hershlag, *Introduction to the Modern Economic History of the Middle East,* p.
211.

the domestic cotton industry increased markedly.[38] By 1939, production had risen to 150 million square meters.[39]

In post–World War I Turkey, the first steps toward government support of industry in general, including the cotton textile industry, were taken in 1927. In that year, the Law for the Encouragement of Industry was enacted. This law provided industrial enterprises with advantages such as tax and customs exemptions or rebates, as well as a favored position with regard to government purchases.[40] More important, when the tariff-limiting clause of the Treaty of Lausanne expired in 1929, Turkey took action to provide high protective tariffs.[41] During the 1930s the industrialization of Turkey was given an additional powerful push through the direct intervention of the state. Because Japan was the dominant supplier of cotton textiles to Turkey by this time, she naturally was the chief loser when Turkey reduced her imports.

Latin America

Although hardly a tremendous success for Britain, the Latin American cotton textile market (see Table 34) did not provide the kind of total disaster she experienced in India, China, and the Middle East. The single most important reason for this relatively good record in Latin America was that British exports to Argentina were maintained at a reasonable level throughout the interwar period. This, in turn, was principally because no protection was offered to Argentinian cotton manufacturers until 1931.[42] It was only after protection was finally provided that any real progress was achieved in the Argentinian cotton

[38] In 1935, Egypt took special action against Japanese cotton and rayon goods. The intention was to impose tariffs in the 80% to 100% range on cotton goods. As a result of Japanese protests, fortressed by the possibility of a reduction in Japanese imports of Egyptian raw cotton, however, bilateral negotiations in search of a compromise were instituted (Uyeda, *The Recent Development of Japanese Foreign Trade*, p. 118).

[39] Issawi, *Egypt: An Economic and Social Analysis*, p. 86.

[40] Hershlag, *Introduction to the Modern Economic History of the Middle East*, pp. 176–77.

[41] Ibid., p. 181.

[42] G. Wythe, *Industry in Latin America*, p. 103.

TABLE 34

BRITISH COTTON TEXTILE EXPORTS TO LATIN AMERICA
(in millions of linear yards through 1918, square yards thereafter)

Year	Latin America	Brazil	Argentina
1913	744	97	...
1914	381	34	88
1915	399	38	122
1916	593	67	196
1917	528	58	173
1918	486	52	183
1919	303	32	168
1920	440	41	162
1921	192	16	103
1922	319	25	149
1923	447	33	173
1924	412	49	148
1925	483	68	158
1926	389	62	113
1927	386	61	131
1928	398	55	149
1929	415	37	144
1930	293	8	120
1931	209	2	93
1932	251	3	116
1933	302	5	146
1934	323	3	161
1935	252	1	134
1936	313	2	116
1937	331	1	127
1938	204	1	98

SOURCE: Various issues of *British Parliamentary Papers.*

textile industry. Furthermore, despite this protection and increasing Japanese competition, the growth of the total Argentinian market kept the level of British exports from falling
very far, even during the 1930s. Britain's position, and that
of other exporters, was helped by the fact that spinning
developed faster than weaving in Argentina. Thus, by the end
of 1939, though the import market for yarn had been virtually
eliminated, only about one-third of domestic cloth consumption
was woven domestically.[43] Clearly, however, developments in

[43] Ibid. Much of the yarn that was previously imported had been used in knitting
mills.

the Argentinian cotton textile industry did not bode well for the long-term future of imports.

In Brazil, the trend toward self-sufficiency noted in the previous chapter continued. Although Great Britain did a respectable job of maintaining, or almost maintaining, her share of the Brazilian import market (long since limited to high-quality goods),[44] the total level of Brazilian imports was severely reduced by the tariff increase of 1929. After that year, Brazil was virtually self-sufficient in all types of cotton cloth. This, of course, was the logical culmination of a trend that had begun in the 1880s.

Argentina and Brazil were not the only Latin American countries to raise barriers to trade in cotton textiles in the early 1930s. In fact, virtually every Latin American country, or at least all those with anything resembling a domestic cotton textile industry, did so. Although British exports suffered from most of these actions, the principal target in virtually every case was Japan. This can certainly be said about the Peruvian and Columbian quota systems introduced in 1935.[45] Japan was also the target of the 50% surcharge placed on cotton textile imports into Ecuador after 1936.[46] Other highly protected Latin American cotton textile industries existed in Uruguay[47] and Venezuela.[48] These actions make it clear beyond a shadow of a doubt that the Latin American countries, like so many other countries in the interwar period, were determined to protect their cotton textile industries from serious foreign competition. By the 1930s, the chief source of such competition was Japan.

Europe and the United States

In the previous chapter, much was said about the United States and various European countries. There is much less

[44] See Daniels and Jewkes, "The Post-War Depression in the Lancashire Cotton Industry," p. 164. Also compare the figures for total Brazilian imports provided by Stein, *The Brazilian Cotton Manufacture*, p. 193, with the figures for British exports to Brazil shown in Table 34.

[45] Wythe, *Industry in Latin America*, pp. 231, 254.

[46] Ibid., p. 236.

[47] Ibid., p. 129.

[48] Ibid., p. 254.

to be said concerning them during the interwar period. These countries had been largely eliminated as markets for British cotton textiles before the outbreak of World War I. The interwar years basically saw a continuation of this downward trend, at least to the extent that Britain had anything left to lose. In the case of the United States, what little remained for Great Britain after World War I was virtually eliminated by a combination of economic depression, Japanese competition, and the Hawley-Smoot Tariff.[49] The Anglo-American trade agreement designed to improve American trade relations with Great Britain was not signed until November 1938 and had little or no effect during the interwar period.

The United States clearly viewed Japan as the most serious competitor facing her cotton textile industry. When this threat was felt to be serious, anti-Japanese measures were taken, both with regard to the domestic United States market and with regard to the Philippines.[50]

France, Italy, and Germany were all poor and contracting markets for British cotton textiles during the interwar period. Indeed, France and Italy to all intents and purposes ceased importing British cotton cloth during the 1930s. During that decade, small but relatively free-trade countries such as the Scandinavian and Benelux countries were actually better, or at least less bad, markets for Britain than were the major powers of Europe.

Other Markets

As far as Britain was concerned, Australia, Canada, New Zealand, and Sub-Saharan Africa were the cotton textile markets that behaved most satisfactorily during the interwar years (see Table 35). The relatively favorable developments experienced in these markets were primarily due to the close political connections that existed with Britain. As a result, Britain was

---

[49] The Hawley-Smoot Tariff raised the average duty on cotton goods from 40.3% *ad valorem* to 46.4%. In terms of value added in Britain or Japan, these percentages were, of course, much higher (see P. W. Bidwell, *Our Trade with Britain*, p. 23).

[50] Uyeda, *The Recent Development of Japanese Foreign Trade*, pp. 107–8, 111–12.

TABLE 35

BRITISH COTTON TEXTILE EXPORTS TO CANADA, AUSTRALIA, NEW ZEALAND, AND
SUB-SAHARAN AFRICA
(in millions of linear yards through 1918, square yards thereafter)

Year	Canada	Australia	New Zealand	Africa
1913	...	...	...	341
1914	75	117	40	281
1915	66	198	48	291
1916	76	228	67	331
1917	72	152	39	397
1918	34	170	37	401
1919	22	75	22	217
1920	58	138	38	234
1921	19	115	18	135
1922	42	228	33	234
1923	54	171	37	263
1924	54	159	31	239
1925	46	170	37	339
1926	46	181	32	270
1927	46	188	35	301
1928	44	143	31	314
1929	38	170	34	286
1930	32	129	30	246
1931	28	122	28	180
1932	27	167	41	274
1933	47	146	37	286
1934	64	142	36	251
1935	60	118	36	354
1936	74	124	35	392
1937	76	152	36	379
1938	64	146	27	229

SOURCE: Various issues of *British Parliamentary Papers.*

able to obtain very favorable treatment for her exports. In
these countries, unlike India, favorable treatment proved to
be enough to maintain cotton textile exports at respectable
levels. The fact that at least some of the countries had no
domestic industries to protect and showed no particular interest
in trying to create them was also of considerable importance
in explaining what happened.

A specific example of the benefits to be derived from political
preference can be seen in the sharp recovery of British cotton
cloth exports to Canada, Australia, and New Zealand after

the Ottawa Agreement of 1932.[51] Equally interesting in its own way is the discovery that the imposition of quotas on Japanese cotton textile exports to some of the British colonies seems principally to have benefited countries other than Britain.[52] Japan was clearly beating everyone when competition was completely free.

The last British cotton textile market deserving some comment is what I have called Other Asia. During the interwar period, this market was completely dominated by the Dutch East Indies (Indonesia). As can be seen in Table 36, the decline recorded for Other Asia is little more than a reflection of developments in the Dutch East Indies. The principal cause of this decline, not surprisingly, was Japanese competition. Not only did the Japanese severely damage British exports, but they also hurt the Dutch homeland.[53] The eventual result of these developments was that the Dutch began to put restraints on Japanese trade with their Asian empire.[54] No more than anyone else were the Dutch prepared to let Japan, or any other country, take over "their" market for cotton textiles.

CONCLUSION

The conclusions that can be drawn from Britain's experience as a cotton textile exporter during the 1920s and 1930s depend to a large extent on the observer's perspective. Thus, for instance, it can be argued that the interwar experience was simply a continuation of pre–World War I trends. Throughout the century before 1914, country after country had started a factory cotton textile industry, usually with the help of tariffs and always at the expense of British exports. The only reason that Britain was able to increase her exports up to 1913 was that this movement toward self-sufficiency had barely started in several major and rapidly growing markets. The most important of these were India and China. When the trend

[51] Canada had raised all her tariffs in September 1930 (ibid., p. 113).

[52] F. V. Meyer, *Britain's Colonies in World Trade*, p. 80.

[53] See Daniels and Jewkes, "The Post-War Depression in the Lancashire Cotton Textile Industry," p. 164.

[54] Uyeda, *The Recent Development of Japanese Foreign Trade*, pp. 99–103.

TABLE 36

BRITISH COTTON TEXTILE EXPORTS TO OTHER ASIA

(in millions of linear yards through 1918, square yards thereafter)

Year	Other Asia	Dutch East Indies
1913	421	...
1914	339	270
1915	282	231
1916	312	257
1917	301	249
1918	214	165
1919	153	124
1920	268	209
1921	189	159
1922	187	136
1923	179	136
1924	192	136
1925	239	192
1926	166	122
1927	190	138
1928	191	143
1929	169	120
1930	95	70
1931	58	39
1932	63	44
1933	33	21
1934	23	15
1935	18	10
1936	33	27
1937	66	60
1938	30	27

SOURCE: Various issues of *British Parliamentary Papers.*

toward self-sufficiency and protection reached these countries after World War I, this was nothing really new. It was, however, a virtual death sentence for Lancashire. The growth of the Indian market had been sufficient to offset the loss of the Italian and Brazilian markets. Nothing could offset the loss of the Indian market.

It must be recognized, of course, that Britain suffered much more severely from the competition of other exporters, especially Japan, after World War I than she had before. Once again, however, it was, or should have been, clear, even before World War I, that Japan as well as Italy and perhaps the United States were becoming increasingly successful as cotton textile exporters. After all, not only was world trade declining as a percentage of world production but Britain's share of world trade was also declining.[55]

Another approach is to examine what chance Lancashire had of prospering, given those events that were outside her control. That is, what could have been accomplished had Lancashire improved her technology and lowered her costs more rapidly than she actually did?

The first question relevant to this approach is to ask what happened to the level of world trade. Clearly, it declined. In fact, total average annual world exports of cotton piece goods in 1936–38 amounted to something less than 90% of the piece goods exported by Great Britain *alone* in 1913. What is equally important, the chance that the actual level of world trade in cotton textiles recorded for the late 1930s could have been increased significantly by exporters offering lower prices than those actually charged seems extremely small. After all, virtually every country on the face of the earth was busy fighting any possible increase in cotton textile imports resulting from lower (i.e., Japanese) prices. In particular, the widespread use of quotas demonstrated a strong determination to resist any increase in low-price imports.[56]

The next step is to consider the extent to which Britain might have increased her steadily shrinking share of world trade in cotton textiles. The possibilities here, too, seem very bleak. It has been authoritatively estimated that of the loss in trade suffered by Lancashire between 1913 and the end of the 1930s, two-thirds was the result of increased self-sufficiency by importing countries and only one-third was the result of increased competition from other exporters.[57] In other words, if Britain had maintained her pre–World War I share of the exports of each quality of cloth to each market she would still have lost two-thirds of what she actually did lose. Thus, even if Britain had been able to reduce her costs by

[55] Robson, *The Cotton Industry in Britain*, p. 2.

[56] These negative conclusions are reinforced by the fact that the level of post-World War II trade in cotton textiles has been below even the low levels recorded in 1936–38.

[57] Board of Trade, *Report*, p. 5.

enough to keep up with Japan, her exports at the end of the 1930s would still have been less than 50% of her exports in 1913.

Doing better than retaining this one-third of what was lost, of course, would have required reducing the pre–World War I share of world trade held by other exporters, especially Japan. The improvements in production techniques or the lowering of wages that would have been necessary to achieve such a result, or both, are difficult even to imagine. This is especially true since the Japanese displayed a considerable determination to expand, not just defend, their cotton textile exports. A British threat to cut seriously into Japan's share of the world export market would undoubtedly have resulted in a strong Japanese response, both economically and politically. Thus, undercutting the Japanese would have been an even more difficult task than might appear merely from looking at the prices they charged. Finally, there remains the fact that even if all other exporters were out of the international market and Britain was able to make all the sales the others had been making (two extreme assumptions), Lancashire would still have been faced with a drop in output compared with 1913.

This reasoning also convinces me that a mass installation of automatic looms in Lancashire prior to World War I would probably have resulted in a worse situation than that which actually occurred. The attitude of the importing countries and the determined competitiveness of the Japanese makes it certain that Lancashire faced a very inelastic demand. Thus, even reducing prices to cover only the low marginal cost of automatic weaving would probably have done little to increase the demand for British cotton goods. Indeed, fewer persons would probably have found employment in Lancashire had there been more automatic looms in use there.

I doubt, however, that British prices would have fallen so low as to cover only the marginal cost of automatic weaving. Before that point was reached, an active export trade in used automatic looms would probably have developed. These looms would have been shipped to countries with growing and, except in the case of Japan, heavily protected cotton textile industries. Such a situation would unquestionably have imposed severe losses on the British firms that had installed automatic looms in the pre–World War I period.

I believe that this discussion has satisfactorily established the conclusion that Lancashire's decline after World War I was principally due to causes beyond her control. By no stretch of the imagination can the decline be charged to "technological" backwardness or a failure to adopt new types of machinery. Although something might have been possible along these lines, the key to the problem lay elsewhere.

It would be possible to conclude this section of the book right here. The basic point I wish to make has already been established. To stop now, however, would be to ignore two important problems relevant to Lancashire's collapse as an exporter. First, why did cotton textile manufacturing spread so easily and why were governments throughout the world so eager to protect this particular industry? Second, why was Britain unable to compete effectively with Japan during the interwar period? These questions will be discussed in the next chapter.

10

COTTON TEXTILES AND INTERNATIONAL COMPARATIVE ADVANTAGE

In this chapter, I shall argue that the principal shifts in the location of the world's cotton textile industry and the principal shifts in the pattern of world trade in cotton textiles are closely related to some key characteristics of the manufacturing processes in the industry. I intend to make this argument for the whole period since the Napoleonic wars through the 1930s. In fact, it could probably be extended even farther back in time.

The first important characteristic of the industry is the nature of transportation costs. Cotton, like most other textile raw materials, changes very little in weight as it is processed. Thus, in spinning the waste rate was perhaps 10 or 11% before the American Civil War and has been around 6% since then.[1] In addition, much of the waste cotton is recovered and processed. In view of the weight added to the cloth by sizing, it is not always clear whether the process of converting raw cotton into cloth decreases or increases the weight of the product. Furthermore, the difference in cost per unit of weight between shipping raw cotton and shipping cotton cloth is not great.

[1] See Blaug, "The Productivity of Capital in the Lancashire Cotton Industry during the Nineteenth Century," p. 377.

These considerations mean that it makes little difference whether cotton cloth is manufactured in a cotton-growing area or in a cotton cloth–consuming area.[2] This footloose aspect of the industry is accentuated by the fact that it is not a great consumer of power or of raw materials other than cotton. This makes the cotton textile industry very different, for example, from the iron and steel industry. In the early part of the nineteenth century, the cotton textile industry was at least partly dependent on water power and on a damp climate. Developments in power technology, especially with regard to steam power and electricity, however, have long since freed the industry from dependence on waterwheels. The development of artificial humidifiers has had a similar effect with regard to climate.

In addition to having low differential transportation costs, the industry also has low total transportation costs. That is, the cost of transporting cloth is a relatively small percentage of the value of the cloth. More important, it is also a relatively small percentage of the *value added* to the raw cotton when it is transformed into cloth.[3] In the case of yarn, especially coarse yarn, this may not always have been true. That is, the cost of transporting coarse yarn may on occasion have been a serious obstacle to its sale (as yarn) in a place far distant from where it was manufactured. This, of course, presupposes that a convenient supply of raw cotton was available in this distant place.

The relationship between value added and transportation costs for textiles has been of importance to world trade for a long time. It is at the very least one important reason why cloth was a major item in medieval and ancient trade. Next to spices, precious metals, and perhaps a few other products, such as steel blades, textiles had the lowest ratio of transport costs to value of any product available. It was this consideration,

---

[2] As applied to wool, the argument also helps explain why Edward III banned the export of raw wool from England.

[3] Strictly speaking, the important point is that transport costs are low relative to the comparative advantage some country is able to develop in producing cotton goods (i.e., the difference in comparative costs). The extent of this advantage, however, is closely correlated with the extent of the economic activity involved, which, in turn, is well measured by value added.

rather than any economies of scale in production or the "importance" of the product, that made textiles the leading item of international trade in most periods of poor communications.

These relatively low transportation costs have at least two implications for the organization of textile production in the modern period. First of all, it means that relatively little is lost if raw cotton (or wool or several other textile raw materials) is shipped from a growing area to a manufacturing area and then, in the form of cloth, to a consuming area without following the shortest route between the growing and consuming areas. Indeed, little is lost if the raw cotton is shipped to a manufacturing area and the resulting cloth is then shipped back to the original cotton-growing area. Thus, if tariffs had not been in the way, Great Britain would probably have supplied the southern United States with cotton cloth manufactured of southern cotton for most, if not all, of the nineteenth century. Instead, New England did it. To some extent, Great Britain did it with Indian cotton. More important, American cotton was shipped to Great Britain, converted to cloth, and then shipped to India to compete with local cloth made of locally grown cotton.

This relationship also goes at least part of the way toward explaining why factory spinning preceded factory weaving in cotton-growing countries with large handicraft industries. As has been noted, transportation costs were a much greater percentage of value added in the case of yarn than in the case of cotton. Shipping raw cotton from India or the United States to Great Britain to be spun into yarn that in turn was to be shipped to India or China involved a relatively heavy transportation burden. Thus, local factory spinners using locally grown raw cotton in India or China had a special advantage in supplying the local handweavers with yarn. Another way of putting this is that in supplying handloom weavers with yarn, British manufacturers had fewer processes with which to offset the transportation advantage of local manufacturers than they did when they competed with the local manufacturers in the sale of finished cloth. This is certainly not the whole explanation of the lead factory spinning so frequently had over factory weaving, for this lead could sometimes be observed in countries with no ready access to raw cotton. Nevertheless, transportation costs undoubtedly played an important role in some cases.

The other consequence of low transport costs is that it tends to make one single country dominate world trade in a given type of textile product. Indeed, in the absence of tariffs and other "artificial" trade barriers, one country might well dominate world *production* of each type of textile product. The reason behind this assertion is that in the absence of any trade barriers at all (including transport costs) there should be one country that has a comparative advantage over all other countries in any particular product.[4]

Naturally, such a sweeping conclusion needs some modification. Thus, for example, if the dominant country is located at some distance from its supply of raw materials, it may have difficulty competing in very distant markets, even if they are unprotected. This is especially true if this distant market has its own raw materials supply. As noted above, this would be most likely to happen with regard to yarn and very coarse cloth. In addition, extreme specialization, either in some particular market or in some particular product, may allow a competing exporter to escape the dominance of the leading producer. Thus, industries specializing in such things as high-quality stockings, lace, handkerchiefs, or particular widths and designs of cloth have frequently been able to compete effectively with the country that dominated world trade in cotton textiles as a whole. What this really means, of course, is that no one country is likely to be able to maintain a comparative advantage in every single type of cotton product. The production skills and market knowledge needed to supply highly specialized products and markets is unlikely to be completely concentrated in the country that has a comparative advantage in the standard grades of cotton cloth. On a more general level, it is possible for one country to be most efficient in the production of

---

[4] This result also requires that average cost does not rise at high levels of output. This condition holds for cotton textiles. In fact, it holds for most products that are not dependent on location near a supply of raw materials or a group of highly skilled workers.

low-quality goods and another country in the production of high-quality goods. Such a situation might occur if one country has a large supply of well-disciplined, hardworking, but not very skilled textile workers and another has highly skilled, but also highly paid, workers.[5] This, of course, is a fair description of the relationship between Japan and Great Britain in the early 1920s.

Finally, a declining national industry that is losing, or has lost, its comparative advantage will not die immediately. Because of the lack of mobility of plant and equipment, as well as skilled workers, a fading industry will usually put up some resistance, presumably by price-cutting, for a period of time. This fight will mean that rates of return on capital and wages will fall below the levels needed to attract new capital or labor into the declining industry. Indeed, manufacturers may only be able to recover part of the original cost of their equipment, and highly skilled workers may get little more than they could earn as unskilled workers in some other occupation.

These theoretical considerations are in close accord with what happened in the world cotton textile industry between 1815 and 1938. Throughout the nineteenth century, world trade in cotton textiles was dominated by Great Britain. During the period 1882–84, Great Britain accounted for no less than 82% of world trade in cotton goods.[6] What is more, Britain came close to dominating world factory production outside of a few highly protected countries.[7] The biggest weakness of the British industry was the extent to which unprotected handicraft industries continued to flourish, especially in India and China. It should be remembered, however, that these handicraft industries benefited from the advantages of poor inland transpor-

---

[5] Presumably they are well paid because other well-paying industries are competing for their services.

[6] Robson, *The Cotton Industry in Britain,* p. 2.

[7] In 1882–84, Britain consumed 37% of all the raw cotton consumed by all the world's cotton mills. Because British goods were of higher-than-average quality and fineness, this represented considerably more than 37% of world manufacturing capacity. In these same years, the heavily protected American industry accounted for over 22% of world mill cotton consumption (Robson, *The Cotton Industry in Britain,* p. 2). In addition, there were important protected industries in a number of other countries, including France, Germany, and Russia.

tation and, at least in some cases, from quality, or at least taste, advantages.[8]

During the years between 1880 and World War I, the British dominance decreased somewhat. In particular, the United States, Japan, and Italy began to emerge as serious rivals in the export of standard types of cotton cloth. In addition, virtually unprotected factory industries began to emerge in India and China. I would argue that these developments reflected the beginning of a shift in comparative advantage away from Great Britain. It will be noted that this competition came first in the provision of yarn for handloom weavers and second in the production and export of low-quality cloth. For reasons that will be discussed below, comparative advantage in cotton textiles, among many other products, first begins to shift in favor of newcomers at relatively low qualities.

After World War I, comparative advantage quickly shifted in favor of Japan. By the 1930s, Japanese cotton textiles were threatening every cotton industry in the world. No better testimony to this can be found than the many countries who enacted special tariffs or instituted quota systems for the avowed purpose of restraining imports from Japan. The 28% (by weight) of all world trade in cotton textiles still held by Great Britain in 1936–38[9] can be credited to her remaining comparative advantage in the production of high-quality goods, discrimination in third (especially Empire) markets and, perhaps most important, the utilization of fixed and semi-fixed resources that could be operated at marginal cost.[10] As for Japan's failure to eliminate all competing exporters other than Britain, only Europe was a serious trade rival by the middle 1930s.[11] Most of this European trade was intra-European, heavily weighted with speciality produts (usually of very high quality), and often protected by discriminatory, especially anti-Japanese, trade

[8] See Kraus, *Cotton and Cotton Goods in China*, pp. 127–28.

[9] Robson, *The Cotton Industry in Britain*, p. 2.

[10] Between 1924 and 1933, British cotton-spinning wage rates decreased by 14% while overall industrial wage rates only decreased by 6%. In addition, the rate of promotion of piecers to spinners slowed markedly, and the rate of unemployment increased (Jewkes and Gray, *Wages and Labor in the Lancashire Cotton Spinning Industry*, p. 50).

[11] Robson, *The Cotton Industry in Britain*, p. 358.

barriers. By the end of the thirties, Japan clearly had the upper hand in almost any freely competitive situation.

The objection might be raised that these shifts in trade patterns were to a large extent the result of exchange rate movements. Thus, it could be argued that Britain's failure was due to overvaluation of the pound in the 1920s and that Japan's success was due to devaluation in the 1930s. Although it is no doubt true that Lancashire was hurt by the overvaluation of the 1920s, the underlying deterioration of the industry's competitive position is demonstrated by the *further* rapid decline that occurred during the 1930s, including the late 1930s.[12] Indeed, in 1938 the export of British cotton cloth was at its lowest level since 1850.[13] This means that in 1938 Britain exported less cotton cloth than she did during the "cotton famine" connected with the American Civil War. Of course, worldwide economic depression and increased trade restrictions also hurt, but they cannot account for all of this decline. Britain's *share* of world trade in cotton goods declined from 39% in 1926–28 to 28% in 1936–38.

As for Japan, the devaluation of the yen in the years just after 1929 certainly helped her export drive of the early thirties. It is also clear, however, that cotton textile exports, despite their relatively heavy dependence on imported raw materials, increased much faster than did other types of exports. In addition, Japanese textile exports were hit by all sorts of trade barriers. Some of these applied to all countries, but others applied only, or with special severity, to Japan.[14] Despite these

---

[12] The sterling-yen exchange rate was stable between 1933 and 1941 (Seki, *The Cotton Industry of Japan*, p. 408).

[13] Robson, *The Cotton Industry in Britain*, p. 332.

[14] G. E. Hubbard has attempted to estimate the effect of Japanese devaluation in the early 1930s by comparing relative devaluation and changes in the wholesale price index in Japan, Great Britain, and the United States. On this basis, he concludes that Japan had obtained a 9.5% advantage on Great Britain between 1929 and 1944 (Hubbard, *Eastern Industrialization and Its Effect on the West*, pp. 100–101). It is not clear how relevant this statistic is to the cotton industry, however. Virtually all the raw cotton used in Japan was imported, and devaluation would not help here. For most cotton goods, raw cotton accounted for more than 50% of total costs (ibid., p. 124). Although the devaluation of the yen up to March 1934 exceeded the devaluation of sterling by 23.7%, Japanese price levels also increased more than British prices. It is probably a considerable exaggeration to say that Japan gained a 10% price advantage over Britain on cotton goods

problems and a worldwide depression, Japan was able to increase her cotton cloth exports from an average annual level of 1,387 million square yards in 1926–28 to 2,511 million square yards in 1936–38.[15] Over the same period, total world trade in cotton goods decreased by about 22%.[16]

While Japan was overtaking Great Britain, a similar development was occurring within the highly protected American market. With foreign products virtually excluded by high tariffs, the American market was a world unto itself. Up until 1870, this market was completely dominated by New England. After that date, southern competition began to be felt, first in low-quality goods. As time passed, the South came to dominate the production of low-quality cloth and to compete seriously in the medium and high-quality trades. By the 1930s, the South had an advantage in practically all qualities. The remaining output of New England was made possible mainly because fixed capital was being consumed and industrially immobile workers had to accept wages that were low relative to New England standards. The situation of the cotton textile industries in Old and New England were very similar at this time.

The logical problem that arises at this point is to explain why comparative advantage shifted away from Great Britain and New England toward Japan and the South. This question, of course, can only be answered after it has been determined which factors affect comparative advantage in the cotton textile industry. The previous discussion has already made it clear that location or accessability of natural resources has little influence on comparative advantage in this industry. That would seem to leave management and entrepreneurship, industrial skill, labor supply, and capital supply.

Compared with most industries, cotton textiles are labor, as opposed to capital, intensive. This is true even if automatic

---

through these changes. The special charges and quotas imposed on Japanese cotton textiles in so many places during the early 1930s must certainly have been enough to offset this devaluation advantage. What is more, between 1934 and 1937 Japanese wholesale prices increased somewhat faster than British wholesale prices while the exchange rate remained constant at 1s. 2d. per yen (Allen, *British Industries and Their Organization,* p. 92).

[15] Robson, *The Cotton Industry in Britain,* p. 358.

[16] Ibid., p. 2.

looms are used. What is more, it has been demonstrated at an earlier point in this book that, at least before World War I, sufficiently low wages made power looms uneconomical (especially if the looms had to be imported). As a result, automatic looms had little impact outside of the United States until after World War I. This relatively low capital intensity was, of course, of relative advantage to capital-poor countries and regions. The trade in used cotton textile machinery that flourished during at least part of the period under review also helped the cause of the low-wage newcomers.

Perhaps even more important than low-capital intensity was low-skill intensity. The possibility of using unskilled workers to advantage, especially in the production of low-quality goods, is documented in virtually every study of a nascent cotton industry.[17] In fact, of course, this also applies to British developments in the late eighteenth century, although by the late nineteenth century technical improvements (e.g., automatic mules and ring spindles) had probably reduced the earlier skill requirements somewhat. This means that compared with other industries with higher skill requirements, cotton textiles were an attractive medium for the South and Japan to use in exploiting their relatively large supply of unskilled labor.

Two other aspects of the industry that helped these particular new producers and that go a long way toward explaining why cotton textiles were almost always the first industry developed by a non-industrial country[18] deserve some mention. The first point has already been made above, that is, that the industry can locate almost anywhere, regardless of transportation costs or climate. This condition was especially important for Japan. Because the South was covered with cotton fields, the only transportation factor that could have hurt its prospects as a cotton textile producer would have been if the manufacturing process *added* substantially to the weight of the cotton processed.

The second, and more important point, is that a considerable

[17] See, for example, Broadus Mitchell for the United States, Morris Morris for India, and G. E. Hubbard for Japan.

[18] The only major exceptions to this rule of cotton textiles first were countries with some major natural resource to exploit. This, for example, would be true of the timber trade in Scandinavia.

market exists for cotton textiles almost everywhere, at least for low and medium qualities. In this context, "considerable" means a sufficient demand to permit full utilization of scale economies. In fact, scale economies are not very important in cotton textiles. That is, fully efficient manufacturing plants do not have to be very large. Certainly, almost any national market is, and has long been, large enough to support efficient plants, except possibly for very high quality and very specialized types of cotton goods.

The dynamic version of this comparative advantage argument is that Great Britain slowly lost the relative advantage she had obtained from her early start in cotton textiles, principally because she began to accumulate capital and develop other industries. The effect of this process was to make labor relatively scarce and relatively expensive. Great Britain's comparative advantage shifted into more and more capital- and skill-intensive industries. Eventually, it became possible for a peasant economy like Japan's to expand its comparative advantage from raw silk and other agricultural products to include low-capital and skill-intensive manufacturing. The result was the development of the Japanese cotton textile industry. This trend was also aided by the development of machinery requiring relatively little labor skill.[19] Japan's advantage lasted at least as long as she was able to move peasants straight from the rice field to the cotton mill. The evidence indicates very strongly that the Japanese cotton textile industry had access to a virtually perfect elastic supply of cheap labor well into the 1930s. Indeed, the rural depression after 1929 improved the relative position of the Japanese cotton textile industry compared with what it had been earlier.[20] During the post–World War II period, the Japanese cotton textile industry has not been able to obtain cheap peasant labor. This development has undoubtedly contributed to the recent deterioration of Japan's competitive position as a supplier of cotton cloth (not relative to Great Britain, however), especially low-quality cotton cloth.

[19] During approximately the same period, a similar trend had been going on within the protected American market. The backward South was able to establish a comparative advantage in cotton textiles.

[20] Hubbard, *Eastern Industrialization and Its Effect on the West*, p. 165.

Relatively cheap labor, however, cannot be the whole story behind the shift of comparative advantage in cotton textiles.[21] After all, Japan was certainly not the country with the world's relatively most abundant supply of labor. Why was Japan more successful than, for example, India, China, or tropical Africa?

Aside from problems of political stability, I think the answer lies in the supply of entrepreneurship and management skill together with the adaptability of the work force to factory conditions. Clearly, many countries in the past, as well as the present, have suffered from an acute lack of these factors of production. To discuss why this is so would be to write a textbook on the problems of economic development. What is clear, however, is that the absence of these factors makes industrialization of any kind virtually impossible. In other words, such a society has a comparative advantage in peasant and plantation agriculture and handicraft industry because these activities require relatively little of the factors that are truly scarcest.

The importance of good entrepreneurship and management has been emphasized by several students of the cotton textile industry, notably Rockwood Chin. As is apparent from the previous paragraph, I fully share the view that these factors are most important. I do not believe, however, that Britain lost her dominant position in the world cotton textile industry because of poor management. Indeed, the whole first part of this book can be viewed as at least a partial defense of British management against a charge of inefficiency. More important is the fact that the nature of comparative advantage makes it very unlikely that poor management was the principal cause of the British decline. There is no question of the fact that Japan had access to a supply of relatively cheap labor. For the supply of managerial talent to be of crucial importance, therefore, Britain must have had a very great shortage of management talent as compared with Japan, *and* the cotton textile industry must have been a relatively management-intensive activity. In fact, I do not believe that either of these hypotheses was, or is, true.[22] On the contrary, I find it more

---

[21] It might, however, be the whole story behind the American shift, for the South was the *lowest* wage area in the United States.

plausible that cotton textiles were a good industry for Japan partly because she suffered from a relative shortage of managerial and entrepreneurial talent compared with previously industrialized countries.

Another possible way of putting the blame on poor British management is to argue that, for historical or other reasons, British cotton textile management was much worse than British management in general and that Japanese cotton management was much better than Japanese management in general. I do not believe that the evidence available supports such a contention. Furthermore, I would argue that any possible relative superiority of Japanese cotton textile management during the interwar period was principally a result, rather than a cause, of Japanese growth and British decline.

One of the problems raised at the end of the previous chapter still remains to be answered. Namely, why are countries so prone to protect their cotton textile industries? The trend toward protected self-sufficiency is one of the most striking features of the industry's history. Some idea of how far this movement had progressed by the early 1930s can be obtained from Table 37. Furthermore, the striving for self-sufficiency had by no means reached its peak by the early 1930s. By 1936–38, only 16% of world factory production of cotton goods entered international trade.[23]

As I have noted more than once, this trend toward autarky would have severely damaged Lancashire's export trade even without the shift in comparative advantage toward Japan. Similarly, Japan was not able to enjoy the full fruits of having become the world's most efficient producer of cotton textiles because of this drop in trade.

The reason that so many countries moved in the direction of protected self-sufficiency in cotton textiles derives from the features of the industry that have already been discussed. The unimportance of transport costs and scale economies means

[22] Cotton textiles may have been management intensive relative to Japan's peasant agriculture but not relative to industry in general.

[23] The share of trade was 55% in 1829–31, 38% in 1882–84, 28% in 1910–13, 23% in 1926–38, and 10% in 1953–55 (see Robson, *The Cotton Industry in Britain*, p. 2).

TABLE 37

SHARE OF HOME MARKET HELD BY DOMESTIC PRODUCERS OF COTTON GOODS IN
SELECTED COUNTRIES IN VARIOUS YEARS

Country and Year	Percentage of Cotton Piece Good Consumption Supplied by Domestic Producers
United States (1933)	99.5
India (1935)	76.5*
China (1934)	87.5*
USSR (1934)	99.9
Japan (1935)	99.9
Germany (1928)	92.9
United Kingdom (1934)	98.5
Italy (1934)	99.2
France (1932)	99.0
Brazil (1929)	93.5
Netherlands (1933)	89.5
Canada (1934)	74.8
Belgium (1933)	92.9
Rumania (1934)	88.1
Switzerland (1929)	88.8

SOURCE: Board of Trade, Working Party Report, *Cotton*, p.243. The table is originally from International Labour Office, *The World Textile Industry* (1937); I have been unable to locate this work.

*Excluding handicraft production.

that almost any country can be the site of a cotton textile industry. The low capital and skill requirements mean that it is usually the easiest industry for a peasant country to develop. In other words, the characteristics of the industry are such as to make it very responsive to tariff protection. This, in turn, means that the static inefficiency of using tariffs to protect a cotton textile industry is lower than for most other industries. Thus, lower tariffs are usually sufficient to induce this particular industry to develop than is the case with most industries.[24] It is true that protecting cotton textiles can become very expensive in highly industrialized, high-wage countries (such as the United States at the present time). In such a situation, however, the political influence of a long-established cotton textile industry still makes protection very likely.

Although the cotton textile industry can flourish almost

[24] The principal exceptions to this rule are industries that face very heavy transport costs (e.g., soft drink bottling or brewing).

anywhere, it usually requires at least some protection. The reason for this, of course, is the unimportance of transport costs. With no protection at all, the dominant exporter would presumably be able to move in and dominate almost any market. This is exactly what Great Britain did during most of the nineteenth century. Only protected markets and remote handicraft regions were able to withstand British competition. Thus, although it is very responsive to tariff protection, cotton textile manufacture is not usually a very good infant industry. In most cases, the child requires protection even after adolescence has been reached. Of course, the level of protection required at this stage may well be somewhat lower than that required at birth.

11

CONCLUSION

This study has arrived at two major conclusions, one negative and one positive. The negative conclusion is that the failure of British management to adopt new machinery, especially ring spindles and automatic looms, at a rapid rate did not play an important part in the decline and eventual collapse of the British cotton textile industry after 1870. The positive conclusion is that a reduction in export demand resulting from forces outside the control of British management was the principal cause of Lancashire's downfall. In addition, a number of other, less sweeping, conclusions were reached in the course of the analysis. Some of these are:

1. Both British and American cotton textile management generally acted in a rational manner in choosing between ring and mule spindles for new installations in the period just before World War I.

2. The relatively aggressive behavior of the American mule spinners unions encouraged the adoption of ring spinning in the United States. The more amiable British mule spinners unions had less of an effect in this direction.

3. The evidence available is at least consistent with the hypothesis that British and American cotton textile managers were rational in their decisions as to whether old mules should be junked and as to whether plain or automatic looms should be used. It is possible, however, that the British were somewhat more cautious than were the Americans about relatively capital-intensive production methods.

4. The British cotton-weaving unions probably retarded the adoption of automatic weaving in Great Britain by their stand on work loads and wage rates for automatic looms.

5. Contrary to the findings of G. T. Jones, efficiency in the Lancashire cotton textile industry increased between 1885 and 1910. This is true even for the 1900–1910 period, for which Jones found a decrease in efficiency.

6. The differences between the increase in efficiency and in labor productivity in Lancashire and in Massachusetts between 1885 and 1910 (or 1914) seem to be explicable without recourse to any supposed British managerial failure.

7. The *pattern* of disinvestment in the British cotton textile industry between the World Wars appears to be generally consistent with rational economic behavior.

8. Ever since at least 1816, British cotton exports have been adversely affected by the growth of protected cotton textile industries in various parts of the world.

9. Starting about 1870 or 1880, Britain's comparative advantage in cotton textiles began to decline relative to a number of countries. The most important of these countries was Japan.

10. Because of the low transport costs faced by the industry, world cotton textile trade is very likely to be dominated by one country at a time. Between the World Wars, Great Britain was replaced by Japan as the world's leading and most efficient cotton textile exporter.

In addition to listing conclusions, some mention should be made of what has *not* been demonstrated, especially with regard to the quality of British management. Nothing definite has been proved about the quality of British management in general; nor has it been demonstrated that British cotton textile management was efficient in all its functions. Indeed, even within the limited sphere of technology it has been noted that British cotton textile management displayed little interest in searching out improvements or encouraging research. Furthermore, management actively supported the policy of short-time work during periods of slack demand. This policy tended to retard capital-intensive innovations.

Taking all this into account, however, the analysis presented in this study makes it seem highly unlikely that poor management was a major contributor to Lancashire's decline. It would have required a truly outstanding managerial performance to have improved Lancashire's international position significantly. If that had happened, however, the proper description of such events would be that outstanding management overcame outside forces that were undermining British cotton textile exports.

If a really sweeping conclusion is desired at the end of this kind of study, it might be claimed that the story of Lancashire's decline has a lesson for all industrialized countries. That is, as industrialization spreads, the more advanced countries will tend to lose their comparative advantage in those industries that can be operated efficiently with a relatively unskilled work force using relatively little capital equipment. Thus, if free competition is maintained, the advanced countries will have to shift out of such industries.[1] In fact, the usual reaction of the advanced countries to such a development has been to offer the affected industry protection in the form of tariffs or quotas. Such action, however, imposes costs on the advanced country. Even more important, it places a serious obstacle in the way of the efforts of the less-advanced countries to industrialize.

The special vulnerability of the British cotton textile industry

[1] Transportation costs, both differential and absolute, would also play an important role in this regard. See the analysis in chapter 10.

arose from the fact that it was primarily an export industry. As a result, it could not be protected by British tariffs. Moreover, because the industry was a major exporter, it was much larger than the cotton textile industries of other countries. Readjustment was thus both necessary and very painful. Of course, the pain was made worse by the fact that the British wool, coal-mining, and shipbuilding industries were all declining at the same time. Indeed, it can be argued that the price Britain had to pay for her early industrialization was that she became specialized in the exporting of low capital– and low skill–intensive staple goods. This meant that sooner or later she would have to choose between a major industrial readjustment and an extremely low and stagnant wage level. In retrospect, once the pain of the readjustment was over, Britain was in a much stronger position than had previously been the case. She is no longer dependent on enormous export industries vulnerable to the kind of disaster that overtook Lancashire.

APPENDIXES

A. PROBLEMS IN THE COVERAGE OF DEPRECIATION AND OBSOLESCENCE ALLOWANCES

A major problem in estimating the net rate of return on capital invested in the replacement of well-functioning mules with rings is deciding which of the necessary conversion expenditures should be depreciated. In principal, the purpose of depreciation and obsolescence allowances is to compensate for the declining value of an investment over time. Eventually, when the equipment or other investment has become worthless, the amounts allocated to cover depreciation and obsolescence should be sufficient either to permit replacement of the investment or to permit the investor to withdraw his invested capital from the enterprise.

Thus, some depreciation allowance should be charged whenever a piece of equipment, building, organizational innovation, or other investment expenditure is expected to decline in value over time. In other words, expectations about future developments are decisive. This is particularly true in a case such as the present where the problem lies between keeping an old method of production or replacing it with a new method.

In order to illustrate the importance of expectations concerning future developments, I shall discuss below four different types of expectations and the type of depreciation and obsolescence policy implied by each one. In fact, of course, actual expectations might have been somewhere in between two of my cases or they might have consisted of a probability distribution involving more than one of my cases.

1. It is thought that the choice is between introducing the new method now or introducing the same method in the same building and at the same total cost sometime in the future. In this case, the problem is solely one of deciding on the timing of the conversion.

2. It is thought that the choice is between installing the new method and using it forever or keeping the old method and using it forever.

3. It is thought that the choice is between using either the new or the old method for a finite period of time. At the end of that time, the firm will be broken up and the residual value of equipment, good will, and so on, will be the same regardless of which method was used at the end.

4. It is thought that both methods currently available will eventually be replaced by a third method and that the cost of adopting this third method will be the same regardless of the method being used at the time of replacement.

These various possibilities clearly imply very different things for depreciation policy. In the first example, depreciation allowances should be limited to things that physically deteriorate with time and use. This presumably applies to all machinery and equipment, since a postponement will mean that newer equipment will eventually be used. This newer equipment, in turn, will presumably be better than older, similar equipment and will not have to be replaced as soon. Physical alterations in buildings also should be depreciated if they are less durable than the building itself. (This is so because if they are less durable than the building, they will eventually have to be done over again.) This, however, is not likely to be the case. Certainly, the costs associated with closing the plant for alterations and recruiting and training the new work force should not be depreciated. These expenses are only being shifted in time, not avoided, when conversion is postponed.

Under example two, it might appear that no depreciation at all should be charged. If both sets of equipment are expected to last forever, there is no need for a replacement fund. Such an expectation, however, is patently ridiculous. The equipment is certain to deteriorate with time and use. This, in turn, means that the equipment embodying the old method will eventually have to be replaced—presumably by equipment embodying the new methods—at some time in the future. This conclusion largely reduces example two to example one.

Example three, however, leads to very different results. In this case, all the expenses of the conversion must be depreciated. If they are not, then at the end of the period of operation all the extra capital needed for the conversion will not be recovered. The investor will not be able to withdraw all the capital he put into the firm.

This alternative of a foreseeable end to operations with either method (or any method, for that matter), might be considered excessively pessimistic. In fact, however, it corresponds better to actual British experience in cotton spinning than does example one. After World War I, large quantities of both types of spinning equipment were junked. On the other hand, it must be granted that ring-spinning firms probably did a little bit better when they were dissolved than did mule-spinning firms.

Example four leads to results similar to those that follow from example three. Unless all the extra expenses have been depreciated, the investor will not be able to recover all his capital outlay when the time comes for conversion to the third method. This conclusion will, of course, be modified to the extent that the costs of adopting the third method are lower if the second method (i.e., rings) has already been adopted. If the cost of adopting the third method is reduced by a sum equal to all the non-machinery costs of adopting method two, then this fourth example becomes essentially identical with example one.

These various possibilities should make it clear that I am being very conservative when I only apply an allowance for depreciation and obsolescence to machinery and equipment. This approach is tantamount to assuming that the only reasonable expectation for a British cotton-spinning manager in the pre-World War I period was that sooner or later he would replace all his low-count mules with rings, without, however, tearing down his factory building.

B. DEPRECIATION RATES ON COTTON TEXTILE MACHINERY

The appropriateness of the rate of depreciation charged is an important factor in judging the soundness of all investment decisions involving a choice between production methods of differing capital intensity. If too high a rate of depreciation has been charged, then the apparent rate of return on invested capital will be correspondingly too low; and the opposite effect will be produced if too low a rate of depreciation has been charged. Within the context of this book, these considerations mean that any judgment about decisions as to whether well-functioning, previously installed mules should be junked and replaced with new rings and decisions as to whether automatic or plain looms should be used depend crucially on the depreciation rate assumed. On the other hand, the rate of depreciation has very little effect on the choice between new mules and new rings.

Unfortunately, it is extremely difficult to determine what constitutes the "appropriate" rate of depreciation. This is true in retrospect and it is even more true in prospect. In all cases, some room must be left for disagreement among reasonable men. Thus, only under extreme circumstances can an investment decision be called "irrational" because it, either explicitly or implicitly, is based on too high or too low a rate of depreciation.

In my calculations, I have used a rate of 10% for "loss,

depreciation, and upkeep" on spinning and preparatory machinery. The reason for adopting this particular rate is that James Winterbottom, an acknowledged authority on cotton textile production during the period being studied, described it as being "generally accepted."[1] Because this rate is higher than other rates frequently alluded to by observers as being the "depreciation" rate, it should be stressed that the Winterbottom rate involves more than just the pure depreciation of the machinery. Loss, upkeep, and repairs can be important items, although I have made no attempt to quantify them. In particular, it must be remembered that though the life of the basic spinning frame or other machine might be quite long, many parts, such as spindles, have much shorter lives. Furthermore, as far as my calculations are concerned, no separate account is taken of the risk of machines being destroyed by fire, natural disaster, vandalism, or any other cause. In other words, I am implicitly including an insurance policy in my "depreciation."

In arguing for a lower rate of depreciation, it could be pointed out that some cotton machinery remained in operation for fifty years or even longer. This could be taken to imply a real depreciation rate of around 2% per annum. It must be remembered, however, that by no means all machines lasted even close to fifty years. In addition, as was noted above, many parts would have been replaced and many repairs carried out before a machine reached the age of fifty.

With regard to weaving equipment (i.e., looms), I followed the practice of T. W. Uttley, an Englishman observing the American cotton textile industry. Uttley uses a 5% rate of depreciation for plain looms. For automatic looms he adds 2 percentage points to account for obsolescence.[2] As Irwin Feller has pointed out, it makes no sense to apply the obsolescence allowance to automatic looms only.[3] If automatic looms become obsolescent, so do plain looms. Uttley can, therefore, be said to have used a rate of 7% for depreciation and obsolescence on looms. I adopted this rate for my calculations. This is not quite the same thing as the 10% I used for spinning equipment, however, because it takes no account of upkeep. What is more, the Draper Company admitted that repair costs were greater on its automatic looms than on plain

[1] Winterbottom, *Cotton Spinning Calculations and Yarn Costs*, p. 271.

[2] Uttley, *Cotton Spinning and Manufacturing in the United States*, pp. 25–26.

[3] Feller, "The Draper Loom in New England Textiles," pp. 340–41.

looms.[4] Thus, although I used the 7% for looms, I am by no means convinced that it is superior to any other figure between 5% and 10%. Indeed, the range may be even larger. This uncertainty, of course, also applies to the 10% figure for spinning equipment that I got from Winterbottom. The special advantage of that figure is that it is specifically reported to be the rate actually used.

An interesting example of how a particular British textile company handled machinery depreciation can be taken from the history of Marshalls of Leeds, the well-known flax spinners. Up until 1827, machine depreciation was carried out on a purely ad hoc basis. In that year, however, a standard depreciation rate of 7.5% per annum was introduced.[5] This rate was raised to 10% sometime before 1858, because in that year it was reduced from 10% to 7.5%. In 1862, it was further reduced to 5%.[6] It is not immediately obvious what rate was most appropriate, nor is it clear exactly what was included in the depreciation rate. It is clear, however, that the reductions of 1858 and 1862 were connected with a policy of raising the book value of the company. In addition to lowering the depreciation rate, the book value of the plant was raised by the stroke of a pen. The historian of the firm describes these measures as "window dressing."[7] Marshalls went into liquidation in 1886.

In its 1912 study of the American cotton textile industry, the United States Tariff Board uses a depreciation rate of somewhat less than 5% for entire cotton mills.[8] This calculation, however, includes buildings as well as machinery. Because buildings are usually depreciated less rapidly than machinery, the rate applied to machinery by the Tariff Board was, in fact, probably 5%. Furthermore, although it is never made absolutely explicit, it does seem clear that the Tariff Board figure includes no allowance for upkeep, repairs, or insurance. Insurance and spare parts supplies are treated as separate cost items, and upkeep is probably included in "works costs."

One final consideration is the time pattern of actual physical depreciation and obsolesence. That is, did the value in use of

[4] Ibid., p. 343.
[5] Rimmer, *Marshalls of Leeds: Flax-Spinners*, p. 196.
[6] Ibid., p. 262.
[7] Ibid., p. 270.
[8] U.S. Tariff Board, p. 467.

the machinery really decline in a straight-line fashion? If it did not, problems arise concerning the calculated rates of return.

To take an extreme example, assume that a piece of equipment generated a constant stream of net income for twenty years and then fell apart (the so-called one-horse shay case). If that were the situation, then the resale value of the equipment would decline by 5 percent per annum (disregarding moving and installation problems). This fact might make it appropriate to charge 5 percent annual straight-line depreciation. It should be noted, however, that the capital tied up in the equipment would continually decline. After the first year (or other appropriate time period), net income would consist of what the equipment yielded plus what could be earned on the funds recovered through depreciation accounting. Thus, over the life of the equipment, the average invested capital would be only about one-half of the original cost of the equipment. Rates of return based on the total cost of the equipment would thus be only about one-half of the actual rate of return.

On the other hand, if the net return on the equipment declined because of wear, increases in upkeep costs, or obsolesence, then the situation is different. In fact, if the net return on the equipment declines at 5 percent per year (straight line), then the extra return earned on the depreciation funds (if at the same rate as for the equipment) would be just enough to maintain the total net return on all the money originally put into the equipment. In this case, however, the resale value of the equipment would decline more rapidly than by 5 percent per year.

The question then is: What did pre-World War I cotton mill managers mean when they charged straight-line depreciation? If they believed that their equipment's resale value declined in a straight line, then they must also have thought that it was of the one-horse-shay variety. In fact, however, it is clear that the physical productivity of cotton textile machinery did decrease with age.[9] In addition, a degree of progressive obsolesence occurred. As noted above, my calculations assume that the time pattern of this decline in net return was approximately straight-line.

Even if the equipment were of the one-horse-shay variety, however, and thus the true rate of return on invested capital was higher than my calculations indicate, the error involved was essentially one of accounting procedure. The cotton mill managers clearly *believed* that it was appropriate to charge interest for the

[9] Ibid., pp. 471–72.

life of the machinery at its original cost. As Paul David has pointed out (in conversation), it is not conceptually clear whether or not this kind of accounting error should be included in the rubric of economic irrationality.

This discussion has not shown that the 10% depreciation apparently charged by British cotton spinners in the pre–World War I period (or the 7% depreciation rate I assign to looms) is an ideal rate. On the other hand, there is certainly no evidence that a manufacturer using this rate (or rates) was in any way irrational or "technologically backwards." The *most* that could possibly be asserted is that these manufacturers may have been somewhat conservative in matters involving the commitment of funds to fixed capital.

C. THE QUALITY OF BRITISH COTTON TEXTILE EXPORTS, 1815–1913

The term *quality* as used in this book is defined as real value per yard of cloth and pound of yarn exported. Thus, a reduction in export quality does not mean that a specific type of cloth has deteriorated. Rather, it means that there has been a shift from more expensive to less expensive types of cloth. It may also mean that the same type of cloth is being exported in a different state—white instead of printed or gray instead of bleached.

The results of the investigation presented in this appendix are a quality index of British cotton cloth exports and a quality index of British cotton yarn exports for the period 1815–1913. The same method used to compute the quality of all British cotton textile exports has also been applied to determine the quality of exports to particular markets.[1]

I

The normal procedure for computing an export quality index is to establish a scale of relative qualities and then weight these qualities by the quantity of each type of goods exported in each year. Because a lack of information made this calculation impossible, I was compelled to use an indirect approach. The first step

[1] This appendix is a much-shortened version of a paper that appeared in the March 1968 *Journal of Economic History*.

in my method of constructing export quality indexes was to find a series of the average f.o.b. prices received per yard of cloth and pound of yarn exported. Fortunately, the "declared" values of exports reported in the British Trade and Navigation Accounts are generally accepted as being an accurate record of f.o.b. export receipts.[2] All that was necessary to get average f.o.b. export prices was to divide the total declared value of cloth or yarn exported by the total number of yards of cloth or pounds of yarn exported. These series were then converted to index form.

Movements in these indexes of unit export price reflect two types of changes. These are changes in the average quality of the mix of goods exported and changes in the prices of the various types of goods exported. Thus, if an index of unit export prices could be deflated by a composite index of the *prices* of the various types of goods exported, the result would be an index of the *quality* of the mix of different goods exported.

To give a simple example, consider a country that exports "good" and "poor" cotton cloth. An examination of her trade statistics indicates that the average f.o.b. export price per yard of cotton cloth exported was $1.00 in 1815 and $2.00 in 1825. The index of average f.o.b. export price thus stood at 200 in 1825 (1815 = 100). If the price per yard of "good" cloth had risen from $1.50 in 1815 to $3.00 in 1825 and the price per yard of "poor" cloth had risen from $.50 in 1815 to $1.00 in 1825, then the composite index of the prices of the types of cloth exported also stood at 200 in 1825 (1815 = 100). If the index of the average f.o.b. export price is divided by the composite index of the prices of the types of cloth exported (henceforth to be known as the cotton cloth price index), the result will be 100 for both 1815 and 1825. The export quality index thus shows average export quality to have remained constant between 1815 and 1825. If, on the other hand, the prices of both "good" and "poor" cotton cloth had tripled instead of doubled between 1815 and 1825, the above calculation would have recorded a decline of one-third in average export quality.

It will be noted that these examples assume that the prices of the different types of cloth exported moved in unison. If the price movements of the various types of cloth exported diverged considerably, then a useful cotton cloth price index could be constructed only with a detailed knowledge of the mix of goods

[2] For discussion of the accuracy of the "declared" values, see A. Imlah, *Economic Elements in the Pax Britannica*, pp. 23–24.

exported in each year and the price movements of each type.[3] In fact, of course, no such detailed knowledge of exports and prices is available for the nineteenth century. It so happens, however, that during the period 1815–1913 the prices of the most important types of cotton gray cloth and cotton yarn generally moved in virtual unison (see Discussion A below). It follows that useful yarn and gray cloth price indexes can be computed from price series of closely specified, representative types of yarn and gray cloth without a detailed knowledge of the composition of exports. Conversely, such detailed knowledge would only result in a slight improvement in the accuracy of the yarn and gray cloth price indexes, and would in no way affect the principal conclusions of this appendix.

For the period 1815–45, the price index used for cloth is based solely on the price of 7/8, 72 reed printing gray cloth. This type of cloth is generally considered to be a typical gray cloth. The yarn price index used for the same period is based on the prices of No. 100 and No. 140 mule yarn. Unfortunately, these yarns are far from typical. The quality index for yarn exports obtained for the period 1815–45 must therefore be viewed with considerable reserve.

For the periods 1845–98 and 1898–1913, both the cloth and yarn price indexes are based on weekly price information for a whole group of products. Between 1845 and 1890, my price index for cotton cloth can be compared with another computed on the basis of the same data by Blaug. Slight differences arise between the two indexes because of a difference in sampling procedure and weighting. Column 1 of Table 39 contains my price index, and column 2 of the same table contains Blaug's index. (For a more detailed description of the construction of these price indexes, see Discussion A.)

The price indexes for cloth that I have calculated refer only to gray cloth. The export figures, however, include large amounts of bleached, dyed, and printed cloth. Furthermore, the data indicate that the export prices of gray and white (plain) cloth and printed and dyed (colored) cloth did not move in unison during the periods 1815–45, 1855–71, and 1900–1913. (The 1855–71 period differs from the other two in that the plain/colored export price ratio had returned to its beginning value by the

[3] The continual changes in the mix of goods exported, by changing the weights in the cloth price index, would also introduce a certain amount of ambiguity into the results obtained.

end of the period.) If the changes in the plain/colored export price ratio were due to changes in the relative qualities of plain and colored cloth exported, no serious problem arises. In this case, average "quality" can be determined simply by dividing the price index of gray cloth into the index of average f.o.b. export prices received per yard (Assumption 1). This quality index was calculated for the entire period and for all subperiods.

A careful study of the problem, however, indicates that changes in the plain/colored export price ratio were probably due to changes in the relative prices of gray cloth and finishing services. To take account of this phenomenon, it was necessary to adjust the average f.o.b. export prices in the dividend of the cloth export quality index. I did this by adjusting the value of colored cloth so as to maintain the plain/colored export price ratio that existed at the start of each period during which the plain/colored export price ratio moved (Assumption 2). For the periods 1815–45, 1855–71, and 1900–1913, there are thus two quality indexes for cloth. Of these, I consider the one based on Assumption 2 to be the most likely result. At least for the period 1815–45, the Assumption 1 results must be viewed as an upper limit. (For a more detailed discussion of the plain/colored export price problem, see Discussion B.)

II

Table 38 shows estimated quality changes in British cotton cloth exports to all parts of the world for the period 1815–45. Column 2 contains the results of Assumption 1 and column 3 the results of Assumption 2. A sharp decline in quality is recorded under either assumption.

These quality changes can be put in better perspective if the world is divided into "high income" (HI) and "low income" (LI) countries. I have included the United States, British North America, Australia, New Zealand, Scandinavia, Germany, France, Switzerland, and the Low Countries in the HI category; All other countries are listed as LI. Under Assumption 1, export quality to the HI countries rose from 100 in 1815 to 107.7 in 1845, whereas export quality in the LI countries fell from 100 to 91.9. There was also a shift in the relative importance of the two market areas. In 1815, the LI markets took 46.2 percent of the yardage exported. By 1845, this percentage had risen to 85.9. Given Assumption 2, quality fell to 91.7 in the HI countries and to 81.7 in the LI countries.

TABLE 38

ESTIMATED QUALITY OF BRITISH COTTON TEXTILE EXPORTS, 1815–45

(1815 = 100)

Year	Gray Cloth Price Index (1)	Cloth Quality Index (Assumption 1) (2)	Cloth Quality Index (Assumption 2) (3)	Yarn Quality (4)
1815	100.0	100.0	100.0	100.0
1816	103.7	87.2	85.7	101.4
1817	84.0	94.2	91.6	108.4
1818	78.0	109.4	107.9	87.0
1819	79.0	101.6	96.8	88.2
1820	63.0	116.0	108.3	89.8
1821	61.0	112.6	106.7	89.0
1822	58.0	108.6	102.2	83.9
1823	56.0	106.4	97.0	83.9
1824	58.0	100.2	92.0	72.1
1825	...	...	...	65.4
1826	42.0	121.9	110.2	71.5
1827	40.0	122.8	110.3	70.2
1828	39.0	122.3	107.1	65.0
1829	35.0	123.1	105.6	59.2
1830	34.8	126.7	108.2	65.4
1831	35.7	112.0	99.7	71.0
1832	34.2	100.6	92.4	71.8
1833	35.7	97.5	89.0	72.4
1834	37.3	94.4	86.7	73.4
1835	40.7	92.6	86.2	64.5
1836	40.0	93.3	86.6	56.2
1837	31.0	107.4	96.5	60.1
1838	33.7	92.6	83.7	60.9
1839	34.5	90.1	80.8	54.0
1840	29.0	98.6	87.3	58.5
1841	29.0	95.5	83.4	64.8
1842	25.2	96.8	84.2	73.8
1843	25.8	88.8	77.4	66.8
1844	26.0	89.6	78.3	66.8
1845	24.8	92.3	80.6	56.7

The single most important factor in this drop was the Indian market. Its quality index dropped from 100 to 60.9 under Assumption 1 and from 100 to 57.4 under Assumption 2. At the same time, India's share of the yardage exported rose from 0.5 percent in 1815 to 21 percent in 1845. Without India, the worldwide quality index would have stood at 94.8 in 1845 under Assumption 1 and 83.4 under Assumption 2.

TABLE 39
ESTIMATED QUALITY OF BRITISH COTTON TEXTILE EXPORTS, 1845–98
(1845 = 100)

Year	Author's Gray Cloth Price Index	Blaug's Gray Cloth Price Index	Cloth Quality Index Author's Price Index (Assumption 1)	Cloth Quality Index Blaug's Price Index (Assumption 1)	Yarn Quality
	(1)	(2)	(3)	(4)	(5)
1845	100.0	100.0	100.0	100.0	100.0
1846	90.8	89.3	104.8	106.6	104.4
1847	96.6	92.4	107.2	112.1	101.3
1848	79.7	80.2	108.0	107.4	116.9
1849	87.8	87.8	95.9	95.9	110.5
1850	102.9	100.8	88.9	90.8	90.3
1851	99.1	96.2	87.5	90.1	88.2
1852	94.3	92.4	91.9	93.8	94.9
1853	99.5	97.7	91.4	93.0	93.5
1854	91.7	90.8	91.8	92.7	96.3
1855	87.0	97.7*	94.0	105.3*	93.8
1856	92.3	90.1	91.9	94.1	88.2
1857	105.7	103.8	83.2	84.7	81.2
1858	100.4	100.0	83.3	83.6	86.4
1859	110.9	106.8	79.3	82.2	78.8
1860	113.3	109.9	77.6	80.0	81.4
1861	111.4	106.9	76.8	80.0	82.9
1862	153.6	153.4	66.6	66.7	65.1
1863	215.1	211.5	62.0	63.0	71.9
1864	243.8	233.6	54.2	56.5	73.4
1865	194.1	187.8	69.7	72.0	79.2
1866	196.6	174.0	69.4	78.4	79.6
1867	142.8	136.6	79.8	83.4	102.8
1868	122.4	119.8	83.7	85.5	121.3
1869	130.2	126.7	81.0	83.3	108.3
1870	122.8	119.8	80.5	82.5	105.0
1871	110.4	106.9	86.2	89.1	113.7
1872	118.2	121.4	85.6	83.4	99.0
1873	115.2	111.5	85.2	88.1	103.3
1874	108.5	107.6	85.4	86.2	102.5
1875	106.5	103.1	85.9	88.7	105.0
1876	95.1	93.9	89.2	90.3	100.6
1877	99.1	96.2	83.8	86.2	98.7
1878	87.9	86.3	91.7	93.4	106.5
1879	80.6	80.9	94.8	94.4	114.0
1880	89.7	88.5	85.2	86.3	98.7

TABLE 39 (*Continued*)

Year	Author's Gray Cloth Price Index	Blaug's Gray Cloth Price Index	Cloth Quality Index Author's Price Index (Assumption 1)	Cloth Quality Index Blaug's Price Index (Assumption 1)	Yarn Quality
	(1)	(2)	(3)	(4)	(5)
1881	91.5	89.3	82.2	84.2	99.8
1882	90.6	87.8	85.0	87.7	102.2
1883	83.9	81.7	88.1	90.5	106.6
1884	83.1	80.9	85.3	87.6	106.3
1885	79.1	77.9	84.3	85.6	107.7
1886	78.4	76.3	79.6	81.8	109.9
1887	80.2	77.9	79.9	81.1	108.4
1888	81.1	79.4	77.7	79.3	105.5
1889	83.4	82.5	74.8	75.6	101.4
1890	83.7	82.5	76.7	77.8	106.0
1891	79.8	...	81.2	...	106.8
1892	72.6	...	83.5	...	116.8
1893	75.5	...	81.9	...	110.2
1894	67.6	...	85.2	...	115.3
1895	64.5	...	87.4	...	111.5
1896	66.5	...	89.3	...	109.8
1897	61.7	...	94.3	...	113.6
1898	61.3	...	91.0	...	109.6

*These results are probably caused by a misprint in Blaug's article.

Yarn quality appears to have deteriorated even more rapidly than cloth quality during this period. The index of yarn quality stood at 56.7 in 1845 (1815 = 100). During the period, however, the price of high-quality yarn was apparently falling less rapidly than the price of low-quality yarn. If the No. 40 mule and No. 30 water yarn prices for the period 1828–45 given by James Mann are used, the quality reduction from 65 in 1828 to 56.7 in 1845 is virtually eliminated (see Discussion A). The most that can be said is that it is unlikely that the entire 35 percent drop in quality recorded between 1815 and 1828 is due to the choice of yarn counts in the price index. In view of the uncertainty attached to these results, I have not bothered to disaggregate them or connect them with the much more reliable results for the post-1845 period.

The results for the period 1845–98 are shown in Table 39. Column 3 contains the results of Assumption 1 using my gray cloth price index. Column 4 shows the results of Assumption

TABLE 40

ESTIMATED QUALITY OF BRITISH COTTON TEXTILE EXPORTS, 1856–71

(Assumption 2, author's price index) 1845 = 100

1856	1859	1862	1865	1868	1871
91.9	83.4	73.1	75.3	83.4	86.2

1 using the gray cloth price index derived from Blaug's work. Column 5 contains the results for yarn.

Table 40 shows the results of Assumption 2 and my gray cloth price index for the period 1856–71. Observe that the values for 1856 and 1871 are identical to the Assumption 1 results for those years.

All the indexes for cloth export quality once again show deterioration over the 53-year period. Column 3 of Table 39 shows an overall decline from 100 in 1845 to 90.7 in 1898. This decline can be partitioned into a decline to 87.6 in the LI markets, an increase to 125.6 in the HI countries, and an increase from 85.9 percent to approximately 90 percent in the yardage going to the LI markets.

Once again, the Indian market exerted a strong downward pull

TABLE 41

ESTIMATED QUALITY OF BRITISH COTTON TEXTILE EXPORTS, 1898–1913

(1898 = 100)

Year	Author's Gray Cloth Price Index	Cloth Quality (Assumption 1)	Cloth Quality (Assumption 2)	Yarn Quality
1898	100.0	100.0	100.0	100.0
1899	100.1	101.9	101.9	96.2
1900	115.0	98.7	98.7	89.0
1901	113.9	100.9	101.8	96.9
1902	109.9	102.7	103.6	97.3
1903	120.6	96.9	97.6	91.6
1904	134.1	93.3	93.7	91.6
1905	132.8	93.9	95.3	96.4
1906	141.8	92.7	96.7	90.7
1907	144.0	96.7	97.6	91.0
1908	130.7	105.7	107.7	101.8
1909	130.6	99.7	101.0	100.4
1910	152.1	93.8	96.0	97.7
1911	164.0	89.5	93.5	100.5
1912	152.0	94.6	95.1	107.9
1913	153.7	97.6	101.4	105.2

TABLE 42

ESTIMATED QUALITY OF BRITISH COTTON TEXTILE EXPORTS 1815–1913

Year	Cloth Quality (Assumption 1)	Cloth Quality (Assumption 2)	Yarn Quality
1815	100.0	100.0	
1845	92.3	80.6	100.0
1885	79.0	69.0	107.7
1890	70.6	61.7	106.0
1898	84.0	73.3	109.6
1913	82.0	74.3	115.3

on average quality. The quality of cloth exported to India fell to 84.5 in 1898 (1845 = 100), while her share of total exports rose from 21 percent to 43.1 percent. Without India, the worldwide quality index would have stood at 99.8 in 1898. The yarn index shows a slight increase in quality over the period. The HI and LI countries shared about equally in this increase. In fact, both improved slightly more than the overall index. An increase in the percentage exported to the LI countries explains this phenomenon.

The results for the period 1898–1913 are shown in Table 41. In this period, there was little or no decline in the quality of British cotton cloth exports. Interestingly enough, quality to the HI countries, especially Canada, Australia, and New Zealand, did somewhat less well than quality to the LI countries. There was also a slight increase in the percentage of cloth exports going to the HI countries. Yarn quality improved slightly as the result of a sharp improvement in HI country quality and a small decline in LI country quality. In addition, the percentage of yarn exports going to the LI countries declined from 55 percent to 36 percent.

Results for the entire period 1815–1913 are shown in Table 42 and Figure 6. As mentioned above, I consider the results of Assumption 2, shown in column 2, of Table 42, to be more accurate than the results of Assumption 1.[4] The quality deterioration shown in column 2 is the result of a decline from 100 to 72.9 in LI country import quality and an increase from 100 to 104.6 in HI country import quality together with an increase from 46.2 percent to approximately 90 percent in the export yardage going to the

[4] Assumption 1 implies that the quality of plain cloth deteriorated from 100 in 1815 to 82.1 in 1845, while the quality of colored cloth increased from 100 to 111.6. Assumption 2, of course, implies that both colored and plain cloth quality fell to 82.1 in 1845.

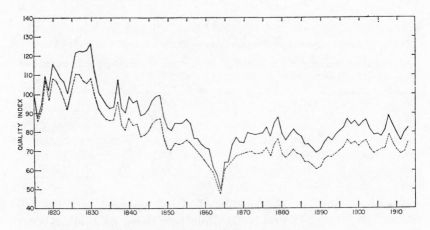

**Figure 6. Quality Index of British Cotton Cloth Exports,
1815-1913. 1815 = 100.
———— Assumption 1; ------- Assumption 2.**

LI countries. Without India, the quality index in column 2 would have gone from 100 in 1815 to 85.9 in 1913.

The quality of yarn exports shown in column 3 increased considerably between 1845 and 1913. This improvement can be credited to a steady quality level in the LI countries, a 25 percent improvement in HI country quality, and a decline from 45.9 percent to 36.5 percent in the share going to the LI countries.

DISCUSSION A

Problems in the Calculation of Price Indexes

The principal problem in obtaining the price indexes used as the denominators in the various quality indexes calculated in this appendix was a shortage of reliable price information. For the period 1815–45, there is really only one continuous and authoritative series for a closely specified type of cloth. This series is for 7/8, 72 reed printing gray, prepared by Alderman Neild of Manchester for presentation to the British Association in 1861.[1] The author's express purpose was to present a representative price

---

[1] A. Neild, "An Account of the Prices of Printing Cloth and Upland Cotton from 1812 to 1860," pp. 491–97. I adjusted the values in the table according to the instructions given by Neild.

index for cotton cloth, and his claim that the cloth involved was in fact "typical" has never been contested.

It is, of course, very dangerous to base an overall price index on a single product, particularly in a period of rapid technological change. There is, however, a good deal of ancillary evidence that gives support to Neild's series. Between 1845 and 1902, the 7/8, 72 printers' is one of six supposedly representative types of gray cloth the prices of which are available on a weekly basis. Throughout this extensive period the price of the 7/8, 72 printers' moved in excellent accord with the prices of the five other types of gray cloth.

There are also fragments of other price series from the pre-1845 period. In his classic history of the British cotton manufacture, Edward Baines presents a price series of "second quality 74's" from 1814 through 1820 and of "third quality 74's" from 1821 through 1833.[2] These series usually agree within a few percentage points with Neild's series. By 1833, the 74 series appears to be a few percentage points above Neild's series. In addition, Ellison reports the price changes between 1815 and 1856 of an unspecified type of calico and an unspecified type of printers' cloth, and these changes are virtually identical with that reported by Neild.[3] In view of this information, I am prepared to accept Neild's 7/8, 72 printers' series as a reasonable surrogate for a more comprehensive gray cloth price index. At the very least, I believe it to be accurate enough to be used in determining general trends in export quality.

With regard to cotton yarn, T. S. Ashton has prepared continuous series, covering the period 1815–45, of the prices received by the firm of M'Connel and Kennedy for No. 100 and No. 140 mule yarn.[4] These, of course, are very high-quality yarns and are far from typical. Furthermore, these series show considerable deviations from the prices of the more standard No. 40 mule and No. 30 water yarn reported by James Mann for the period 1828–45.[5] Because they are the only series available for the entire period, I have nevertheless used the No. 100 and No. 140 prices. In view of these facts, the results of this calculation must be scrutinized with great reserve.

[2] E. Baines, Jr., *History of the Cotton Manufacture in Great Britain,* p. 356.

[3] Ellison, *The Cotton Trade of Great Britain,* p. 61.

[4] T. S. Ashton, "Some Statistics of the Industrial Revolution in Britain," pp. 214–34.

[5] J. A. Mann, *The Cotton Trade of Great Britain,* p. 96.

As has already been indicated, the situation improves considerably in the period after 1845. In that year, the *Economist* began publishing the weekly prices of four different types of raw cotton, two types of yarn, and six different types of gray cloth. The prices of the same set of closely specified goods continued to be published until the end of the century.

The six different types of gray cloth consisted of three different types of shirtings, two types of printers' cloth, and one type of long cloth.[6] The range of their prices usually exceeded 2 to 1. Furthermore, the purpose of publishing this information was, of course, precisely to give a general view of the gray cloth price situation.

I constructed a separate annual price index for each of the six types of cloth by drawing one weekly price per quarter for each type. This sampling procedure clearly makes some error inevitable. Nevertheless, the six indexes are remarkably well synchronized. (Usually at least four, often five, and sometimes all six are within five percentage points of each other, even during the violent price fluctuations occasioned by the American Civil War.)[7] Furthermore, for most of the period there are frequent changes in the rank ordering of the price index values. By the late 1870s, however, the most expensive type of cloth (one of the three shirtings) begins to be consistently a few index points above the rest. However, because of the high price of the first and because the *Economist* had at least occasional trouble in obtaining quotations on the second, I doubt that these two types of cloth were as important as the other four.

I formed an overall index by the simple expedient of adding the six separate indexes and dividing their sum by six. This is equivalent to assuming that equal sums were spent on each type of cloth. Thus, the volume of each type of cloth assumed to be exported is inversely proportional to its price.

Some check on the effects of this sampling procedure can be obtained by comparing my summed series with a gray cloth price index based on the same data calculated by Marc Blaug for the

---

[6] The six types were: (1) 26 in., 66 reed, Printer, 29 yds., 4 lbs. 2 ozs.; (2) 27 in., 72 reed, Printer, 29 yds., 5 lbs. 2 ozs.; (3) 39 in., 60 reed, Gold End Shirtings, 37 1/2 yds., 8 lbs. 4 ozs.; (4) 40 in., 66 reed, Gold End Shirtings, 37 1/2 yds., 8 lbs. 12 ozs.; (5) 40 in., 72 reed, Gold End Shirtings, 37 1/2 yds., 9 lbs. 8 ozs.; and (6) 39 in., 44 reed, Red End Long Cloth, 36 yds., 9 lbs.

[7] The individual indexes are included in a mimeographed appendix available upon request from the author.

period 1845–90.[8] Instead of calculating a separate price series for each type of cloth, Blaug summed *all* the weekly price quotations in shillings and divided by the total indicated pound weight. He thus obtained a series of the average price in shillings per pound of gray cloth, based on the assumption that an equal number of pieces of each type of gray cloth was produced. This procedure thus puts a relatively greater weight on the high-priced goods than does my weighting scheme. I believe my weighting scheme is more realistic, particularly with regard to exports. Blaug does, however, have the advantage of 312 observations per year as opposed to my 24 observations. This is of particular advantage during periods of considerable price fluctuations.

Blaug's results, converted to index form, are shown in column 2 of Table 39. They are very similar to my summed index shown in column 1. Some variations are, of course, to be expected, owing to differences in weighting, sampling procedure, and rounding, as well as possible computational errors by both parties. There is some tendency for my index to be above Blaug's. By the end of the comparison period, this difference seems to have settled into a 1 to 2 percent upward bias. Although part of this difference may be attributable to differences in weighting, there does seem to be some discrepancy due to my limited sampling procedure.

Unfortunately, these price series begin to behave very strangely starting in 1898 or 1899. For the first time, there are inversions in the ranking of *absolute* prices. By 1902–3, it is difficult to put any faith in the series at all. The editors of the *Economist* clearly shared this opinion, for in 1903 they substituted the prices of a new bundle of cotton goods. When this change took place, the prices of the new goods were quoted back through 1898.

This new bundle of goods consisted of two types of raw cotton, three types of yarn, and four types of gray cloth: one printers' and three different shirtings.[9] These new cloth price indexes are quite well synchronized starting in 1902. Unfortunately, between 1898 and 1902 they show a good deal of divergence. Thus, though I felt free to use the new price series to construct a gray cloth price index between 1902 and 1913, the period 1898–1902 pre-

---

[8] Blaug, "Productivity of Capital in the Lancashire Cotton Industry during the Nineteenth Century," pp. 376–78.

[9] The four cloths listed were: (1) 32 in., Printers', 116 yds., 16 by 16, 32s and 50s; (2) 32 in., Shirtings, 75 yds., 19 by 19, 32s and 40s; (3) 38 in., Shirtings, 38 yds., 18 by 16, 10 lbs.; and (4) 39 in., Shirtings, 37 1/2 yds., 16 by 15, 8 1/4 lbs.

sented a serious problem. Neither series is "well behaved" during this period, and their summed indexes diverge noticeably. After studying the alternatives, I chose to stop the old series in 1898 and to start the new series at that point. The overlap is thus only one year. The main reason for this choice is that the old price index increased rather sharply from 1898 to 1899, while the new index and the average export price to all ten markets I distinguished remained virtually constant. This particular method of connecting the two indexes results in a somewhat lower price index (i.e., a somewhat-higher-quality index) than would result if the whole overlap period 1898–1902 were used. As a result of these problems I must confess to some misgivings about the gray cloth price index I used for the period 1898–1913.

As was mentioned above, starting in 1845 the *Economist* also published price series for cotton yarn. In the period 1845–1902, the two yarns quoted were a No. 40 mule and a No. 30 water twist. The advantage of this choice is that it includes yarns produced by two different methods. On the other hand, there is very little spread in counts. This does not seem to be a serious problem, however, because, for the period 1845–82, the *Economist* series are extremely well coordinated with the prices of very-high-quality yarns given by Ashton.[10] The only exception to this occurred during the American Civil War when the prices of high-count yarns rose less rapidly than prices of low-count yarns. My index may thus slightly understate the quality of yarn exported during the Civil War period. In any case, the two price series given by the *Economist* are remarkably well synchronized. In 1898, they stood at 63.5 and 63.3, respectively (1845 = 100).

For the period 1898–1913, the yarns described were a 32 twist, a 40 weft, and a 60 Egyptian twist. These prices are somewhat less well synchronized than those for the earlier period. In connecting the two series, I used the same procedure as for cloth.

DISCUSSION B

*The Problem of Variations in the Plain/Colored
Export Price Ratio*

The price indexes discussed above and in the text of Appendix C apply only to gray cloth. As noted in the text, however, cloth

[10] See Ashton, "Some Statistics of the Industrial Revolution in Britain."

exports did not consist exclusively of gray cloth. In fact, the majority of all cloth exported between 1815 and 1913 was at least bleached. This would present no problem if the price of finishing cloth moved in unison with the price of gray cloth. Unfortunately, it is virtually impossible to investigate finishing prices directly. Some notion of the relative prices of gray cloth and finishing services can be secured by looking at the average price of various types of exports. The ratio of the average price of gray and white (plain) cloth exported over the average price of printed and dyed (colored) cloth exported (with 1815 = 100) changed as follows: 1815 = 100.0; 1820 = 88.4; 1826 = 81.4; 1830 = 74.3; 1835 = 88.2; 1840 = 79.4; and 1845 = 74.0. Between 1845 and 1856, this ratio remained virtually constant. During the American Civil War, however, it rose sharply. With 1856 = 100, the ratio was 102.1 in 1859, 122.0 in 1862, 115.6 in 1865, 106.6 in 1868, and back to 100 in 1871. After the Civil War, the ratio remained virtually constant until 1900, and then rose slightly up to 1913.

The problem here lies in determining what caused these fluctuations in the plain/colored export price ratio. Unless the relatively more rapid fall in the price of plain cloth up to 1845 was the result of its quality actually deteriorating relative to the quality of colored cloth, merely dividing the average export price of all cloth by a price index for *gray* cloth will tend to exaggerate average export quality.

One possible explanation for the decline in the plain/colored export price ratio during the period 1815–45 is that plain cloth exports tended to concentrate more and more in low-quality markets. Using the average quality computed for ten different British cotton textile markets (see text above) for 1815 and 1845, it is possible to explain approximately 15 percent of the decline in the plain/colored export price ratio by the greater concentration of plain cloth in low-quality markets in 1845 than in 1815. If the relative price of plain cloth fell for some other reason than a relative decline in quality, however, the markets with a heavy concentration of plain cloth will have their quality indexes biased downward. This means that the above calculation is undoubtedly biased upward. One way of eliminating this bias is to assume that, in each separate market, plain cloth quality and colored cloth quality moved in unison. Once the quality indexes have been corrected by this assumption, none of the decline in the plain/colored export price ratio can be explained by the growing concentration of plain cloth exports in low-quality markets.

Some indication that part of the decline in the plain/colored export price ratio was really due to a relative decline in plain cloth quality can be obtained from the "official" export statistics. These figures indicate that the shift away from muslins, fustians, and the like toward calicoes had a greater effect on the average "official" value of plain than of colored cloth exported. This was so because almost all muslins were exported plain. Thus perhaps 10 percent of the relative decline in plain cloth prices can be attributed to the general shift toward calicoes.

This evidence suggests that only a small percentage of the decline in the plain/colored export price ratio can be attributed to a relative decline in the quality of plain cloth exports. The only other reasonable explanation of the observed phenomena is that the price of gray cloth fell more rapidly in the period after 1815 than did the price of finishing. The most likely source of such a divergence in prices during this period is technological change. It is well known that the period 1815–45 witnessed a veritable revolution in gray cloth production. In addition to major improvements in the preparatory processes, spinning machinery was made larger, more efficient, and more automatic during this period. More important, by 1845 British cotton weaving was dominated by efficient power looms. In the finishing processes, however, there was really only one major development, the improvement and widespread adoption of machine printing. Interestingly enough, the period of most rapid growth of machine printing appears to have been the early 1830s, the same period during which the plain/colored export price ratio temporarily recovered from 74.3 to 88.2.[1] It is generally agreed that the rate of technological improvement in gray cloth production fell off after 1845.[2]

The relative increase in the export price of plain cloth during

[1] For a general description of technical developments in the finishing industry, see G. Turnbull, *A History of the Calico Printing Industry of Great Britain.* The evidence as to the period of most rapid spread of machine printing is unfortunately somewhat vague. It is clear that printing increased extremely rapidly in the 1830s. In 1821, 7,000,000 pieces were printed, as opposed to 8,600,000 in 1830; 16,000,000 in 1840; and 20,000,000 in 1850 (ibid., p. 81). It is also clear that there was a great rush into printing after the removal of the excise on printed calicoes in 1831 (Baines, *History of the Cotton Manufacture of Great Britain,* pp. 282–84). Although there had been a drawback on exports, the rapid growth of the industry undoubtedly resulted in increased mechanization and technical improvement. At least by 1842, the previously flourishing art of block printing was on its last legs (Turnbull, *A History of the Calico Printing Industry of Great Britain,* pp. 211–12). This very same period also witnessed the introduction and rapid growth of machine printing in the United States (see Ware, *The Early New England Cotton Manufacture,* pp. 94–95).

[2] This general view of technical developments is in accord with the description

the American Civil War cannot be attributed to changes in the distribution of plain and colored cloth between high- and low-quality markets. Nor can I see any way of explaining it through changes in technology. Rather, the likely explanation lies in the acute shortage of raw cotton experienced during this period. Prices of cotton goods rose, not because there was a shortage of manufacturing capacity, but because there was a shortage of raw material. Price series available from the Civil War period indicate that the price of raw cotton rose more rapidly than the price of yarn, which, in turn, rose more rapidly than the price of gray cloth.

The slight upturn in the plain/colored export price ratio between 1900 and 1913 can possibly be attributed to two developments in the finishing trades: the first was the development and rapid adoption of the so-called vat dyes, and the other was the consolidation and rationalization that took place in the industry.[3] It is, however, difficult to draw any definite conclusions about this period.

In the light of this discussion, I have, as noted in the above, constructed two different cloth quality indexes for the periods 1815–45, 1855–71, and 1900–1913. The first index assumes that changes in the plain/colored export price ratio actually represent changes in the relative quality of plain and colored exports. This index is obtained simply by dividing the average declared export price by the gray cloth price index (Assumption 1).

The other calculation assumes that changes in the plain/colored export price ratio do not represent relative quality changes. Instead, the quality of colored cloth is assumed to fluctuate in unison with the quality of plain cloth. I made this correction by adjusting the value of colored cloth so as to maintain the price ratios of 1815, 1855, and 1898, respectively (Assumption 2).[4]

Of these two indexes, I feel that the second is more accurate. Any downward bias it contains because of the shift to calicoes should be offset by the fact that some of the plain cloth exported was finished to the extent of being bleached.

---

given by Deane and Cole (*British Economic Growth*, p. 192). It also accords well with Blaug's results ("The Productivity of Capital in the Lancashire Cotton Industry during the Nineteenth Century," pp. 360, 366).

[3] See Turnbull, *A History of the Calico Printing Industry of Great Britain*, chaps. 8, 9.

[4] It would, of course, be equally legitimate to adjust the price of plain cloth so as to maintain the price ratios of 1845, 1864, and 1913. Because this approach would assume a different fixed-price ratio, it would give somewhat different results than my method. The difference turns out to be so small, however, that it can be safely ignored.

D. BRITISH EXPORTS OF COTTON CLOTH TO SELECTED COUNTRIES, 1815–1913

The following data have been extracted from various annual volumes of the Trade and Navigation Accounts of the *British Parliamentary Papers*. They are based on the quantities and values (in current prices) declared at the time of export. They are subject to a number of possible types of error. First of all, some exports may not have been recorded. There was no incentive to under-report, however, so this is unlikely to be a large source of error. Errors of collection, addition, and typography may have entered at several different stages. More important that these possibilities, however, are problems of geographical definition and re-exportation.

Before the unification of Italy and Germany, British exports to these regions were listed separately for individual ports and/or subregions. Unfortunately, ports and subregions importing relatively small amounts were usually lumped into the "other destination" category. Because I consistently ignored this category, my early estimates for Germany and Italy are probably somewhat low. What is worse, the number of ports and subregions listed varied from year to year. Thus, the size of the downward bias in my figures also varies from year to year.

It is also certainly true that some of the cloth was re-exported from the declared destination. This is probably the case especially with regard to Germany, particularly during the Crimean War. It may also have played some role with regard to the French figures before 1861. Although some of the cloth declared for export to France while the prohibition of English cotton cloth was in effect may have been put into the hands of smugglers, some was probably consigned to a free port and then re-exported.

TABLE 43

BRITISH COTTON TEXTILE EXPORTS TO VARIOUS COUNTRIES, 1815–1913

(in thousands of yards and thousands of pounds sterling)

Year	UNITED STATES		FRANCE		GERMANY		ITALY	
	Volume	Declared Value	Volume	Declared Value	Volume	Declared Value	Volume	Declared Value
1815	70,813	4,332	193	20	29,561	2,765	11,734	1,009
1816	35,621	2,266	221	26	32,731	2,319	10,976	747
1817	32,005	1,731	144	14	40,543	2,700	17,017	1,326
1818	40,364	2,240	76	9	42,110	2,854	29,059	1,818
1819	19,387	1,007	45	4	37,284	2,064	31,677	1,810
1820	24,183	1,156	18	2	47,658	2,707	26,192	1,320
1821	38,931	1,868	14	1	40,477	2,161	22,088	1,019
1822	37,767	1,666	18	2	41,456	2,094	44,641	1,946
1823	35,997	1,536	8	1	35,858	1,749	28,291	1,177
1824	41,380	1,801	114	5	34,798	1,577	33,392	1,293
1825	45,259	2,074	117	7	37,141	1,714	27,357	1,003
1826	30,135	1,301	408	18	38,672	1,377	28,085	929
1827	52,857	2,258	365	16	43,697	1,541	28,113	905
1828	36,200	1,612	79	6	39,511	1,326	32,823	994
1829	32,552	1,346	...	...	...	...	...	...
1830	49,352	2,056	139	7	43,817	1,175	53,287	1,706
1831	68,588	2,519	947	35	41,522	941	38,165	1,036
1832	31,509	1,049	826	29	51,480	1,163	47,695	1,116
1833	45,142	1,386	1,544	46	49,534	1,189	47,672	1,088
1834	45,631	1,394	2,318	61	50,532	1,294	60,684	1,563
1835	74,963	2,393	2,432	72	43,572	1,191	34,682	951
1836	62,042	2,115	3,534	88	37,458	977	57,441	1,406
1837	17,482	595	2,440	59	43,171	1,008	42,607	1,009

TABLE 43 (*Continued*)

Year	UNITED STATES Volume	UNITED STATES Declared Value	FRANCE Volume	FRANCE Declared Value	GERMANY Volume	GERMANY Declared Value	ITALY Volume	ITALY Declared Value
1838	38,493	1,206	2,607	60	39,040	887	62,512	1,337
1839	37,236	1,145	2,722	59	38,910	847	39,314	843
1840	32,073	899	2,839	64	45,588	920	58,866	1,119
1841	40,291	1,191	3,427	71	48,756	945	56,296	1,115
1842	12,924	360	4,136	73	41,790	758	53,404	902
1843	21,251	604	3,271	61	48,274	814	77,472	1,109
1844	29,424	804	3,046	64	49,652	833	58,193	952
1845	31,237	838	2,506	54	43,621	752	54,424	865
1846	37,106	942	2,691	57	43,651	744	70,725	1,141
1847	105,423	2,305	2,004	42	40,623	690	37,698	635
1848	70,840	1,367	2,871	45	38,601	606	64,765	882
1849	87,160	1,704	3,218	62	43,048	668	85,449	1,211
1850	104,230	2,128	5,043	123	47,350	797	71,145	1,135
1851	76,580	1,571	3,928	98	48,424	836	96,258	1,405
1852	110,995	2,121	3,808	89	41,874	716	69,617	999
1853	193,329	3,608	...	...	...	...	...	...
1854	163,455	2,830	5,038	110	54,203	870	39,910	598
1855	184,588	3,150	7,028	135	71,179	1,102	54,175	757
1856	207,289	3,772	9,461	149	42,080	515	60,613	874
1857	177,842	3,071	17,404	250	54,676	1,045	58,970	895
1858	154,818	2,610	11,510	191	56,336	1,014	108,317	1,524
1859	225,147	3,995	9,471	173	65,009	1,147	65,746	932
1860	226,778	3,849	10,823	206	73,627	1,323	78,960	1,259
1861	74,680	1,254	31,322	479	67,521	1,196	114,588	1,821

TABLE 43 (*Continued*)

Year	United States		France		Germany		Italy	
	Volume	Declared Value	Volume	Declared Value	Volume	Declared Value	Volume	Declared Value
1862	97,293	1,840	33,799	526	45,531	1,005	64,560	1,183
1863	71,049	1,598	17,238	441	37,562	954	65,226	1,534
1864	63,055	1,653	19,016	502	27,521	818	42,590	1,237
1865	122,384	3,012	21,405	596	54,034	1,313	52,133	1,237
1866	112,504	3,242	55,381	1,266			70,146	1,661
1867	86,922	2,205	39,948	926	82,616	1,861	56,026	1,137
1868	74,832	1,883	39,687	929	83,436	1,787	61,688	1,108
1869	99,780	2,398	41,612	989	74,248	1,631	78,902	1,488
1870	132,308	3,067	29,894	724	57,337	1,212	49,433	932
1871	129,621	3,505	86,854	1,688	78,655	1,792	69,427	1,210
1872	131,618	3,492	106,731	2,148	94,232	2,037	73,186	1,224
1873	109,533	2,716	108,163	1,884	52,752	1,272	85,671	1,397
1874	105,340	2,563	119,191	2,074	58,886	1,459	71,050	1,097
1875	79,898	1,899	87,748	1,622	58,660	1,353	90,301	1,329
1876	54,871	1,276	88,754	1,630	53,763	1,092	89,987	1,349
1877	61,175	1,319	63,588	1,333	78,075	1,304	81,525	1,270
1878	48,692	1,130	63,890	1,319	67,284	1,122	70,802	1,069
1879	51,595	1,191	56,592	1,148	53,473	963	67,581	940
1880	77,916	1,749	56,331	1,103	43,406	779	60,574	880
1881	67,980	1,543	53,838	1,031	41,822	716	65,023	1,310

TABLE 43 *(Continued)*

Year	United States		France		Germany		Italy	
	Volume	Declared Value	Volume	Declared Value	Volume	Declared Value	Volume	Declared Value
1882	73,864	1,759	60,849	1,093	38,510	680	75,951	1,046
1883	60,865	1,628	58,377	1,095	47,043	797	89,741	1,245
1884	52,561	1,460	50,712	1,023	48,784	822	86,718	1,119
1885	46,076	1,217	45,052	877	44,693	759	85,567	1,058
1886	45,057	1,140	35,472	681	45,358	676	85,051	965
1887	44,029	1,055	34,592	600	43,765	626	119,961	1,364
1888	40,313	879	33,379	585	30,923	482	46,191	572
1889	49,109	1,015	29,452	513	33,117	515	70,291	856
1890	58,812	1,299	30,368	534	31,821	518	55,939	760
1891	54,737	1,303	39,542	711	39,493	592	53,723	723
1892	60,731	1,429	23,744	461	38,298	531	42,213	579
1893	64,324	1,529	29,509	522	45,273	610	34,908	482
1894	46,125	1,080	22,991	429	36,093	521	20,642	314
1895	64,996	1,585	21,297	449	49,604	680	26,498	333
1896	55,913	1,400	24,410	454	66,251	906	12,037	196
1897	65,512	1,509	17,459	333	61,006	835	9,771	160
1898	51,683	1,249	13,467	262	59,912	813	7,983	140
1899	75,343	1,806	16,443	302	50,721	745	7,068	119
1900	67,326	1,709	25,791	420	56,010	858	9,544	149
1901	50,937	1,407	20,834	398	67,341	1,014	6,214	117
1902	68,685	1,960	21,328	413	70,185	1,057	6,158	119
1903	72,327	2,048	17,553	336	60,649	953	6,363	134
1904	52,391	1,568	17,759	325	60,129	1,006	7,904	171
1905	65,563	2,021	14,875	288	65,842	1,093	8,746	194

TABLE 43 (*Continued*)

Year	United States Volume	United States Declared Value	France Volume	France Declared Value	Germany Volume	Germany Declared Value	Italy Volume	Italy Declared Value
1906	78,735	2,216	15,038	301	72,659	1,238	11,048	248
1907	98,376	2,772	21,416	418	85,918	1,557	17,697	349
1908	59,034	1,611	17,394	361	69,945	1,334	14,381	339
1909	75,881	1,977	14,609	351	72,785	1,307	12,674	258
1910	60,657	1,792	15,269	439	85,664	1,747	13,480	333
1911	57,125	1,859	13,904	424	92,698	2,094	12,825	341
1912	48,100	1,713	14,129	405	88,679	2,058	10,859	299
1913	44,415	1,572	12,764	377	76,372	1,801	10,243	287

Year	Brazil Volume	Brazil Declared Value	India Volume	India Declared Value	China Volume	China Declared Value	Japan Volume	Japan Declared Value
1815	15,823	1,015	1,356	131	...	...	...	...
1816	15,829	915	1,705	143	...	...	...	...
1817	20,071	1,028	5,317	394	...	...	...	...
1818	27,308	1,634	8,851	566	...	...	...	...
1819	14,837	775	7,128	453	...	...	...	...
1820	18,692	925	14,326	817	...	...	...	...
1821	19,147	920	19,946	1,099	...	...	...	...
1822	16,899	706	20,742	1,097	...	...	...	...
1823	32,694	1,285	23,292	1,134	...	...	...	...
1824	34,239	1,350	24,470	1,097	...	...	...	...

TABLE 43 (*Continued*)

Year	BRAZIL		INDIA		CHINA		JAPAN	
	Volume	Declared Value	Volume	Declared Value	Volume	Declared Value	Volume	Declared Value
1825	40,514	1,551	23,042	1,013	...	...	...	...
1826	24,928	812	26,166	1,021	...	...	...	...
1827	37,196	1,119	36,168	1,355	1,581	66	...	...
1828	63,098	1,967	37,567	1,395	...	...	...	...
1829	...	...	39,734	1,267	...	...	...	...
1830	46,204	1,369	52,180	1,550	...	...	...	...
1831	26,272	681	43,386	1,183	...	...	...	...
1832	60,578	1,280	51,834	1,312	...	...	...	...
1833	68,903	1,608	45,756	1,152	...	...	...	...
1834	65,424	1,427	38,972	944	6,381	152	...	...
1835	58,831	1,439	51,777	1,338	11,217	289	...	...
1836	72,810	1,670	74,281	1,973	12,820	370	...	...
1837	48,768	987	64,214	1,528	10,964	272	...	...
1838	80,454	1,599	80,085	1,781	22,134	519	...	...
1839	75,966	1,516	100,950	2,286	16,675	386	...	...
1840	76,848	1,451	145,084	2,964	13,478	238	...	...
1841	73,875	1,408	145,881	2,729	24,609	421	...	...
1842	44,882	787	155,507	2,480	27,619	469	...	...
1843	66,265	1,049	215,862	3,183	46,086	654	...	...
1844	83,481	1,311	239,493	3,709	98,798	1,457	...	...
1845	87,076	1,393	229,261	3,347	108,449	1,633	...	...
1846	107,704	1,581	231,698	3,236	78,693	1,024	...	...
1847	84,908	1,431	149,414	2,394	60,515	847	...	...
1848	70,452	1,015	185,376	2,301	67,508	809	...	...

TABLE 43 (*Continued*)

Year	Brazil Volume	Brazil Declared Value	India Volume	India Declared Value	China Volume	China Declared Value	Japan Volume	Japan Declared Value
1849	107,463	1,461	295,444	3,438	78,301	880	...	...
1850	102,980	1,511	314,453	4,128	73,209	892	...	...
1851	134,421	1,960	360,667	4,349	114,975	1,407	...	...
1852	124,178	1,831	352,637	4,242	140,922	1,649	...	...
1853	...	...	357,281	4,457	98,603	1,206	...	...
1854	99,387	1,392	516,510	5,832	41,644	498	...	...
1855	124,962	1,664	467,374	5,097	74,032	786	...	...
1856	154,491	2,086	477,950	5,451	112,657	1,330	...	...
1857	182,783	2,765	469,958	5,715	121,575	1,572	...	...
1858	124,724	1,825	791,546	9,300	138,459	1,821	...	...
1859	108,426	1,643	968,149	12,043	193,867	2,753	...	...
1860	156,135	2,299	825,066	10,519	222,874	3,153	...	...
1861	168,287	2,477	797,844	10,018	243,645	3,176	...	...
1862	107,862	1,859	514,089	8,057	80,722	1,266	...	...
1863	91,063	2,033	558,322	12,185	46,074	1,150	...	...
1864	87,765	...	475,989	11,550	73,426	2,015	5,906	164
1865	114,779	2,717	561,089	11,073	125,801	2,769	26,367	606
1866	167,931	3,961	627,231	12,540	187,174	4,383	26,790	652
1867	146,665	2,850	741,406	12,239	227,822	4,262	29,626	606
1868	151,016	2,675	925,847	13,265	328,212	5,516	22,754	394
1869	215,997	3,866	712,519	10,422	308,816	5,663	18,907	366
1870	146,467	2,620	909,613	12,660	394,605	6,141	34,852	540
1871	165,310	2,911	1,021,391	13,085	468,975	6,509	34,972	453
1872	185,818	3,426	995,533	13,385	402,077	6,373	28,058	446

TABLE 43 (*Continued*)

Year	BRAZIL		INDIA		CHINA		JAPAN	
	Volume	Declared Value	Volume	Declared Value	Volume	Declared Value	Volume	Declared Value
1873	159,117	2,886	1,109,846	14,919	349,745	5,295	23,368	359
1874	172,786	2,955	1,264,926	15,801	393,263	5,303	20,330	275
1875	197,522	3,309	1,231,407	15,079	396,318	5,303	39,622	604
1876	179,221	2,814	1,293,415	14,299	447,799	5,023	45,676	625
1877	177,437	2,680	1,446,430	15,971	367,326	4,407	27,110	423
1878	169,878	2,403	1,295,398	14,080	340,084	3,986	42,230	648
1879	203,288	2,641	1,327,435	13,766	462,284	4,807	61,618	763
1880	233,112	3,248	1,812,692	19,699	447,706	5,266	61,371	877
1881	223,038	2,980	1,796,683	19,245	523,666	5,974	63,325	793
1882	221,210	2,979	1,663,674	18,259	401,837	4,613	52,920	611
1883	204,969	2,581	1,799,575	19,020	370,545	4,103	45,303	529
1884	208,991	2,609	1,791,062	17,647	394,583	4,186	45,355	498
1885	190,096	2,189	1,796,242	16,762	523,924	5,291	45,412	495
1886	241,022	2,679	2,237,610	19,598	455,823	4,570	34,629	383
1887	215,365	2,517	1,964,450	17,967	552,743	5,625	65,404	698
1888	214,959	2,521	2,196,823	19,774	574,548	5,890	77,857	788
1889	178,002	2,146	2,129,669	18,737	474,426	4,629	82,579	844
1890	212,641	2,503	2,190,166	19,918	570,297	6,029	63,310	707
1891	109,037	2,082	1,967,772	18,064	534,129	5,747	61,120	677
1892	278,899	2,881	1,974,638	16,448	497,475	4,961	75,180	778

TABLE 43 (*Continued*)

Year	Brazil Volume	Brazil Declared Value	India Volume	India Declared Value	China Volume	China Declared Value	Japan Volume	Japan Declared Value
1893	265,756	3,084	1,981,330	16,661	365,406	3,659	68,308	712
1894	227,819	2,630	2,418,876	19,273	425,340	3,886	71,512	752
1895	194,485	2,179	1,839,878	13,634	528,145	4,620	96,033	910
1896	166,747	1,863	2,143,106	17,128	542,815	5,402	105,284	1,265
1897	134,922	1,363	1,892,243	14,707	445,182	4,211	94,047	996
1898	208,446	1,967	2,246,049	16,991	486,332	4,320	104,950	1,038
1899	132,562	1,360	2,319,637	17,816	554,282	5,268	93,851	963
1900	104,934	1,196	2,018,538	17,127	456,195	5,030	119,455	1,597
1901	70,160	800	2,372,011	21,197	491,072	5,853	63,368	802
1902	128,252	1,411	2,123,145	18,032	574,777	6,101	109,116	1,330
1903	152,462	1,678	2,127,461	18,595	477,692	5,629	67,364	864
1904	134,841	1,623	2,374,874	22,609	548,974	7,651	42,372	609
1905	131,509	1,612	2,538,704	24,150	799,733	10,197	128,724	1,604
1906	124,167	1,676	2,506,669	24,498	647,425	9,257	110,286	1,600
1907	143,906	1,963	2,571,993	26,908	553,373	9,036	121,241	1,928
1908	87,761	1,208	2,241,490	24,058	498,293	7,256	113,884	1,708
1909	90,611	1,213	2,172,549	20,990	572,443	7,314	113,908	1,390
1910	155,322	2,348	2,343,290	24,482	471,334	7,271	100,393	1,419
1911	160,068	2,465	2,521,324	28,722	647,450	6,869	92,206	1,384
1912	127,018	2,013	2,964,313	32,234	527,565	8,105	74,761	1,339
1913	96,538	1,651	3,216,450	37,349	716,533	11,733	50,187	1,051

BIBLIOGRAPHY

The following bibliography is limited to works referred to in the text. Those items that I consider, by some subjective standard, to have been very important sources of data or analysis are marked with an asterisk.

Aldcroft, D. H. "The Entrepreneur and the British Economy, 1870–1914." *Economic History Review*, August 1964.

———. "Introduction." In D. H. Aldcroft, ed. *The Development of British Industry and Foreign Competition, 1875–1914*. London: George Allen & Unwin, 1968.

*Allen, G. C. *British Industries and Their Organization*. 4th ed. London: Longmans, Green, 1959.

Ashton, T. S. "Some Statistics of the Industrial Revolution in Britain." *The Manchester School*, May 1948.

———. *An Economic History of England*. London: Methuen, 1960.

Ashworth, W. *An Economic History of England, 1870 to 1939*. London: Methuen, 1960.

Baines, E., Jr. *History of the Cotton Manufacture in Great Britain*. London: Fisher, Fisher & Jackson, 1835.

Bidwell, P. W. *Our Trade with Britain*. New York: Council on Foreign Relations, 1938.

Blackwell, W. L. *The Beginnings of Russian Industrialization*. Princeton, N.J.: Princeton University Press, 1968.

Blaug, M. "The Productivity of Capital in the Lancashire Cotton Industry during the Nineteenth Century." *Economic History Review*, April 1961.

*Board of Trade, Working Party on Cotton. *Report*. London: His Majesty's Stationery Office, 1946.

Bowker, B. *Lancashire under the Hammer.* London: Hogarth Press, 1928.

Bowley, A. L.. *Wages in the United Kingdom in the Nineteenth Century.* Cambridge: Cambridge University Press, 1900.

*British Census Office. *Census of Production 1907.* Vol. 1. London: His Majesty's Stationery Office, 1908.

British Foreign Office. *Economic Conditions in Turkey, 1932.* London: His Majesty's Stationery Office, 1932.

*British Foreign Office, Department of Overseas Trade. *Economic Conditions in Turkey to April, 1930.* London: His Majesty's Stationery Office, 1930.

*British Ministry of Production. *Report of the Cotton Textile Mission to the United States of America.* London: His Majesty's Stationery Office, 1944.

* *British Parliamentary Papers.* Trade Accounts for various years.

Burn, D. L. *The Economic History of Steel Making.* Cambridge: Cambridge University Press, 1940.

Burnett-Hurst, A. R. "Lancashire and the Indian Market." *Journal of the Royal Statistical Society,* Part 3, 1932.

Burnham, T. H., and G. O. Hoskins. *Iron and Steel in Britain, 1870–1930.* London: George Allen & Unwin, 1934.

Chapman, S. J. *The Lancashire Cotton Industry.* Manchester: University of Manchester Press, 1904.

*Chapman, S. J., and T. S. Ashton. "The Sizes of Businesses Mainly in the Textile Industries." *Journal of the Royal Statistical Society,* April 1914.

Chang, Y. K. *Foreign Trade and Industrial Development of China.* Washington: The University Press of Washington, D.C., 1956.

Chin, R. *Management, Industry, and Trade in Cotton Textiles.* New Haven, Conn.: College and University Press, 1965.

*Clapham, J. H. *The Economic Development of France and Germany, 1815–1914.* Cambridge: Cambridge University Press, 1921.

Clark, C. *The Conditions of Economic Progress.* London: Macmillan, 1940.

Clark, W. A. G. *Cotton Fabrics in Middle Europe.* Bureau of Manufactures, Special Agents Series, No. 24. Washington: Government Printing Office, 1908.

———. *Cotton Textile Trade in the Turkish Empire, Greece, and Italy.* Bureau of Manufactures, Special Agents Series, No. 18. Washington: Government Printing Office, 1908.

*Clough, S. B. *The Economic History of Modern Italy.* New York: Columbia University Press, 1964.

*Copeland, M. T. *The Cotton Manufacturing Industry of the United States.* Cambridge, Mass.: Harvard University Press, 1912.

*———. "Technical Development in Cotton Manufacturing since 1860." *Quarterly Journal of Economics,* November 1909.

Cotton Factory Times. 17 June 1904; 9 September 1904; 3 April 1908; 24 July 1908.

Daniels, G. W., and J. Jewkes. *The Comparative Position of the Lancashire Cotton Industry and Trade.* Manchester: The Manchester Statistical Society, 1927.

*———. "The Crisis in the Lancashire Cotton Industry." *Economic Journal,* March 1927.

———. "The Post-War Depression in the Lancashire Cotton Industry." *Journal of the Royal Statistical Society,* Part 2, 1928.

Deane, P., and W. A. Cole. *British Economic Growth, 1688–1959.* Cambridge: Cambridge University Press, 1962.

Dunham, A. L. *The Anglo-French Treaty of Commerce of 1860 and the Progress of the Industrial Revolution in France.* Ann Arbor: University of Michigan Press, 1930.

———. *The Industrial Revolution in France, 1815–1848.* New York: Exposition Press, 1955.

Ellison, T. *The Cotton Trade of Great Britain.* London: Effingham Wilson, 1886.

Farnie, D. A. "The Textile Industry: Woven Fabrics." In Charles Singer et al., eds. *A History of Technology.* Vol. 5. London: Oxford University Press, 1958.

Feller, I. "The Draper Loom in New England Textiles, 1894–1914: A Study of Diffusion of an Innovation." *Journal of Economic History,* September 1966.

———. "The Draper Loom in New England Textiles: A Reply." *Journal of Economic History,* December 1968.

Florence, P. S. *Economics of Fatigue and Unrest, and the Efficiency of Labor in British and American Industry.* London: George Allen & Unwin, 1924.

*Frankel, M. "Obsolescence and Technical Change in a Maturing Economy." *American Economic Review,* June 1955.

Gibson, R. *Cotton Textile Wages in the United States and Great Britain.* New York: King's Crown Press, 1948.

*Gray, E. M. *The Weaver's Wage.* Manchester: Manchester University Press, 1937.

Henderson, H. D. *The Cotton Control Board.* Oxford: Clarendon Press, 1922.

Henderson, W. O. *The Lancashire Cotton Famine.* Manchester: Manchester University Press, 1934.

Hershlag, Z. Y. *Introduction to the Modern Economic History of the Middle East.* Leiden: E. J. Brill, 1964.

Hobson, J. *Incentives in the New Industrial Order.* New York: Thomas Seltzer, 1923.

Hou, Chi-Ming. "Economic Dualism: The Case of China, 1840–1937." *Journal of Economic History,* September 1963.

———. *Foreign Investment and Economic Development in China, 1840–1937.* Cambridge, Mass.: Harvard University Press, 1965.

Hubbard, G. E. *Eastern Industrialization and Its Effect on the West.* London: Oxford University Press, 1935.

Imlah, A. *Economic Elements in the Pax Britannica.* Cambridge, Mass.: Harvard University Press, 1958.

Issawi, C. *Egypt: A Social and Economic Analysis.* London: Oxford University Press, 1947.

*Jewkes, J., and H. Champion. "The Mobility of Labour in the Cotton Industry." *Economic Journal,* March 1928.

*———, and E. M. Gray. *Wages and Labor in the Lancashire Cotton Spinning Industry.* Manchester: Manchester University Press, 1935.

*Jones, G. T. *Increasing Returns.* Cambridge: Cambridge University Press, 1933.

Kindleberger, C. P. *Economic Growth in France and Great Britain, 1851–1950.* Cambridge, Mass.: Harvard University Press, 1964.

———. "Foreign Trade and Economic Growth: Lessons from Britain and France, 1850–1913." *Economic History Review,* December 1961.

Knowlton, E. H. *Pepperell's Progress.* Cambridge, Mass.: Harvard University Press, 1948.

Kraus, R. A. "Cotton and Cotton Goods in China, 1918–1936: The Impact of Modernization on the Traditional Sector." Ph.D. dissertation, Harvard University, 1968.

Lamb, R. K. "The Development of Entrepreneurship in Fall River, 1813–1859." Ph.D. dissertation, Harvard University.

Landes, D. S. "Technological Change and Development in Western Europe, 1750–1914." In H. J. Habakkuk and M. Postan, eds. *The Cambridge Economic History of Europe.* Vol. 6. The Industrial Revolutions and After, Book 1. Expanded and republished as *The Unbound Prometheus.* Cambridge: Cambridge University Press, 1969.

Leveson, I. F. "Reductions in Hours of Work as a Source of Productivity Growth." *Journal of Political Economy,* April 1967.

Levine, A. L. *Industrial Retardation in Britain.* New York: Basic Books, 1967.

Lindsay, H. A. F. "Discussion on Mr. Burnett-Hurst's Paper." *Journal of the Royal Statistical Society,* Part 3, 1932.

Lockwood, W. W. *The Economic Development of Japan: Growth and Structural Change, 1868–1938.* Princeton, N.J.: Princeton University Press, 1954.

London Economist. January 1845 to December 1938.

Lucas, A. F. *Industrial Reconstruction and the Control of Competition: The British Experiments.* London: Longmans, Green, 1937.

*McCloskey, D. N. "Productivity Change in British Pig Iron." *Quarterly Journal of Economics,* May 1968.

———. *Economic Maturity and Entrepreneurial Decline: British Iron and Steel.* Cambridge, Mass.: Harvard University Press, forthcoming.

———, and L. G. Sandberg. "From Damnation to Redemption: Judgments on the Late Victorian Entrepreneur." *Explorations in Economic History,* Fall, 1971.

Mann, J. A. *The Cotton Trade of Great Britain.* London: Simckin, Marshall, 1890.

Marshall, A. "Fiscal Policy of International Trade." In *Official Papers.* London: Macmillan, 1926.

———. *Industry and Trade.* 4th ed. London: Macmillan, 1923.

———. *Principles of Economics.* 8th ed. London: Macmillan, 1920.

Marx, K. *Capital.* New York: Modern Library, 1936.

Meyer, J. "An Input-Output Approach to Evaluating the Influence of Exports on British Industrial Production in the Late 19th Century." *Explorations in Entrepreneurial History,* October 1955.

*Mitchell, B. R. (With the collaboration of P. Deane.) *Abstract of British Historical Statistics.* Cambridge: Cambridge University Press, 1962.

Mitchell, B. *Industrial Revolution in the South.* Baltimore: Johns Hopkins University Press, 1930.

———. *The Rise of the Cotton Mills in the South.* Baltimore: Johns Hopkins University Press, 1921.

Morris, M. D. *The Emergence of an Industrial Labor Force in India.* Berkeley and Los Angeles: University of California Press, 1965.

———. "Towards a Reinterpretation of Nineteenth-Century Indian Economic History." *Journal of Economic History,* December 1963.

Musson, A. E. "The Great Depression in Britain, 1873–1896: A Reappraisal." *Journal of Economic History,* June 1959.

Myers, R. H. "Cotton Textile Handicraft and the Development of the Cotton Textile Industry in Modern China." *Economic History Review,* December 1965.

*Neild, A. "An Account of the Prices of Printing Cloth and Upland Cotton from 1812 to 1860." *Journal of the Statistical Society of London,* December 1861.

Nyman, R. C. *Union-Management Cooperation in the "Stretch Out."* New Haven, Conn.: Yale University Press, 1934.

Nystrom, P. H. *Textiles.* New York: D. Appleton, 1916.

Paslovsky, L. *Economic Nationalism of the Danubian States.* New York: Macmillan, 1928.

Pearse, A. S. *The Cotton Industry of India.* Manchester: International Federation of Master Cotton Spinners' and Manufacturers' Associations, 1930.

Phelps-Brown, E. H., and S. J. Handfield-Jones. "The Climacteric of the 1890's: A Study in the Expanding Economy." *Oxford Economic Papers,* October 1952.

Phelps-Brown, E. H., and B. Weber. "Accumulation, Productivity, and Distribution in the British Economy." *Economic Journal,* June 1953.

Pollard, S. *The Development of the British Economy, 1914–1950.* London: Edward Arnold, 1962.

Pratt, E. R. *Trade Unionism and British Industry.* London: John Murray, 1904.

Redford, A. *Manchester Merchants and Foreign Trade. Vol. II. 1850–1939.* Manchester: University of Manchester Press, 1956.

Rimmer, W. G. *Marshalls of Leeds: Flax Spinners, 1788–1886.* Cambridge: Cambridge University Press, 1960.

*Robson, R. *The Cotton Industry in Britain.* London: Macmillan, 1957.

Rostow, W. W. *The Stages of Economic Growth.* Cambridge: Cambridge University Press, 1960.

Ryan, J. "Machinery Replacement in the Cotton Industry." *Economic Journal,* December 1930.

*Salter, W. E. G. *Productivity and Technical Change.* Cambridge: Cambridge University Press, 1966.

*Sandberg, L. G. "American Rings and English Mules: The Role of Economic Rationality." *Quarterly Journal of Economics,* February 1969.

*———. "The Draper Loom in New England Textiles: A Comment." *Journal of Economic History,* December 1968.

*———. "Movements in the Quality of British Cotton Textile Exports, 1815–1913." *Journal of Economic History,* March 1968.

Saul, S. B. "The Engineering Industry." In D. H. Aldcroft, ed. *The Development of British Industry and Foreign Competition, 1875–1914.* London: George Allen & Unwin, 1968.

Sayers, R. S. *A History of Economic Change in England, 1880–1939.* London: Oxford University Press, 1967.

Seki, K. *The Cotton Industry of Japan.* Tokyo: Japan Society for the Promotion of Science, 1956.

Smith, R. *The Cotton Textile Industry of Fall River, Massachusetts.* New York: King's Crown Press, 1944.

Snyder, C. "A New Index of the General Price Level from 1875." *Journal of the American Statistical Association,* June 1924.

Statistical Yearbook for India. Various years.

*Stein, S. J. *The Brazilian Cotton Manufacture.* Cambridge, Mass.: Harvard University Press, 1957.

Svennilson, I. *Growth and Stagnation in the European Economy.* Geneva: United Nations, 1954.

Sweezy, A. "The Amoskeag Manufacturing Company." *Quarterly Journal of Economics,* May 1938.

Taussig, F. *Some Aspects of the Tariff Question.* Cambridge, Mass.: Harvard University Press, 1918.

————. *The Tariff History of the United States.* New Rochelle, N.Y.: G. P. Putnam's Sons, 1892.

Temin, P. "The Relative Decline of the British Steel Industry, 1880–1913." In H. Rosovsky, ed. *Industrialization in Two Systems.* New York: John Wiley & Sons, 1966.

Tippett, L. H. C. *A Portrait of the Lancashire Cotton Textile Industry.* London: Oxford University Press, 1969.

Todd, J. A. *The World's Cotton Crops.* London: A & C Black, 1915.

Turnbull, G. *A History of the Calico Printing Industry of Great Britain.* Altrincham: John Sherratt & Sons, 1951.

Turner, H. A. *Trade Union Growth, Structure, and Policy.* Toronto: University of Toronto Press, 1962.

Tyson, R. E. "The Cotton Industry." In D. H. Aldcroft, ed. *The Development of British Industry and Foreign Competition, 1875–1914.* London: George Allen & Unwin, 1968.

United States Bureau of the Census. *Census of Manufactures, 1905.* Vol. 3. Washington: Government Printing Office, 1905.

————. *Census of Manufactures, 1914.* Vol. 2. Washington: Government Printing Office, 1919.

United States Bureau of the Census. *Bulletin No. 160.* 1926.

*United States Congress, House of Representatives, United States Tariff Board. *Cotton Manufactures.* 62d Congress, 1st session, 1912. House Document No. 643.

United States Department of Commerce, Bureau of Foreign and Domestic Commerce. *The Cotton Spinning Machinery Industry.* Miscellaneous Series, No. 37. Washington: Government Printing Office, 1916.

United States Tariff Board. *See* United States Congress.

United States Tariff Commission. *The Japanese Cotton Industry and Trade.* Washington: Government Printing Office, 1921.

United Textile Workers Association. *Inquiry into the Cotton Industry, 1921–1922.* Blackburn, England: United Textile Workers Association, 1923.

Utley, F. *Lancashire and the Far East.* London: George Allen & Unwin, 1931.

*Uttley, T. W. *Cotton Spinning and Manufacturing in the United States of America.* Manchester: Manchester University Press, 1905.

Uyeda, T. *The Recent Development of Japanese Foreign Trade.* Tokyo: Japanese Council, 1936.

Veblen, T. *Imperial Germany and the Industrial Revolution.* New York: Macmillan, 1915.

Ware, C. F. *The Early New England Cotton Manufacture.* New York: Houghton Mifflin, 1931.

*Weber, B., and S. J. Handfield-Jones. "Variations in the Rate of Economic Growth in the U.S.A., 1869–1939." *Oxford Economic Papers,* June 1954.

Whittam, W. *Report on England's Cotton Industry.* Bureau of Manufactures, Special Agents Series, No. 15. Washington: Government Printing Office, 1907.

*Winterbottom, J. E. *Cotton Spinning Calculations and Yarn Costs.* 2d ed. London: Longmans, Green, 1921.

Wood, G. H. *History of Wages in the Cotton Trade.* Reprint of *JRSS* article. London: Sherrett & Hughes, 1910.

————. "The Statistics of Wages in the Nineteenth Century. Section V. Changes in the Average Wage of All Employed with Some Account of the Forces Operating to Accelerate or Retard the Progress of the Industry." *Journal of the Royal Statistical Society,* June 1910.

Wright, S. F. *China's Struggle for Tariff Autonomy, 1843–1938.* Shanghai: Kelley & Walsh, 1938.

Wythe, G. *Industry in Latin America.* New York: Columbia University Press, 1945.

*Young, T. M. *The American Cotton Industry.* London: Methuen, 1902.

*Zevin, R. B. "The Growth of Cotton Textile Production after 1815." In R. Fogel and S. Engerman, eds. *The Reinterpretation of American Economic History.* New York: Harper & Row, 1971.

INDEX

Africa, North, 143

Africa, Sub-Saharan, 169, 200
  imports of British cotton textiles, 144, 146, 200–201

Aldcroft, D. H., 9, 70–71, 133

Alsace, 157–58, 160

American Civil War, 5, 6, 144, 157, 160, 248, 251

American cotton textile industry
  exports of, 155–56, 169
  managerial behavior in, 11, 63–65, 221–22
  protection of, 151–53, 200
  Northern states
    efficiency improvement in, 8, 12, 93–94, 111–12, 119
    labor productivity growth in, 113–16
    labor unions in. *See* Labor unions, American cotton textile industry
    managerial behavior in, 89 n, 90 n, 154–55
    origin of, 149, 151
    production levels of, 151–52
    reduction of work week in, 112, 114
    work force, composition of, 114–15
  Southern states
    growth of, 13, 153–54, 214
    labor force in, 154

American Cotton Yarn Association, Ltd., 127

Amoskeag Manufacturing Company, 90 n, 130

Anglo-American Trade Agreement of 1938, 200

Argentina
  imports of British cotton textiles, 197–98
  protection of cotton textile industry, 197–98

Arkwright, R., 18–19

Ashton Brothers of Hyde, 80–81

Ashton, T. S., 245, 248

Ashworth, W., 94

Asia, Other
  definition of, 143
  imports of British cotton textiles, 146–48, 202–3

Australia, 238
  imports of British cotton textiles, 200–201

Austria, 181

Austria-Hungary, 181

Automatic weaving
  advantages of, 68
  cost of looms, 79